Hell of a Journey

Hell of a Journey

ON FOOT THROUGH THE SCOTTISH HIGHLANDS IN WINTER

Mike Cawthorne

MERCAT PRESS
EDINBURGH
www.mercatpress.com

First published in 2000 by Mercat Press
Reprinted 2001
James Thin, 53 South Bridge, Edinburgh EH1 1YS
www.mercatpress.com

ISBN 184183 0054

To my mother and father

It was no summer Progresse. A cold coming they had of it, at this time of the yeare; just the worst time of the yeare to take a journey, and specially a long journey.

Lancelot Andrews, 1622

Here is the start and here the end
Of many a mountain day,
And what do we buy that we should spend
Our time this tinker way.
We buy what never the fool shall please
Nor over the knave have power,
The things that are one with the wind and the trees
And a fire at Altanour.

Sydney Scroggie

Set in Italian Garamond at Mercat Press
Printed and bound in Great Britain by
Redwood Books, Trowbridge, Wiltshire

Contents

Illustrations

Maps

Biographical note

Born in London, Mike Cawthorne taught for many years in Birmingham, and now lives in Scotland. *Hell of a Journey* is his first book.

Acknowledgements

The meticulous, hand-drawn maps are the work of Toby Whitty, to whom I am indebted. I would also like to thank Francis Byrn for his excellent overview map. Eugene Coyle offered advice on the manuscript.

During the course of the journey the following provided assistance in some way: Jon Cawthorne, Antony and Ursula Ranger, Paul Winters, Andy Smithson, Gavin Davidge and Clive Dennier.

I am also especially grateful to Seán Costello, and all the staff at Mercat for their support and encouragement.

Prologue

ANYONE TOILING up the Ben Nevis tourist path that day might have seen them. A man and two young boys, brothers. They were an odd sight. The man carried a stick and wore a tweed jacket, patched at the elbows. One of the boys dragged his feet and shivered involuntarily. But the eye would likely be drawn to the younger, for he was draped in a jersey many sizes too big. The hem hung loosely about his legs, the sleeves sagging so low they almost brushed the scree.

Presently they entered a strange world of mist, chill winds and falling snow. Snow in August! The mind of the boy in the jersey was on fire. Had they not just come from a green sunlit valley, through leafy woodland and bracken? And now this, a desert of grey rock, a moonscape, so alien he could not comprehend it. Then, nearing the old summit observatory, he saw something even more incredible. The ground simply vanished. Curiosity drew him towards the edge, close as he dared, and transfixed, he peered into a snow-covered gully. It dropped straight into the bowels of the earth, without end. Something must have been stirring in his childish imagination because, appalled and fearful though he was at the sight, he knew that life could never be the same again.

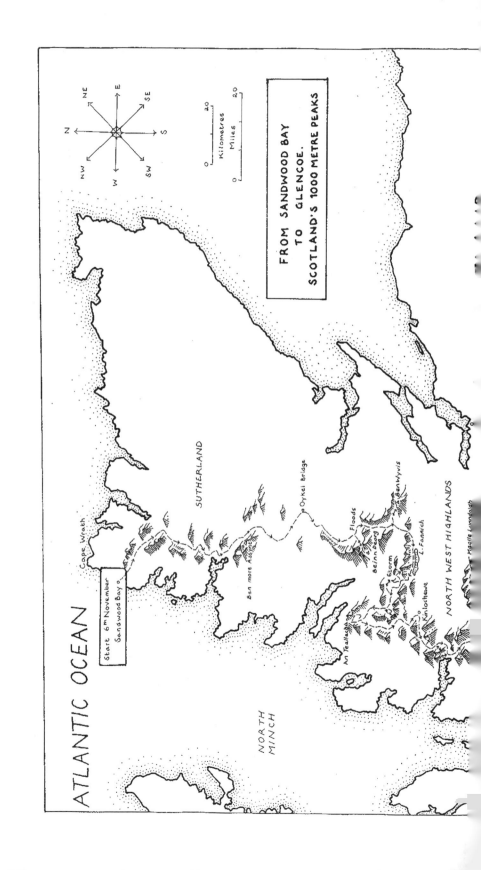

FROM SANDWOOD BAY
TO GLENCOE.
SCOTLAND'S 1000 METRE PEAKS

ATLANTIC OCEAN

Cape Wrath

Start 6ᵀᴴ November
Sandwood Bay o

SUTHERLAND

Ben more Assynt

Oykel Bridge

Floods

Beinn Dearg

Ben Wyvis

Gorm

L. Fannich

An Teallach

Kinlochewe

NORTH WEST HIGHLANDS

Maoile Lunndaidh

NORTH
MINCH

Kilometres

Miles

N
NW NE
W E
SW SE
S

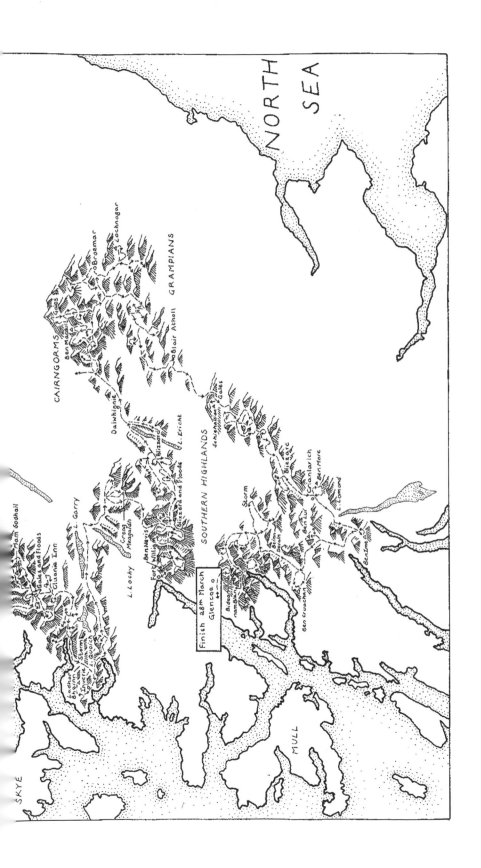

Introduction

EVERY LONG journey has a history and inspiration behind it. The trek I began in November 1997 evolved from the memory of another which I had undertaken more than a decade before. On a whim in May 1986, with a friend, Dave Hughes, I set out to climb Scotland's Munros—284 mountains above 3,000 feet—in a single sweep. With no support or planning, or even adequate equipment, we should have failed, but somehow by the end had covered 1,800 miles on foot and ascended nearly half a million feet. Perhaps naivety banished our worries. Clad only in jeans, jumpers and fishermen's jackets, we may have appeared like roaming vagabonds, but, unburdened by worldly cares, we lived as lords. A nostalgic turn of mind must later have embellished those weeks and months in the hills because, despite the sheer physical struggle and the war we waged against weather and midges, in hindsight it seemed like one continuum of magic.

During subsequent years I went overseas to the Greater Ranges, first to the Alps and North America, then onto equatorial ice in Africa, and through the desert mountains of Northern Pakistan. I continued to explore the Scottish Highlands intimately, finding delight in the discovery of lower peaks and glens, reclimbing my favourite hills, visiting at all seasons and in all weathers. But enjoyable as these experiences were, few of them quite matched the joy that had unfolded day by day and came back over the years from that long walk over the Munros. There was something inevitable about what followed.

Without travelling overseas what, I wondered, amounted to the wildest and toughest journey one could undertake, something new and untried? I defined my own criteria: it had to be mountainous, alone, entirely on foot, and unsupported. And for sheer severity it would be undertaken through an entire winter. The Munros were considered, but quickly dismissed; 284 winter mountains on foot and with no back-up seemed a madman's charter, only a fool would attempt it. Nor did I have any wish to recycle what for me had been a unique experience. I needed a different route and a fresh idea.

In these days of metrication, the 1,000-metre peaks presented a more appropriate challenge. There were few enough to make it a possibility, but plenty for it to be worthwhile. A detailed look at the map was a revelation: 135 peaks that stretched in an unbroken chain through the heart of the Scottish Highlands, from

Sutherland to the Eastern Cairngorms, down to Loch Lomond, west to Glencoe. Every mountain range would be included, every significant peak would have to be climbed. My route wove together the finest of Scottish scenery, linking every portion of wilderness, and unifying it all at the wildest time of year.

For a long while the idea slumbered, put into hibernation by a new career and a need to be financially secure. Then one Easter I returned to work after a week in the Highlands and handed in my notice.

In 1986 the preparation was easy—we didn't do any. A winter journey would be entirely different. More clothes were required, layers of thermals, a wind-proof fleece, and, for the extremities, thick, heat-retaining garments. I would have to lug around an ice-axe, crampons, have a good bivvy bag for likely benightments, carry extra food for emergencies. Boots would have to be heavier and more rigid for warmth and support. Crucially, my tent would need to withstand a storm-force wind, and my sleeping bag keep me comfortable at −15°C. I already had good gear but saved valuable grams by replacing much of it with lighter items. Unfortunately there was no time to test this new equipment properly, and it was not without some misgivings that I crammed it all into my rucksack.

Then there was the question of food, or, more to the point, how to carry it. The required daily consumption of 4,000 calories roughly equates to a kilogram of food, plus fuel. As my route led me away from village shops and hotels for up to a fortnight at a time, there could be no question of hauling on my back ten or more kilos of grub, perhaps through deep snow or in the dark of a winter night. The early Antarctic explorers had the answer: food caches. And so, three weeks prior to starting, I set about the bizarre task of burying four months' supplies at strategic points along the route. Besides food, I buried fuel, candles, batteries, maps, first aid, reading material; in fact any item that might help make surviving a Scottish winter a little less than the dreadful experience it threatened to be.

I harboured no illusions about winter. At various times I have been stranded by snowstorms that raged for days, have been forced to bivvy or burrow for survival into snowdrifts. Once, for three days, torrents of snow-melt trapped me the wrong side of a river in the Skye Cuillin. The meterological data speaks for itself. Storms are common. In a normal winter season above the thousand-metre level, winds of gale force could be expected every second day, precipitation is markedly higher, daytime temperatures considerably lower. The resulting wind chill can be as low as −30°C. Given 'average' conditions my plans were, at best, provisional. A severe, stormy winter would have them in shreds.

Blizzards are the most lethal weapon of a Scottish winter and can provoke an almost pathological fear in hill-walkers. Most years there are tragedies. In a vicious cocktail of falling snow and spindrift it is easy to stagger over a cliff-edge, drop through a cornice, or trigger an avalanche; easy to lose vital body heat and succumb to a creeping hypothermia. Cairngorm blizzards in particular have shocked many with their Arctic severity. The polar explorer Apsley Cherry-Garrard knew all about this menace: 'Fight your way a few steps from your tent and it will be gone. Lose your sense of direction and there is nothing to guide you back. Expose your hands and face to the wind, and they will soon be frostbitten.'

Reliable equipment, adequate food, careful route-planning, a good level of fitness, these can all be prepared for. But what of the psychological terrors of winter, the long nights, sixteen or seventeen hours of darkness? There would be stress from poor weather, and a perceived danger, either real or imagined, that could paralyse you with worry. And there would be loneliness. How does one prepare for these?

Winter for me was largely uncharted territory, my previous experiences of it patchy. I had climbed barely a hundred mountains in full winter conditions, had rarely gone alone, and never for more than a week. To consider rationally the consequences of an injury or serious error of judgement when days from any-where was sobering. But at another level this uncertainty was a prime motivation for going. By confronting my own fears, and perhaps by overcoming them, could I then hope to discover something new and fresh about life? The journey would supply an entire range of anxieties, and there could be no better testing ground than the great colosseum of the mountains.

There was something else. In a technological age of great material comfort, we are still, incredibly, plagued by unease, a sense of disenchantment at the heart of things, however we define it. We bolt our doors, ignore the stranger, swallow our pills. And, paradoxically, the greater our comfort the more profound our dis-quiet, or boredom. The French poet Baudelaire called it the 'horror of home'. Travel is one means of escape.

Above all there is that ultimate lure, the dream of winter: to tread a narrow, corniced crest on a day of blue shadows and low sun; to witness a full moon rise from a summit ridge; to see a hundred peaks on days of utter clarity when they appear as frozen waves, and night skies so brilliant with stars they seem smudged. There is a curfew of silence save for the muffled squeak of your boots through deep powder, then later you marvel at the aurora, great searching beams of green, blue and orange above the snowy Cairngorms. Days of perfection which defy analysis, irreducible, appearing almost as visions, yet we know them and will go to great lengths to have them again.

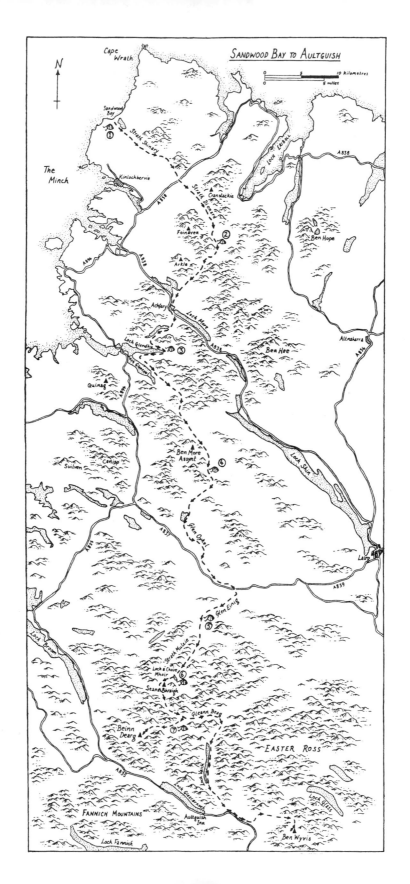

1

Solitary in Sutherland

EVEN FOR reluctant urban dwellers the Ordnance Survey Cape Wrath map is shocking in its sparseness. Brutal Clearances and harsh economic realities have emptied this beautiful land of all but a few tenacious communities, and it is a lonelier place now than at any time since prehistory. A few single-track roads link a handful of tiny settlements: Durness, Scourie, Kinlochbervie, some isolated crofts, the odd hotel. Much of this vast acreage is under water: either bog, or the thousands of lochans that lie scattered like blue confetti. But a primeval atmosphere is created by bold mountains of quartz and gneiss, climbing 900 metres or more straight from sea level, remnants of a geological past too remote even for the imagination to grasp.

'*Camping*! At this time of the year!'

The post-bus driver spat the words out. Grimacing, he dumped my large ruck-sack onto the gravel verge, then watched as I struggled to haul it onto my shoulders. He looked at me gravely.

'Out for long?'

'About a week,' I said, trying to appear casual.

It was not an idle question, but to say 'five months' or 'all winter' would have been absurd. After all, there was no guarantee I would last a fortnight, let alone till March the following year. I was the only passenger, but we had said nothing to each other during the three-hour ride from Lairg. Perhaps circumstances had excavated a trench of difference between us, separating our immediate reference points. Like millions of people at that moment he was merely doing an honest day's work. In the coming months, while he plied these lonely roads delivering and collecting mail, transporting the carless and elderly, I would be locked into a fantasy of adventure, of benefit to no one, and causing concern in many.

A few months ago I had taught my last lesson to a lively group of second-year pupils at an inner-city school in Birmingham. 'Why are you leaving?' they wanted to know.

Why was I leaving? What motivates someone to resign from a secure worka-day routine, to leave behind family, friends and colleagues, forego the pubs and parties, to exchange a comfortable salaried existence for the loneliness and dark of a Scottish winter? It was a good question. A week ago I had all the answers, but now on the remote north-west tip of Britain and quite alone, I was not so sure.

The post-bus left in a cloud of diesel fumes.

Though barely midday, being November it would be completely dark in about four hours. I set a brisk pace. The day was sunless and mild, and a salty breeze was coming off the Atlantic, breaking the surface of a grey lochan into a mass of ripples. Oldshoremore, a tiny collection of whitewashed crofts, was deserted. A frenzy of barks shattered the quiet, a wolfish looking dog raced towards me, then sprang back, nearly strangling itself on its tether. I passed through a gate with the sign 'Sandwood Bay 4½ miles'.

The track degenerated to a boggy, heavily eroded path; gaiters became necessary. I walked into the gloom of late afternoon. Another mile, and the faintest of twilight helped me up to a small col, from where I saw a sudden gleam in the distance: a line of white breakers, a broad expanse of sand bounded by a dark headland. In half an hour I was fumbling about in torchlight seeking a smooth pitch for my tiny shelter. Tomorrow I could begin.

Sandwood Bay is justly popular, a band of gold sandwiched between endless miles of impenetrable coastline. The bay is owned and managed by the John Muir Trust, a conservation body established in 1983 whose main aim is to 'acquire and manage key wild areas'. Undoubtedly they are one of the more enlightened movements in Scottish conservation, for, whilst seeking to protect and repair damaged environments, the JMT are sensitive to the needs of local communities. Their low-key approach to management is congruent with the ideas and aspirations of many who love wild places. They do not promote their properties—no car parks, visitor centres, or way-marked paths—they do not even publicise their ownership. My route would take me through a number of JMT properties during the course of the winter.

It may appear illogical to begin a journey on the north-west coast when your first mountain, Beinn Dearg, lies six days' walk to the south. But an irrational journey demands perhaps a symbolic beginning, and for a whole catalogue of reasons Sandwood Bay was packed with symbolism. This was the final destination during many family holidays to Scotland, and the vivid recollections of childish adventures among the dunes and rock pools form some of my earliest memories. Time had not lessened its magic.

§ § §

A balmy, onshore breeze and overcast skies greeted me on my first morning. As I dismantled camp the air filled with moisture, the mist fell, a drizzle started. I went down to the beach. Revisiting landscapes of your childhood can be a melancholy experience, but my mind could dwell only on the unknown future, the weeks and months that stretched out in front of me. Probably my expression registered an intensity quite out of keeping with this morning of gentle mists and unseasonable mildness. I stood in the foam for a moment, then turned, faced south, and climbed back up the sand dunes. Adjusting a strap I heard voices and turned to see a couple running towards the bay. The young woman looked over and waved. These were the last humans I was to see for nine days.

My mind still jangling with all manner of thoughts, I pushed inland heading south-easterly up Glen Shinary, leaving behind in minutes the rumble of breakers and the salty air. Over 20 kilos was resting on my back, all my winter equipment and as much food as I could carry. There would be my food caches, of course, but I would not pass a shop for a fortnight. Ahead lay some of the loneliest country in Britain.

Glen Shinary ended in a quagmire of a watershed, the negotiation of which added an extra hour's effort to the day. Crossing the deserted Durness–Ullapool road I discovered that the path up Strath Dionard was now a freshly-laid Land Rover track. While I protested at yet another intrusion into the wild it did ease me along, the rain and drizzle becoming less wearisome. Mist hung in layers along the ice-polished flanks of Cranstackie, and ahead the clouds formed innumerable bands of soggy grey. The sunless afternoon now grew suddenly dim, allowing me only a few minutes to pitch my tent before an advancing autumnal night thrust me into complete darkness.

Always after arriving at a location in the dark you awake to a fresh landscape, and the first gaze from the vestibule was a revelation. I was situated in a deep, glacial trough. To my right the eastern flanks of a great mountain—Foinaven— were sheets of grey, twisted rock, quite forbidding in the gloomy dawn. Above, the sky was a ruffled blanket but with emerging smudges of blue. There was no breath of wind and no sound. Not being one for pre-dawn starts, I lingered over breakfast and was away as the first rays filtered in from the east.

A walk along the west side of Loch Dionard was a joy. Absolute stillness reigned, the surface of the loch like plate glass. A rowan tried to rid itself of clinging russet; the rocks and erratics strewn about the grass were so pale they resembled the ribs of dead animals. The grass was a hundred shades of gold, the mosses so many shades of green.

Oddly, the map has no mention of the stalkers' path that helped me to a corrie lake, and thence over a spectacular pass at the southern perimeter of Foinaven. The heavy pack pulled at my shoulders, but the weeks of hard training had given me reserves of stamina, and these would only improve as the walk progressed. The grey-blue ramparts of Arkle came suddenly into view, sunlit and spectacular in dimension. There is an impressive scale to things here, the mountains climbing from near sea level to 800 or 900 metres, their summit ridges often protected by weeping crags and vaults of scree. It is a wild and unfrequented country. Winter was far from my mind that gloriously sunny afternoon, warm enough for a shirt only. I indulged in a short tea stop by Loch Stack, having sailed down from the heights with the spring and bounce of someone fast-tuning to his environment.

My route took me past the deserted hamlet of Achfary, up very steep ground, onto a featureless and nameless plateau before dropping equally steeply to wetland and more trackless country. At the mouth of an anonymous loch I sank to my knees in peat bog in the maze of ditches. The effort and lack of any rhythm was consuming precious daylight hours and, like yesterday, the day degenerated into a race against the clock. I have an almost irrational fear of being caught out in the dark, especially alone and in unfamiliar terrain. Rounding a shoulder, I jogged down on tired legs to Loch Glendhu and the sea. I camped among piles of smelly weed, then later, much later, was lulled to sleep by the lapping of wavelets along the shore.

It is strange to wake to nobody but yourself, to see no other human when you unzip the vestibule for the first time and cast about, no other tent, no boat in the bay, no one to talk to. Just another overcast day, a light, muggy breeze from the sea, a few squabbling gulls.

Mornings have always meant people: people hogging the bathroom, crowding the kitchen, making small talk with mouths full of burnt toast and cereal. And then through city traffic to school, probably the most sociable and populated of all places, where conversing and interacting are second only to breathing. After years which have been so crowded with people, how would I cope for any length of time being completely alone? I would meet people for sure, but strangers, and most encounters would be brief: 'Come far?', 'Been out long?', 'Got far to go?' Idle talk. And there would be whole days, like yesterday, when I spoke to no one at all.

Perhaps of all the days this winter, today would hold the least chance of a human encounter. Otherwise my route had everything: remote, rocky inlets, wild mountain scenery, then a compass bearing across one of the last great wildernesses. Much of the route was trackless, all of it new.

Fanned by moist, warm air from the Atlantic, the birchwoods straggling the southern shores of the loch were an ecologist's paradise: an exotic collection of ferns, dwarf shrubs, moss, frills of fungi, large boulders painted in all manner of lichen. Picking a line through this jungle was a nightmare. I rounded the peninsula and clambered to a high point. A few brief minutes of milky sunshine, then cloud like a grey sheet was slowly drawn up from the south, veiling the sun and bringing spots of drizzle. The atmosphere darkened noticeably. Below, Loch Glencoul, with its high, vertiginous sides and overshadowed by brooding mountains, resembled more a Norwegian fjord than a Scottish sea-loch.

I dropped to the water's edge and approached a derelict-looking house. The old place had not seen a caring hand for many years. Inside, floorboards and plaster were missing from a warren of ground-floor rooms. Broken glass had been piled casually in corners, and I saw my reflection in a mirror through a film of soot. Once doubtless a grand lodge, lavishly furnished, where great fires raged all day to keep out the damp, now it was being consumed by the wilderness which pressed in on all sides. It emitted a heavy, oppressive air and propelled me on my way, up a fine path and into a thickening drizzle.

The path which had begun nowhere ended nowhere, tipping me into the middle of a quaking bogland. Ahead was an unnamed wilderness, a huge collecting basin for hundreds of square miles of rainfall. It is both a fortress and a trap. Defended on three sides by broken quartzite mountains and ribbon lakes, swollen rivers quickly cut off its southern exit. There is not the faintest echo of the outside world, and one's natural inclination is to hurry across the trackless miles to seek the line of a stalkers' path, not because it would ease movement, but because it is something human to grasp on to.

The mist now clung around me like a white shroud, compelling me to trust my compass implicitly. But it was simply not possible to adhere to any bearing and walk in anything like a straight line. Countless deep troughs of oozing peat, some with precipitous sides, threw me off on weary detours. Others lured me into their muddy depths where I sank to my knees, staggering and gasping up the far side. Many times I was back in the misty bogs of the High Rwenzori in Central Africa, where six miles a day is considered good progress, and I half expected the ice bowl of Mount Stanley or Speke to emerge through a cloud window. There was a scarcity of solid earth and no landmarks until I stumbled upon the black waters of Crom Loch Mòr, though occasionally a fleeting glimpse revealed a wider landscape, a weeping cliff or a vein of shiny quartz. Reaching the path which I knew to straddle the lower slopes of Ben More became the day's sole objective.

I found the path almost exactly where I had crossed it fifteen years ago. Barely out of school I had set off with a classmate on a five-week walking adventure, a journey I had been planning since the age of eight. At the end of a long day, so hot the tarmac on the road by Loch Shin was melting, we found ourselves in a nightmare of ditches and bog. Desperately tired and sunburnt we sought a place to camp, but vicious midges urged our exhausted limbs on and up to a giddy pitch high on Ben More Assynt. Here there was a cool breeze for scorched faces, icy spring-water for parched throats, and an unbelievable view across a mountain landscape lit up by the fire of sunset.

A protracted stop for a hot drink was a mistake, for, despite the subsequent miles of rough going, I never really managed to warm up properly again. Cold rain now came down heavily and I was dripping and very tired by the time darkness fell. Pitching even a simple tent always seems to take longer in the rain, and my damp clothes quickly became cold while I fumbled with knotted guy lines and dithered to place pegs. Inside, and now shivering quite uncontrollably, I stripped to pull on dry thermals, dived into my sleeping bag, all the while eating peanuts and chocolate. In thirty minutes I was overheating, but I knew all about hypothermia, how quickly it can strike, how innocent its early stages are. Today served up a timely warning.

It had stopped raining by morning. Everything dripped with condensation. I was perched on a tiny knoll in a sea of heather, the heather itself in a larger sea of mist which gathered itself into layers. Nothing broke the silence. I even packed quietly. The path led past ranks of conifers and became a track. Ahead were the buildings of Benmore Lodge, but there was no human shadow or barking dog. Just blue smoke pluming from a chimney.

Continuing south the track ended abruptly among thick forestry. While the map indicated a path 400 metres due south, which would take me down to Glen Oykel, there was the small matter of dense ranks of Sitka Spruce to contend with. After a couple of false openings I wove through a hopeful gap, but this grew narrower and tighter, forcing me to lurch lower and lower until I was practically crawling, being raked all the while by wet branches. And this was how I emerged finally into daylight, a sodden thing covered in needles, crawling and cursing, stumbling towards the river to douse my head, yelling invective.

A midday sun burned through the mist painting Strath Oykel an emerald green, the river meandering across its flood-plain a crane-neck of silver. My haste was prompted by my appetite. With the promise of my first food cache at Oykel Bridge, I found myself salivating at the thought of the rather ordinary tins of fruit I knew to be stashed there. Just beyond the Ullapool–Bonar Bridge road I scaled a high forestry fence, rummaged among some small boulders and unearthed a white polythene sack. I delved into the contents like a child on his birthday, and ate till bursting. I moved on for Glen Einig. A fine clear afternoon had developed, the Ben More Assynt range diminishing behind me, now sunlit and shrugging off a beret of cloud. To the east a mist bank was edged in sunset pink, while straight ahead were acres of swelling moorland and the promise of high mountains beyond.

A clear night had allowed the temperature to plummet, and an early glance outside revealed the moorland dusted with frost. From my camp on a grassy shoulder overlooking Strath Mulzie, I could see blue, snowless mountains, in particular the far-flung Munro of Seana Bhraigh and her pointed neighbour Creag an Duine. This morning I felt slightly troubled. After four days of hard going my right knee—my bad knee—now complained with a dull ache. For years I had lived with a knee which swelled painfully after a game of football but nevertheless had always seemed to manage a week's trekking. Whether it would cope with four or five months of punishment I could not tell—it had never been tested— but I reckoned the next few days would be crucial. Martin Moran's first attempt at the winter Munros was curtailed due to a damaged knee. During our Munro walk in 1986 we overcame many minor injuries: bruised muscles and tendons, overworked knees, strains, even a chipped bone in the ankle. For this journey, and accepting conventional wisdom, I armed myself with a single ski pole, and today limited my ambitions to six trackless miles, aiming for a lonely loch in the shadow of Seana Bhraigh.

On the footbridge over the River Einig I idled a few minutes, marvelling at some migrating salmon thrashing a tortuous path up-river. My day also, though short, was wearisome. Bored with private roads, I went cross-country. I passed the ruin of Upper Letters, contoured a small hill, then struggled over a boggy watershed before dropping to land gently by Loch a' Choire Mhoir. A similar location in an English National Park would attract thousands. Moorlands and mountains meet emphatically, the soft, heather-clad hills giving way abruptly to scree slopes, which climb to corries and green cliffs. The twin summits of Seana Bhraigh and Creag an Duine have a grandeur one normally only sees in the Greater Ranges.

Rising only 927 metres, Seana Bhraigh was not on my list of peaks to climb, yet that seemed a poor excuse to bypass one of my favourite hills. Seana Bhraigh has a paradoxical quality. Approach from the south and she appears as an insignificant blip at the edge of a high plateau. But today, coming from the north, I climbed a real mountain, pulling up a ridge for 600 metres which ringed a fine corrie. North-west was a heart-rending vista, a landscape from the imagination: the Coigach Hills, Stac Polly, Suilven and Canisp all seemingly strung in a row, floating on a sea of moorland like a line of tall ships.

The view shrank towards a misty summit where there had been a light dusting of snow. I moved swiftly, for the wind strengthened as it swung round to the west and now harried me the miles down to Gleann Beag. The bothy was a fine refuge. There was just time to search for wood among nearby peat hags, and I hauled back a pile of soaking roots so wet I could not imagine they would ever ignite and glow with a rekindling heat. But they did.

Six days out and my brain was still coming to terms with the scarcity of light. For much of the time it was like living in a dimly-lit cave. Days were noticeably growing shorter, some days seemed barely to get light at all, as if under the influence of a strange lunar shadow. Mornings struggled to brighten, and cloud cover meant twilight began soon after 2 p.m., any brightness then seeping from the afternoon like a door slowly being shut. It was completely dark by five, and from that time until past eight the following morning I lived by torch or candlelight in a flickering world of eerie shadows. And outside, during those early moonless nights, it was so dark I could not register even a hand in front of my face.

That night I was woken more than once by the rush of wind over the roof and the ceaseless drumming of rain. In the grey light of dawn I counted six new waterfalls on the crags opposite, tassels of white emerging from the thick cloud base. I could happily face the wetness, but when I was out collecting water and a gust nearly toppled me, I decided that Beinn Dearg, my first 1,000-metre peak, could wait.

The day was far from sedentary. Wet hours were spent foraging for wood which was then chopped and stacked. Every haul was rewarded with a scalding mug of tea which I drank dripping, face flushed, condensation steaming the window. And when I grew tired of wood-gathering I wandered up the valley for a mile or so, where every burn was muddy and angry, the River Beag transformed from the gentle flow I had splashed across yesterday to a wild and rabid thing.

The ever-shortening days posed the obvious problem of how to pass the long dark evenings. A spell of inactivity quickly fills the mind with all manner of anxieties: about the poor weather, a failing schedule, dwindling supplies. Paddy Buckley, writing in the Scottish Mountaineering Club Journal, vividly describes how on a twelve-day trek he went from bothy to bothy but encountered no one. To combat the deepening solitude he would whistle grand classical concertos, or sing and dance his way through a hundred English Morris tunes.

Of course in a bothy the problem is halved. I would invest much time in the delicate art of nurturing and feeding a good fire, an activity which was fast becoming an all-consuming obsession. While by day the bothy interior appeared grubby and drab, at night it was magically transformed by a fire and candlelight into a medieval palace, the flames throwing a warm glow onto the panelled walls, occasionally blazing up like a flare to illuminate the whole room. And I would gaze at it transfixed, as Silas Marner would at his gold. That night, despite not climbing any mountains nor seeing another soul, it was a well-fed and contented gangrel that blew out the candles and was put to sleep by the arpeggio of rain across the roof.

My tiny altimeter showed a rise in pressure, which explained the general absence of noise: the rain no longer clattering, the wind having moderated, and the elements mostly quieter. After breakfasting by candlelight, I meticulously packed a day sack: spare thermals, fleece, bivvy bag, a day's food plus emergency supplies, camera, knife, map, compass, altimeter, headtorch, ice axe; enough to survive the cruellest night. It weighed about eight kilos.

Approaching from the east there is no recognised route up Beinn Dearg, certainly no path. It is a stiff pull to a gently sloping watershed pitted with ditches, a tricky contour past two lochans, then a steep climb into the clouds. After the floods of yesterday there were fleeting patches of blue sky, and, for a few precious moments, a spray of sunshine on waves of empty moorland, wine-red to myriad shades of brown. Grey outcrops above glistened with green slime and run-off; and there was a hint of overnight snow on the tops. A herd of red deer watched my movements then danced away across sunlit puddles. I nearly trod on a mountain hare high on Dearg's northerly slopes, its white coat flashing between dark boulders. The final hundred metres was a struggle up slippery wet snow, inches deep.

From 1,084 metres on a clear day there is a vast panorama: the Sutherland peaks to the north diminish, while Ben Wyvis, the Fannichs and An Teallach are the hills of tomorrow. A good eye would identify the Cairngorms over 60 miles to the south, a range I might reach by February. But today the mist and snow made this an anonymous spot, indistinguishable from a hundred summits. Somehow it seemed an appropriate place to start my mountain days. My first peak also represented a psychological hurdle and, in buoyant mood, I retraced my steps, the terrain now easy to cross, the peat ditches no longer any effort. Chased the final mile by an icy shower, I arrived back dripping and exhausted.

As always, once I had stopped moving a chilly dampness took hold and I became convulsed in shivering fits. To keep warm I went out again, this time to drag a huge slime-covered trunk from the bog, hands numb in the wind, my expensive jacket smeared in glutinous peat. But I cared not. Very soon there would be a fire, dry clothes, a steaming brew. Nothing else mattered.

About to pull the door shut I instinctively cast about, half expecting a figure to appear, a hooded walker lumbering up the valley perhaps, or someone dropping from the flank behind. But nobody came and I spent my eighth day alone. This solitude, being a strange and novel experience, had at first fuelled minor worries and intensified doubts, but as each day passed and no one appeared I grew more settled. I could thrive in this harsh environment, knowing that however cold, wet or hungry I became, I would soon be warm, dry and satiated. My previous life of modernity had fallen away, reduced by a primitive need to survive. The outside world was not merely irrelevant, it no longer existed, all my energies now being focused on the basic essentials of survival. And increasingly these became intoxicating pleasures—when tired, how much more inviting was rest, when hungry, how much more palatable the food. Later the cloud tore itself into holes, and the light of the moon came flooding through the small window like a great beam from space.

The River Beag drains easterly, first swelling to become the River Carron then spilling its waters gently into the North Sea. Scotland so narrows at this point that it is possible to walk from coast to coast on a long summers' day, a trek of about thirty miles. Half that distance separated me from the Aultguish Inn, and the luxurious prospect of bed, baths, cooked meals and conversation. My original plan to traverse fifteen miles of moorland to Ben Wyvis had long since disintegrated in the face of continuing poor weather and my remaining paltry supplies.

A short way down the glen is a large, prominent boulder, an erratic left by a melting glacier. Seven years ago this boulder probably saved my life. I had walked in alone, hauling a week's food over the thirteen miles, and while bus times had dictated a late start, it had been a benign winter's day, the hills resplendent and sun-dappled. With little warning it started to snow, lightly at first, but a strong headwind sprang from nowhere, blowing clouds of flakes into my face. Having no tent I went on for the bothy. The track ended, darkness fell, and I was soon reeling in deep drifts. Now a full blizzard was raging, and as happens in a blizzard, I grew disorientated and fearful. After an hour of struggle I began to hallucinate, seeing strange images, hearing shrill voices that bellowed and pleaded, and I caught myself shouting back. Was this, I wondered, my life flashing before me? By chance, to my right across the river, I had seen the vaguest outline of a boulder, and in ten minutes had made a secure bivvy in its shelter, the snow whistling past. With no tent and in such conditions I have often wondered whether I would have survived a night in the open. I fancy not.

This morning the weather was merely unpleasant. Spears of rain and a cold gusty wind conspired in an attempt to make the hours to the Aultguish devoid of enjoyment. During the fiercest showers and for what seemed an age I moved with my hood bound tight, head down, a cold dampness already on my back, neck and shoulders, and my mind wandering to faraway places and dwelling on unrelated thoughts. And in between showers, when mountain slopes could clearly be seen, I was moved by the hues of brown, red and green which contrasted and blended into a multitude of exquisite shades, like an Appalachian Fall.

After days of wilderness Lower Gleann Beag was a rude reminder of the ravages of man. Though doubtless for sound economic reasons, the hand of the Hydro Board was everywhere: damming rivers, bulldozing roads, constructing weirs and ugly pipelines. They had been untidy too, as strewn beside the track were slabs of concrete and a jumble of rusting iron.

The glen continued east; I swung south, round the long shoulder of Meall a' Chaorainn, over a small watershed and into open, exposed country. Just beyond the large dam at Loch Vaich and a mile and a half from the main road, a white Toyota van slowed to a halt. With rain pinging off the roof, a bearded, middle-aged gentleman leaned half-out of the window.

'You'll be wanting a lift to the road head?'

'No thanks, I'm walking.' I grinned at him.

'Aye, I can see you're walking. But are you wanting a lift?'

'No thanks.'

For a moment he stared at me, saying nothing, then pushed the gear lever and sped away.

§   §   §

Like a scene from a movie, a stranger enters the bar and the room is suddenly quiet as a core of locals turn and stare. They keep staring. Only the television is speaking, blaring away inanely. Later, having been shown to a room, I could fully appreciate their overreaction. My mirror reflected an ill-shaven face partly obscured by a tangle of windblown hair. But more disturbing was my complexion, for somehow I had managed to smear my face with charcoal, or soot, so that my appearance was made stranger still.

Aultguish was home for two nights; the day in-between I dealt with some unfinished business a little to the south. I climbed Ben Wyvis and drew a line under this first section. Ben Wyvis can clearly be seen from the streets of Inverness where she appears as a slumbering giant, by far the highest peak visible from any large British town. Four miles of main road took me past Inchbae Lodge and up through a fire-break in a prosaic ring of conifers. A strong, southerly wind gave a considerable wind chill, hounding my approach to the summit ridge; but the dreadful forecast failed to materialise. Fine views north suggested my original planned route across a heathery wilderness looked child's play, poor exchange for the miles of tarmac and screaming vehicles. Roadwalking has little to commend it:

the litter-covered verges, noise and fumes only reminding me of the busy commercial world I had left behind. Careful planning fortunately made this the only stretch of main road I was to follow in four months.

§   §   §

The taps gushed with a murky brown liquid, filling the bath with water you might normally find in a peaty lochan. I went to see the landlady.

'It has therapeutic qualities,' she assured me, 'they use it on health farms. Great for aches and pains.'

And indeed it was.

2

First Storm

IT WAS the middle of November, and for a mind incurably tied to an annual pattern of events—terms, exams, holidays—this time of year always meant a visit to Dovedale in the Peak District National Park. For a hundred or so adolescents it was their first experience of real countryside. They came from the grimy heart of a Midlands conurbation, that well-known area between the city centre and inner ring road, where derelict factories and poor housing exist cheek-by-jowl with superstores and incinerators, and where dual carriageways rumble all night. And now, suddenly, a land of limestone towers—like minarets they seem—of arches and caves so high in the rock face they must have been chiselled out by an ancient race of giants. Here was something different, as much a culture-shock for these youngsters as a visit to a far planet. For staff as well, this honey-pot limestone gorge always seemed the highlight of the autumn calendar.

Janion, a pretty South African waitress, served up breakfast, and I did not dwell too much on where else I might have been that morning. The only guest in the dining room, my eyes wandered across the road to where ash-grey moorland piled up. This was in fact the tail-end of a mountain region whose names had been with me since childhood: Fannichs, Fisherfield, Slioch, An Teallach, 'Whitbread Wilderness'; all places I had heard and dreamt of a decade before ever seeing them for myself. By now they seemed to have all the old familiarity of friends long-known.

Even by Highland standards the region is remote. A straight-line journey from the Aultguish west towards the sea might cover forty or so miles before crossing a metalled road or chancing upon habitation. Fortunately I had many times undertaken long, meandering treks across this mountain wilderness and felt I knew the area reasonably well.

The weather remained changeable. Last night's forecast ominously showed a huge area of low pressure brewing in the west. Troughs and fronts would soon be queuing up to charge in from the Atlantic, and while I intended climbing only half a dozen peaks, I realised it might be a week before I made Kinlochewe.

Leaving the hotel I was saddened to discover that a new conifer plantation

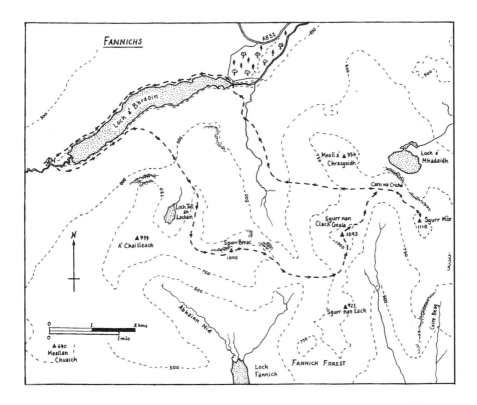

will soon smother the rolling inclines and stream courses of the moorland fringing the road. Its boundary fence pointed me more or less in my intended direction, eastwards up a burn, through a narrow col between low hills, across a peaty bogland, then finally to the Fannich Lodge track where I unearthed a food cache. Arrival in the Fannichs from the east is always announced by the operatic presence of An Coileachan, in particular her towering Garbh Choire Mòr, 'Big Rough Corrie', now brilliantly spotlit by a low sun against a wall of dark cloud. In an hour the sun became haloed. I expected a downpour, and soon got it.

The rain, when it fell, came with a monsoon-like intensity, quickly finding ways through my Gore-Tex armoury, streaming down my face, seeping inside my cuffs. Fannich Lodge—I knew from past visits—was only four miles from a place where I might stop for the night, by a ruined cottage. But, as ever, memory had shortened those last miles. I had forgotten the twists and turns, the sudden inclines, how the track climbs frustratingly into the dark of an old plantation when reason suggests it should be following the lochside. Emerging into the open again my spirits soared: the sky suddenly cleared, the rain became a spray of silver drops. Warm light the colour of hay bathed the hills; pine needles on the trees glittered like glass, and Slioch sprouted through a gap in the hills freshly rinsed and hung out to dry.

Expectantly I rounded the final bend. A roofless burnt-out shell of a house came into view. Grass and moss had got a foothold around the old fireplace, tiny roots loosening the cement and adding, along with the weather, to the relentless attrition of the standing walls. In another decade they will have likely collapsed. Just then, in the ebbing light, it was impossible to associate this ruin with my first and finest recollection of these mountains.

Perhaps because they always seem fresh and vibrant, youthful impressions tend to be the most enduring. A few days before Hogmanay two of us had come this way on our very first winter foray. Train times and hours of daylight had not been in harmony, and we found ourselves walking into darkness, harried the last few miles by bruising snow showers. We caught the resinous woodsmoke hours before a house took shape from the night. As we approached the porch, boisterous voices and a sudden outburst of manic laughter came from inside. In the gloomy, smoke-choked room our eyes watered painfully as we squinted to see the source of all the commotion. A small, animated group was huddled around the fire. The great bearded one feeding the flames with a monster log turned and grinned, 'Welcome to the Nest of Fannich'.

Subsequent days I remember as much for the manifold characters, their stories and songs which filled the long evenings and—for us—opened up new worlds, as for the gales and blizzards which continually lashed the hills outside. One night some years later we had come over the pass from the north and, in disbelief, found a scene of devastation: the Nest had been gutted by fire. It felt as though an old friend had died. I nearly wept.

With the demise of the Nest, the west end of Loch Fannich had become an even lonelier place. I'd not been back in eight years. Close by was an outhouse, probably a stable for estate ponies, and although doorless, it provided adequate shelter. I fashioned a window with a piece of plastic and threw straw into the corner. Later, when I was snug inside my sleeping bag with a scalding mug of tea, there was a modicum of cheerfulness about the place.

A southerly gale sprang up in the early hours, and from then on the booming of the wind allowed only for a fitful sleep. By morning it had churned the surface of Loch Fannich into a mass of white streaks, while inside, eddies of wind left straw and dust on my breakfast things. With the high summits effectively stormbound, the Fannichs would have to wait. I might have stayed put, climbing my mountains from this base tomorrow, but the dung-covered floor and general grubbiness was incentive enough to push northwards, seven miles over an exposed bealach, to seek the shepherd's cottage beyond Loch a' Bhraoin.

It was a wild and exciting crossing. Violent gusts threatened to topple me at the height of the pass and confirmed my wisdom in staying off the tops. The cottage was a fine refuge. No sooner had I settled with a brew when outside came the grinding of a low-geared vehicle, growing ever louder until it drew up outside the front door.

Through the window I saw two men in combat-style clothing with blood on their jackets. The blood was from three or four freshly killed hinds which lay slumped on the back of the all-terrain Argocat. Despite appearances they had a friendly, genial manner, expressing surprise at finding a walker out in such conditions. The older one said the estate would be closing the cottage due to continued vandalism, muttering something about 'Duke of Edinburgh louts'. I was suddenly aware of the graffiti on the back wall, much of it innocuous, but there were also obscene drawings of the kind you might find in a public lavatory. Some wood panelling had been ripped out, probably for firewood. To be fair, the lodging had been badly neglected by its estate owners. The wooden mantelpiece around the fireplace, held to the wall by a length of string, was about to collapse, while the front door was only just secured by some folded wire. The men gone, I rolled a stone to make it fast.

Some birch wood I had collected by the loch shore gave an excellent fire. Outside, the wind was as fierce as ever: great sobbing gusts that hammered at the door like an angry mob, knocking grit down the chimney and even threatening to put in the windows.

Next day the wind appeared to have moderated a little, but this perception later proved to be entirely wrong. It was on this morning that I realised fully the stark challenge of the coming months. Any other trip and I would have stayed low, perhaps crept along the glen to the next bothy, or remained here in this one, head buried in a good book, happily oblivious to the hostile world outside. But I had run out of options. There were neither supplies nor time left to delay an assault.

From the south shore of Loch a' Bhraoin I struck up for the long sweeping spur which would lead me to my first top, Sgurr Bhreac. Clouds were streaming across the summits like snow plumes. By creeping up the lee side of the crest it was just possible to avoid the worst gusts. However protection ran out at the tiny col a little below the summit where, as always, the most extreme gusts are found. The wind raged through the gap unchecked, freezing me rigid, knocking me momentarily to my knees. Picking myself up I clambered a few metres over some wet rocks to a small cairn, shaken and troubled by the violence of it all.

In my desperation to descend I blundered down the wrong ridge, heading north instead of east. A dangerous traverse through craggy terrain rectified the error, and in less than an hour I was at the pass I had crossed the day before. Despite a number of visits I had forgotten the scale of these mountains. On a calm, sunny day they can be daunting, but now, in the midst of a storm, they appeared gigantic and menacing, surely beyond my feeble grasp.

There was nothing in the least pleasurable about my hours on that high crest, nothing remotely sublime. It was sheer struggle; my tenure on the ridge was like a thin thread which might snap at any moment. All day I was tossed hither and thither, banged about like a piece of flotsam while a continual racket filled my ears, leaving me reeling and dizzy. The torment was always whether I should continue, struggling on and up to the next peak, when common sense dictated an immediate retreat.

Conscious of how slow my progress was I tried to set deadlines for each new landmark: thirty minutes to the next col, ten to the crest, another ten to the summit. Sgurr nan Clach Geala was reached in about fifty minutes from the pass but the wind on this occasion had helped, giving sails to my legs and pushing me forward. This peak is probably the finest of the Fannich range, its buttressed east face a winter playground for the solitude-seeking climber, the mountain a long way from anywhere.

Sgurr Mòr, at 1,110m one of the highest tops of the North West Highlands, was still unclimbed. I dropped below the mist and had a glimpse of her aquiline profile rising about a mile to the east. Once again violent eddies compressed by two peaks, swept across the col, and again progress was possible only by keeping to the lee of the ridge. I skirted beneath a minor top, then, with time slipping away, struck up for the main summit. But the ridge was steep, and, exposed to the full force of the storm, progress along it was dangerous, if not impossible. A little contouring found me some shelter, but here the increased steepness meant it became a tricky scramble up greasy rakes, the ground falling away at my feet to boulder fields and scree. At last the angle eased and a cairn appeared. It was too risky to walk the final metres so I sank to my knees and crawled.

As if to share a little of my relief, the clouds lifted a touch. I could see green fields beside Loch Broom, pools of rusty light and the distant blue mountains of Sutherland. It would be dark in an hour. The wind still rapped my back in frenzied gusts and there were still many rough miles to cover; but I was brimful of satisfaction at having salvaged a day from such foul conditions. I had battled and slain, my quarry the three peaks I had climbed. I free wheeled to Loch a' Bhraoin like a buccaneer.

In the morning I took stock: worn holes in the heels of my socks, a large tear in my gaiters. Somehow I had managed to break my compass and leave my headtorch on, so now I was without light to walk by. And it was the third day of gale-force winds.

Leaving the cottage I went west and entered the heart of this wilderness. Fixing my tent in the shelter of a small knoll, I clambered up steep slopes to reach Mullach Coire Mhic Fhearchair (1,019m) via the narrow and giddy east ridge, a delight were it not for the wind. A sunless view unfurled to the south and west, across the wastes of Kinlochewe and Letterewe forests, beyond the breast of Slioch to the quartzite architecture of Torridon. For all the multitude of square miles in view I could see not the slightest human mark, not a road or house, nor a man-made track. This peak is often climbed with its neighbouring Munros of Beinn Tarsuinn, Sgurr Ban and Beinn a' Chlaidheimh, but with limbs weary from yesterday I was glad none of these reached my arbitrary threshold of a thousand metres.

Once down, and with my tent hastily packed away, I swung northwards past the troubled waters of Loch an Nid, seeking my night's rest at Shenavall bothy, still four miles away. The gusts gave little respite but at least they bellowed in from the south, lunging at me from behind like an impatient crowd. During one particularly violent blast, birch trees shook with a frenzy, heather and grassland rippled, the roar rising in pitch until I felt the world was about to be engulfed in a fit of hysterics. The earth seemed afflicted with a kind of madness.

Light was fast draining from the day when ahead there appeared a gleam at the lonely house of Achneigie. I had expected the place to be locked and abandoned. Passing the front door I hesitated, unsure whether to investigate. Tingling with anticipation, I shuffled into a short, pitch-black hallway, then fumbled with the handle of the inside door. I entered a dimly-lit room.

A stocky, middle-aged man was slumped on the floor, spooning a meal by the glow from a single candle. His gear was strewn haphazardly around him. My voice, so little used, spluttered and choked like an old engine, but it betrayed a genuine enthusiasm for meeting someone who shared the same obsessions. It was my first exchange with a fellow hill-goer since leaving Sandwood Bay fourteen days ago, and so used by now was I to my own solitude, I had almost forgotten such people existed. He had first walked through this area thirty years ago, and lamented generally about how crowded the hills had become.

The novelty of my first meeting held me chatting when, torchless, I should have been using the last glimmers of twilight to locate Shenavall. Though broad and well used, in the gloom the path was barely discernible and hard to follow. Many times I tripped and nearly stumbled, and with no detail for the mind to latch onto, perceptions of both space and time became strangely distorted: the murky profile of An Teallach—perhaps a mile away—seemed touching distance; a few minutes passed as a good half-hour. Another featureless outcrop loomed and I appeared to walk straight into it; but where was Shenavall? I stumbled blindly over open ground to my right, crossed yet more burns, squelched through a bog and, like a drunk, became entangled with a rowan bush. I cried out as my boots found unyielding boulders. The bothy appeared as the faintest outline against the immense blackness of An Teallach.

Shenavall I found to be a noisy, troubled place that night, the wind moaning across the roof and creeping in beneath doors which groaned on rusty hinges. One door, having no latch, slammed incessantly until I jammed it with a boulder and glued it fast to its frame. A couple of rodents, excited at the new arrival, scratched across wooden floors, adding to the cacophony of disturbing sounds.

Another wild day followed and banished all thoughts of negotiating the An Teallach ridges. Instead I busied myself foraging for wood and exploring the vicinity. Shenavall and its environs is not a place one easily forgets. Situated in the heart of the hills, juxtaposed between broad tree-studded straths and wild, looming mountains, it conveys the impression of an untouched wilderness and a rather exaggerated sense of isolation. To gaze south, across the boggy trough and past the sad ruin of Larachantivore, is to feast your eyes on something exquisite: the grey-stained Beinn Dearg Mòr and Beinn a' Chlaidheimh; and in-between, the green strath of Gleann na Muice which narrows until swallowed by a cluster of Munro peaks. Their lower slopes I would need to breach when moving south in a couple of days.

For much of the century just past the land had almost been forgotten. The owner, Colonel Whitbread, while discouraging visitors, also fought off mineral development and afforestation. Even the Ordnance Survey only completed their work here in the 1970s, the new maps elevating a number of peaks to Munro status. Tom Weir in *Highland Days*, written just after the war, describes how he befriended the family at Carnmore, perhaps then the remotest occupied house in the country. Today there are no permanent dwellings and the region is as empty now as it must have been in prehistory.

I explored eastwards along Strath na Sealga and reconnoitred the route south. Sadly much of the birch and alder woodland here is moribund, overgrazed by deer and domestic animals. It had been another sunless day, save for a distant hill glowing a brilliant yellow for a few minutes, followed by a strange, lingering twilight.

After I had put a match to the kindling, a beam from a headtorch came through the window. A kerfuffle ensued at the door—which I had barricaded—as someone forced away the boulder. The bearded face of Geoff Cohen appeared in the candlelight. Geoff, a seasoned mountaineer, was fine company, and that evening in our quiet conversation we seemed to visit most of the world's ranges, from the Andes and Rockies to the Karakoram and Indian Himalayas.

An Teallach is the magnet that pulls most here, and when seen from a Fannich peak there is perhaps no mountain to compare with it in Britain. Growing from a sea of plain moorland, it becomes a multi-ridged massif the shape of a three-pronged fork, one ridge weathered into fantastic pinnacles. It is mesmerising, and I prayed for just one fair day.

Five days after leaving Aultguish the winds finally blew themselves to sleep. My prayers answered, I had a day of unalloyed magic. While Geoff made off for Beinn Dearg Mòr I climbed with ease into morning sunshine, gaining the main ridge a little east of the infamous 'bad step' or Corrag Bhuidhe Buttress.

Not being a reader of guidebooks I was suddenly confronted by this near-vertical drop during my first traverse with a school friend one sultry August day many years before. Mindful that a slip here would surely send us hurtling towards the corrie lochan 400 metres below, we first lowered our heavy sacks down, then managed a painstakingly slow and nerve-jangling descent.

Today it was easier going up. The ridge narrows to weathered sandstone blocks, some building to weird pinnacles, others holding an almost level walkway. To avoid the rock pitches I teetered along ledges, seeking a high, safe line as close to the true crest as was feasible for a non-climber. There are many ways over An Teallach, all good. From the dizzy overhang of Lord Berkeley's Seat it was a simple scramble to Sgurr Fiona (1,059m). A bright sun dazzled me but, tempered by an easterly breeze, gave precious little warmth. Westwards the Summer Isles basked in a languid sea, then across a blue expanse appeared the distant purple of the Isle of Lewis and Outer Hebrides. From north to east recognisable peaks interrupted the horizon, from the grey-etched hills of Assynt to the shapely Beinn Dearg group where I had stood a week before.

The difficulties all now behind, I romped over my second summit, Bidein a' Ghlas Thuill, in an easy-going mood. Then I managed to fall. It was the easiest thing, a lapse of concentration, my boot on a loose stone, and I spun out of control, tumbling a few metres and landing painfully on my right side, ski pole clattering down a good deal further. There was no damage beyond a little bruising but I was a quite shaken and needed some minutes to gather myself.

A slip in perfect conditions seemed a salutary warning and I proceeded with greater caution. A jarring descent over hard-set scree led past the still waters of Loch Toll an Lochain and back to Shenavall, now dark and empty once again.

The spell of settled weather persisted, and stealing across the mile wide of wetness to Gleann na Muice with morning light on the surrounding mountains was undiluted joy. Absolute stillness and perfect quietness reigned, save for the slide of boots over dewy grass and the rhythmical click-click of my pole. A lapwing skimmed along, some browsing deer seemed unconcerned at my passing. It was impossible to walk for long without gazing back at An Teallach, every minute the light on her sandstone ridge turning a deeper shade of pink. For some hours I seemed to follow a meandering burn on the faintest of paths, across gravelly terraces and alluvial banks of thyme and sage, always in chilly shadow, while above, and casting down, were sunlit flanks and yellow screes. South to Kinlochewe is one of the finest cross-country treks I know, eight hours of mostly trackless going, unspoilt and as beautiful as you could wish for.

Pulling up to the 500-metre watershed, a low sun, now at its zenith, and so bright that at times I staggered along blindly, forced my gaze downwards. This was a day of unbroken sunshine, as if the Creator had yet to fashion clouds. Four strenuous miles of bog and boulders took me round the east end of Lochan Fada and into the gorge of Gleann Bianasdail, then a fine path for the miles to Kinlochewe.

Slioch reared to my right, another of the spectacular mountains in Wester Ross, and once the scene of an extraordinary story of survival. One February a few years ago a friend of mine left his car in Kinlochewe and set off alone to climb Slioch. Unseasonal mild weather had stripped away much of the snow, and the forecast was good. On the summit, however, while leaping about to keep warm he slipped on loose rocks, fell awkwardly and sprained an ankle.

Unable to walk and in intense pain, he half-shambled, half-crawled to seek shelter in a hollow a few metres away. He settled for the night wrapped in a plastic bivvy sack. The night passed, and all the next day he waited for the sounds of help: the thud of a chopper, shouts from a search team, a walker who could raise the alarm. A second night passed, another day came and went, but there was no rescue. At home in Lancashire, no one reported his absence, and six miles away, in Kinlochewe, his abandoned car aroused little curiosity. (Who, at any rate, leaves notes beneath windscreens during these days of car crime?)

All his food gone, he struggled to keep warm. Incredibly, the weather stayed mild, but when on the fifth morning, and in a weakened state, he was woken by an icy wind and falling snow, he left everything and began inching painfully down the mountain. By rolling, crawling, and hobbling he somehow managed the descent to the lochside as darkness fell. It had taken seven hours. Next morning, starved, exhausted and frostbitten, he crawled the final two miles towards Kinlochewe, slipping in and out of consciousness, and was discovered that evening by a farmer a few hundred metres from the village. He was flown immediately to Inverness and made a remarkable initial recovery, but would eventually suffer grievously with amputations of his frostbitten toes and the long weeks of convalescence.

It was impossible to imagine those agonising hours as I trundled the same miles along the riverside in the glow of sunset, brushing past alder groves and last summer's bracken, in as buoyant and happy a mood as I could remember.

Kinlochewe is more a hamlet than a village, a huddle of buildings around a junction where the Inverness road meets the one from Strathcarron. Little traffic comes this way in winter, and perhaps a dozen people in all were crowded into the hotel bar—'crowded' because that is what it appeared to me after the empty mountain lands. A fish farmer over from Torridon, Dundee medical students, a couple from 'down south', the affable staff, we all seemed to know each other by last orders, generating much noise, as if to challenge the empty silence of the surrounding hills. Outside, a sharp frost already whitened the tarmac, and beyond the mountain silhouettes a million bright eyes stared down impassively.

The Torridonian giants of Beinn Eighe and Liathach could doubtless easily be climbed from the road, but in the spirit of the journey I disappeared into another trackless wilderness; I would tackle these peaks from the post-glacial lands to the north. It is merciless terrain. After leaving the fine path through the Beinn Eighe Nature Reserve progress and rhythm were frustrated by all manner of protruding things: sinewy heather like bed springs, erratics, boulder-fields, a succession of moraines, loosely winding burns, all needing hours of patience and concentration. Ice lingered on rock pools, and all day an east wind spoke of the coming winter.

From my tortuous approach Beinn Eighe appeared a loosely clenched fist with knuckles of white quartz and fingers of sandstone. A palm cradled the perfect mountain amphitheatre of Loch Coire Mhic Fhearchair which, I hoped, would offer a wild and idyllic camp. Like a roaming spotlight, a shaft of afternoon sun played down the acres of scree, then high again on a sandstone buttress. Another hour and I set about securing my pitch in a freezing wind which filled the flysheet like a spinnaker. From my eyrie, which I feathered with a down bag, I could survey contentedly the lochan-studded miles I had travelled, then, westwards, the wastes of Flowerdale and Shieldaig forests where few ever venture. Tomorrow I could look forward to a little support: Paul Winters and Andy Smithson up from Lancashire. And tomorrow was also my birthday.

By dawn the wind had eased. Ruadh-stac Mòr (1,010m), the highest point on Beinn Eighe, is the finger which extends out from the main ridge. A small path twists through glacial rubble around the lochan, over brick-red sandstone with skins of jade-green moss, then up a gully of loose scree. In around 50 minutes I was up on the iron-frozen summit. Ruadh-stac Mòr would normally have sufficed as a day's outing in late November but the calm conditions gave an opportunity to pick off the eastern end of Liathach, the jewel of Torridon.

Early photographic images of Liathach must have stirred the Victorian imagination, and almost every first-time visitor since will have seen her somewhere before, on a calendar, book cover, or greeting card. Viewed rising from Loch Clair on the Kinlochewe road, she is one of the most familiar sights of scenic Britain. It is a good thing, perhaps, that An Teallach is a safe 20 miles to the north as two mountains of such character could not flourish side by side.

The north-east ridge, broken by terraces and greasy ribs, gave a gripping scramble. Lichen of vibrant colours, turquoise-green and yellow ochre on grizzled blocks, and wildflowers—liverworts and starry saxifrage—invested the climb with interest. A final slope of angular scree and I stood on Spidean a' Choire Leith, Liathach's eastern Munro. Most, having toiled the thousand metres or so from sea-level, would now move cagily westwards, beginning one of the finest ridges on mainland Scotland. From here the crest splinters into pinnacles, the notorious Am Fasarinen, and is flanked by plunging drops. Certainly no place to be caught out in the dark.

I went down at speed, collected my pack and followed the excellent newly repaired path to the road. A pair of headlights emerged from the darkness. A car slowed and Paul Winters' grinning face appeared above an electric window. Andy was behind the wheel.

'Cawthorne! You're one sad nutter,' was the greeting I received in broad Lancashire from my old climbing friend. 'It could only be *you* out walking in the dark. Glad you never taught my kids. Get in.'

Rock music and hot air spilled out from the interior, and I suddenly felt very weary. Car travel never seemed more enticing.

'No thanks. Remember, it's strictly walking.'

We arranged to meet later at the nearby bar.

'Don't forget it's my birthday. You're buying.' I shouted as the car sped away.

I pitched on a thick bed of heather, so soft it rendered my sleeping mattress quite superfluous. Later, we celebrated in the rather low-key atmosphere of the Beinn Damph bar, the three of us making up half the clientele. The lively company and prospect of hot baths at Strathcarron on the morrow had provided an immense boost to morale.

On the Monday a gusty east wind brought gun-metal clouds and the threat of rain. Worse seemed in store. While Paul and Andy went off for Beinn Eighe, I headed up the western peak of Liathach, Mullach an Rathan, which was much like climbing a ladder, for it was punishingly steep. There were two main sections, the first through bands of sandstone, then finally up interminable scree, loose and gravelly, and into a biting wind which needed all my layers of clothing to repel. The summit was a narrow perch of quartz, a dramatic place on this day of shredding mist and snow flurries. My eleventh top closed the Torridon chapter, and I went down eager to pack and be on my way south to the magic lands of Monar, Mullardoch and Affric.

The right of way from Torridon to Strathcarron was a delight, and reminded one of just how fine a good path could be with its smooth surface and gentle gradients. It climbs from sea level to 500 metres with consummate ease. There is the satisfaction of completing a through-route, of linking two great valleys, and riding a line high among these unique landscapes. Maol Chean-dearg with her castellations and flowing screes is the unchallenged queen of this region, an omnipresence, her looming shape filling my horizon until I dropped from the col at a scorching pace and into the twilight of late afternoon.

Perhaps in the short distance from An Teallach to Maol Chean-dearg are all the components of a perfect mountainscape, as if these ancient rocks have been weathered across some vast timescale to a kind of ripeness. Paul Theroux, in *Kingdom by the Sea*, on seeing the Highland landscape for the first time, said: 'I stared at it and decided that it was ferocious rather than pretty, with a size and texture that was surprisingly unfinished.' But surely the opposite is true, that the Highlands have reached an apex of completion, and on so many days there is an elemental beauty so perfect that not a rock nor blade of grass seems to be misplaced.

3

Chasing Blue Shadows

IT IS ironic that in a nation so crowded is to be found one of the great blank spaces of Europe. Between Strathcarron and Glen Shiel is an area the size of the Lake District, 500 square miles, but as empty as the Scandinavian tundra. We are fortunate that it is still prime mountain wilderness, where bulldozed roads and commercial forestry have yet to proliferate. Perhaps for an eye not accustomed to such scenery there appears a certain savage monotony about the place, ridge piled upon ridge, peaks and naked crests choking almost every view. You might begin your exploration by nibbling at the edges—tackling the Five Sisters, or the Munro hills south of Achnashellach—as most do, or you can pack a week's grub and traverse the heartland in a myriad of ways, as I have always done. Then, after a few visits, there is a pattern and sense to things. Names can be applied: Monar, Affric, Lapaich, Mam Soul; and the raw data from maps and guidebooks become the components of real mountain days and the rich store of memories.

For me the area posed a huge logistical problem. For 170 mostly pathless miles, and twenty-three peaks, there would be no accommodation beyond a few spartan bothies, no phones, no public roads. In 1986 this region put us through the most gruelling test. Plagued by midges and poor weather, we had been delayed and were forced to ration our supplies. Finally, after ten days, we staggered out exhausted and half-starved. That was summer. Another time in February I became trapped in a remote bothy for the better part of a week, first pinned indoors by blizzards, then with floods and torrential rain cutting off escape routes, all my food gone and long overdue at work. Now, with December only a matter of a few days away, I had few illusions about the task ahead.

Mrs Levy, our garrulous host, considered the mountains which had been her backdrop for twenty years.

'Reckon there'll be snow by the end of the week.'

Paul was sceptical:

'How can you tell?'

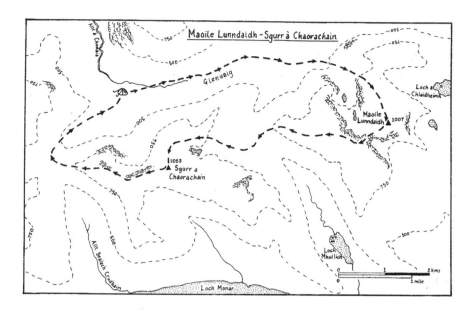

'Oh, just a feeling.' Mrs Levy frowned. 'It's been too mild. It can't last. *How* long did you say you would be out for?'

Of course, Mrs Levy did have a point. Winter was late, and when it finally did come, it would probably be like the arrival of that long overdue bus. Three or four or other buses would be right behind it.

We went east. Perhaps subconsciously I had slowed to accommodate my friends, but the path climbing from Strathcarron seemed like an escalator which conveyed you up in one effortless motion. The railway line, road and scattering of houses vanished, and ahead, from the narrow pass, was a melancholy view of wild, bare mountains with vaguely familiar names: Sgurr na Feartaig, Beinn Tharsuinn, Bidein a' Choire Sheasgaich. Now descending, we were met by a thin, chilly breeze and a sweep of sunshine transforming the grassland into burnished hay. Cloud shadows roamed the strath below. As with a trek in the Greater Ranges there was a sense of stealing into unknown lands, and we all felt the exhilaration that comes at the start of a journey.

A steady climb brought us to a 600-metre bealach where three tumbling ridges met. It was now much greyer and windier, the light being squeezed from the afternoon by a sinking blanket of cloud. We dropped a few quick miles and pitched our tents by the river in Glenuaig. Here there was a grassy terrace so smooth it might have been a manicured section of a St Andrews fairway. Mice had been at the food cache but the perishables were intact, and I reckoned there should be enough to see me through to Strathfarrar.

Next morning, leaving the tent, we moved up Glenuaig, past a shuttered lodge and to a broad watershed. Glenuaig is littered with dismal ruins and old drystone walls, reflecting a time when people and cattle, rather than sheep and deer, thrived here. An aura of sadness hangs over much of this region, a sense of dereliction, and on grey days one notices only the moss-covered shells of once busy communities and endless graveyards of forests. It requires an imaginative turn of mind to see this bogland—as it must have been until fairly recently—beautifully clothed in the bottle-green of Caledonian Pine.

Recent years have added to the degradation of this environment. I envy those who knew the land before the hydro-board tamed the valleys with their dams and weirs. Loch Mullardoch was once two separate lochs sitting comfortably in the lap of Glen Cannich. Now in its place is an oversized reservoir whose artificial shoreline is controlled by turbines, sluice gates and the fluctuating demand for electricity.

We went up the long, monotonous slopes of Maoile Lunndaidh. The day promised little beyond low cloud and a cold, fierce wind. At the summit, and some way ahead of the others, I crawled into my bivvy bag and waited. Maoile Lunndaidh, 'Bare Hill of the Boggy Place', has qualities not immediately apparent when one is huddled for warmth in the lee of its cairn. The graceful sweep of its summit plateau echoes that of a Cairngorm landscape; while its magnificent southern corrie, Toll a' Choin, is replete with a West Highland grandeur.

'You look like a fat, green slug.'

Paul appeared through the mist with Andy close behind. Both were bent and straining into the wind.

'Get a bearing and get us out of here. It's bloody freezing.'

We were fully exposed to the gale-force winds for another mile, navigating by compass across the plateau. Dropping below the cloud base we caught a sodden glimpse of Loch Monar. By this time Andy had had enough and retreated to the tents; Paul followed my hunched outline up the long northern spur of Sgurr a' Chaorachain. With no views, we stared as much at our own footfalls as we did ahead, and might have collided with three looming figures were it not for their dazzling multi-coloured jackets: fluorescent orange with yellow, bold greens and reds. In the usual manner of meetings on the hills our exchange was oddly abbreviated.

'Going for Chaorachain?' one asked.

'Yeah, not far is it?'

'Ten minutes. Great ridge.'

'You guys doing Lunndaidh?'

'Hoping to,' one said, scrutinising his watch.

'Good luck.'

These encounters always bring a degree of comfort to the insecure walker, for here was mutual confirmation that there were others, equally crazy, who considered this cold, windswept mountainside a good place to be just then. They were the first people I had met on the hills in three weeks.

From the summit at 1,052 metres the crest continued westwards along to Sgurr

Choinnich, another Munro. This was the finest walking of the day, a mile of narrow ridge where for once we forgot the cold and discomfort and focused on safe foot placements, delighting in the exposure of a misty highway a long way from anywhere. And when descending the broken ridge to just beneath the cloud base, the immensity of the landscape was suddenly revealed: great green flanks dropping to boulder fields, a river threading a white line far below, and scrolls of mist wrapped round a spur like swaddling.

The reward for being out all day in such poor conditions comes in the first blissful moments when you are back in your tent, the effort and movement finished with, the damp feet forgotten. And though you lie motionless, for an hour or so, blood is still pumped about your extremities with a frenzy so that your legs and feet buzz and tingle. Later, immobilised in the warmth of your sleeping bag, there is the hiss of a gas flame, the taste of a piece of chocolate saved for this moment, and, above all, an inexpressible sense of peace. Three mountains climbed, target achieved, and easy, lazy hours stretching out ahead: drinking tea, eating a huge meal, mulling over plans for tomorrow, reading by candlelight. Whenever I camped, week after week, these rituals hardly changed, and the sheer novelty of extracting such pleasure from simple necessities never waned.

One outstanding benefit of winter camping is the sentence of rest that long nights impose. I woke fully recovered, if not quite raring to go. I had the day marked down as relatively easy: fifteen miles mostly in the shelter of glens. My planned route took me round the bulk of Maoile Lunndaidh, south to Loch Monar, then on for Strathfarrar and a rendezvous with Paul and Andy tomorrow. Here a private road gives limited public access to this wild region.

Of course, the logical way through this area would be to travel east—or west—taking advantage of the great valleys that slice through the mountains. Any southbound walker always comes up against the grain of the land: high passes to breach, great freshwater lochs ten or more miles in length, to circumvent, and much of the walking is trackless and boggy.

Even tracks do not help sometimes. A lazy landowner had mechanically tried to widen the old stalkers' path to the bealach, presumably to allow the passage of an all-terrain vehicle, but had merely turned it into a muddy ditch. At the watershed I crossed into a different estate, the path now faint and little used. Where the trail meets the placid waters of Loch Monar, I gobbled down a bowl of soup—resembling pond weed but tasting delicious—then pushed on for Monar Lodge and into a thick bank of fog.

After hours with only the elemental whispers of nature for company there came the grinding of a van engine and spit of tyres on gravel. Some dogs, having picked up my scent, erupted into a commotion. I hoped they were securely tethered. The bedlam must have aroused those at the lodge because I thought I saw a figure peep from behind some curtains. In more than a fortnight this was the only inhabited dwelling I would pass. I camped a mile beyond the Monar dam.

Although not a pessimistic person, I had been troubled by a recurring dream of late: snow-laden winds shrieking down from the summits, drifts suffocating progress, rivers swollen to bursting, and I was alone, very small, crushed by the violence of it all. They were chilling, highly realistic scenarios, and, as with some dreams, when you wake, so vivid are their images that they blend in with your conscious thoughts. This morning I woke with a strange sense of foreboding, like a premonition. Whether this mood had been evoked by the continual grey days, had come from the remnants of some dream, or was the emergence of festering doubts about my crazy plans, I could not tell, but I felt it was linked with my general expectation of what was ahead in the coming months.

The overnight cloud which had prevented a frost now released a steady rain. A breeze stirred the trees in the woodland opposite. When Paul and Andy arrived I was still wrapped in my sleeping bag, and concluded it was harder to rouse one-self on a cold, damp morning when camping, than if emerging washed and well fed from a local bed and breakfast.

'Not ready? Good. That should give us a head start.' Paul, having popped his head into my vestibule, immediately withdrew at the rich and strange smell. His enthusiasm for this grey and wet day was unbounded. Having driven 600 miles to climb a few Munros he was going to enjoy himself irrespective of what the weather might deliver. With Andy he headed off for the Farrar peaks.

A fine path follows the gushing Allt Toll a' Mhuic, gorge-like in places and straddled by winter skeletons of birch. I moved fast as I did not want my friends hanging about in the cold half way up a mountain, and today also would likely be my last with company until Christmas. An hour brought me to a fine corrie lake but there was no sign of them, nor were there, as far as I could see, any fresh bootprints. Were they doing this round in reverse, I wondered? I climbed into the mist above the corrie. Another fifteen minutes and Paul's chirpy voice came down from above, guaranteeing company.

Conditions had deteriorated rapidly since we left the glen, and now as we broached the summit ridge, then moved onto our first peak, Sgurr Fhuar-thuill, a full gale brought in cold and stinging rain. Undeterred as we were, a stubborn, battling attitude was nevertheless needed. Cols were the worst. Here the topography compressed a gust into a shrieking funnel in which we fought to remain upright, and unlike the day on the Fannichs the wind today came with a wintry cold. Unprotected flesh, cheeks and fingers became numb; hands grew feeble until I thumped life back into them. While the air temperature was still above freezing, the wind chill made it many degrees below. A halt of more than a few minutes led to spasms of shivering, so we kept moving, working hard on the ascents and running down the easy crests.

In such vile conditions, cocooned by an outer shell pulled tight about your face, ears filled with the roar of the wind, eyes focused down on lumbering foot-falls, you simply blank out the external world and slip into a kind of numbness, as if in a dream. This is a kind of insanity you think, and you laugh at yourself because there must be a thousand reasons to be somewhere else. You laugh at your friends just behind, mad as well, because their crab-like actions are comic. Are they drunk? They appear as a couple of ghostly figures, aliens—green and faceless. They seem to be dodging bullets as in the closing scene of *Dad's Army*. It was in this dazed state, after our second summit, Sgurr a' Choire Ghlais, that we fled down the wrong ridge. For minutes it felt good; the wind was on our backs, we had sprouted wings and were flying. Andy continued this flight down to the road, but for myself and Paul it required forty minutes of steep and dangerous contouring to make amends and regain the true ridge, as once again we were pummelled remorselessly from front and side.

Reaching Carn nan Cobhar's bouldery summit, I crouched in the lee of some stones, rummaged in my sack for food and watched for the shape of Paul to appear. Strange, I thought, he was being trailed by a dog, a bedraggled red setter with ears like shrivelled fig leaves. The dog lolloped over, thoroughly fed up, and wistfully eyed my tin of mackerel. The dog's master, a tall sinewy gentleman of advanced years, emerged from the opposite direction.

He fired questions: 'Is this Carn nan Gobhar? How far to Sgurr Fhaur-thuill? How long did it take you?' Rain dripped from stubble on his chin and streamed down his cagoule, the type worn by old fishermen. He seemed tough and leathery, oblivious to the conditions. We were shocked to discover he intended climbing two further Munros. 'Bloody maniac,' Paul said as the man disappeared into the mist again, the dog meandering along after him.

This time trusting to compass and not our instincts, we located the steep south ridge, and from there it was a final slog over spongy moss to Sgurr na Ruaidhe. All day I had managed to stay warm despite the chilly dampness, but now I quivered a little with cold, and realised I was a long way from my tent on a quite foul Saturday afternoon. We jogged down into the expansive Corrie Mhuillidh, dropping below the cloud base and onto the private road. Andy's headlights appeared through the gloom. Paul dived into the warm interior with a shout of 'See you for Hogmanay'. The red tail lights vanished and once again I was alone.

The rain had all but ceased during the few miles back to the tent, and I even managed to dry out a little. Below, spidery trees were set against a still gleaming River Farrar which now held only a memory of light from the day. Our friend with the dog? At around six I saw a needle-point of light still far up on the Farrar ridge.

Some days are distilled magic, giving an experience far transcending the normal boundaries of expectation, and for a while, it seems, you exist in another realm. Such days come upon you quite suddenly and are unrelated to the general run of days, sandwiched, as they often are, between the usual blankets of cloud and wetness. And because of their transient nature, they cannot be fully grasped, for it would be like trying to hold onto a dream on waking; you jabber like a fool afterwards but the right words always elude your tongue. Even photographs dilute the memory. How sad to read of mountaineer Doug Scott, acknowledging he no longer remembers the view from the summit of Everest beyond the confines of the haunting blue transparency captured by his camera.

On a rare appearance the sun came filtering through the pines, warming the tent interior and dispelling the night chill. I had woken with the dreaded thought of another wild day, especially as I would now be heading over high mountains into the empty heart of this area. But I need not have worried. Crossing the Monar dam revealed a marvellous western prospect: hills of autumnal brown, their summits dusted white and mirrored in the tranquil loch waters, and overhead a sky peppered with pale blotches of cloud.

A couple of cars were parked where the hydro-board road finished and became a footpath—probably walkers, though I saw no one all day. Another hour, and I set up camp on a gravel river terrace by a confluence, a meagre patch of green sward in a desert of heather. I might have climbed my mountains and been down well before sunset, but lounged for a while reading, and set off with about three hours of daylight remaining.

Sgurr na Lapaich grew from sunlit pines and the wide sweep of Garbh-choire to a fine, pointed summit brushed with snow. The stalkers' path which had tackled the initial steepness with finely engineered inclines, now petered out when it found the corrie. Some bootprints led up Lapaich's west ridge but the summit was deserted. The air was supercooled and perfectly still, the ground hardening as a frost gripped.

From the summit, waves of hills rolled away in almost every direction, chalky-white crests receding to gloomy troughs. In a wide arc from west to south were ranks of unclimbed peaks all jostling for prominence. A sobering view. I knew these mountains well, but the low winter sun and snow had exaggerated their scale, and they appeared as monstrous upthrusts from an unknown land, out of bounds.

I should have moved on quickly for I needed An Riabhachan, but the light held me enthralled. The thinnest veil of mist drifted across the summit, filtering the sun so the shadows were now soft and luminous. And, by the second it seemed, the light was changing: intensifying, then weakening, as the sun slipped behind a cloud wisp. The thread of a burn became a rivulet of shiny steel, incandescent, and the northern hills, their corries and flanks and ridges, bruise-coloured in the final minutes before sunset.

Chasing the last shadows up An Riahbachan, I reclined by a large rime-encrusted cairn. The sun now gone, the mountains still clung tenaciously to the vestiges of brightness, unwilling to accept the coming night, and for a brief minute a strange phosphorescence prevailed, giving everything expressive outlines as if engraved on dark glass. In the weeks and months ahead I would never see a like display. Starlight saw me back to the tent. It was the last day of November.

'The silence roared in our ears; it was centuries of heaped up solitude,' was how polar traveller Carsten Borchgrevink reflected on a long winter trapped in the Antarctic. My world also was entirely without sound. During the night the temperature sank to uncomfortable depths, and for fifteen hours I locked myself in the warmest recesses of my thick, down bag. Condensation peeled off in thin, icy flakes when I touched the vestibule. With a detached air I considered my frozen boots and gaiters—carelessly left outside. I poked at the frosted socks which had the texture of canvas and, with a shudder, realised they were soon to be wrapped round my warm, dry feet.

Over breakfast came a familiar sound of something soft brushing the nylon, a faint rustling. I lay back and listened. The sound dispelled an entire catalogue of worries. The first snows of winter were coming down on the wings of a soft breeze, not driven by storms as I feared. It would disrupt the day's travel for sure, making the hours long and weary, but it carried no malevolence. In an hour it transfigured the landscape so the smallest detail became a thing of beauty; rough angular boulders were now softly moulded, streams muffled into silence; and it was cradled by the branches of rowans and suspended above ground by an endless canopy of heather.

Contouring the long, northern flank of An Riabhachan would be difficult on such terrain at the best of times, for the route is dissected by a labyrinth of ditches and crossed by burns. But today, as I fumbled with my compass in thick mist, the snow added a web of deception. It concealed deep troughs, the bogs and ice-covered stones, making minefields of boulders. Although the temperature remained below freezing, I was sweating profusely from the intense effort. There was no chance of any rhythm, just a careful placing of each muffled footfall, a patient, methodical progress westwards.

The peak of An Socach (1,069m) is essentially a continuation of the An Riabhachan ridge, and from where I stood it was a jaunt of some 600 metres. But it was still snowing heavily, and if I pitched my tent would I find it on my return? I dropped to a lower altitude, by which time it was too late for an ascent.

Overnight showers left about 20cm of level snow, which, by morning, was beginning to drift in a strengthening wind. Intermittent sunshine brightened the ascent, pools of white light streaked across the spacious Ling watershed, over iced lochans, up snowy flanks. The clouds stubbornly refused to leave the higher summits.

My map only hinted at the craggy, complex nature of An Socach's southeastern corrie. Through whirling snow I caught a glimpse of a cauldron of white-stained rock holding a tiny frozen lochan, and on this wintry day of spindrift and shifting cloud, a remoter, less frequented enclave of wilderness was hard to imagine. There was no question of romping down, much as I would have liked to after a grinding ascent, for the drifts covered a treachery of boulders. Far beyond the orbit of any habitation, a twisted ankle here was unthinkable, meaning miles to crawl to any-where, and I was not expected to phone for another nine days.

During idle moments in the years preceding my trek, I had contemplated a series of images of a winter journey. Among the scenarios involving blizzards, floods and epics, that of a figure ploughing a furrow across an endless lonely space was probably the most enduring. And now here I was putting white miles between myself and the Ling Basin, stealing up a pass, pushing southwards once again, the world silent save for the tinkling of a burn whose blue pools mirrored an empty sky and pink snows. Past the deserted Iron Lodge I cleared snow from a bank overlooking the River Eichaig, pitched, and settled to another freezing night.

With the first hard frosts of the winter came the problem of dealing with frozen footwear. Some climbers wrap their boots in plastic and sleep with them on, but as I could not abide such lumpy long-term bed partners (there was barely enough room as it was), I resigned myself to dealing with stiff boots. I thus established a morning ritual of defrosting them over a gas flame. Securing the stove between my knees, and holding the boot above, I would slowly massage and bash softness back into the steaming leather. This morning it took about twenty minutes.

Until quite recently Upper Glen Eichaig was threaded with occupied dwellings. Now all are deserted, and in the sixteen years since I first passed this way they have suffered a rapid deterioration: the whitewash streaked with moss and algae, tiles fallen, gables rotting, and the once tidy gardens now piled with animal excrement.

The emptying of Glen Eichaig is sad but there have been other more depressing changes. Not so long ago an innocuous stalkers' path climbed the steep slope behind Iron Lodge, taking you a few rough miles eastwards to the lonely head of Loch Mullardoch. Here the shadows cast are by some of the remotest Munros in the Highlands: Mullach na Dheiragain, Beinn Fhionnlaidh, yesterday's An Socach. But there is now an ugly disfigurement. Apparently with impunity, the landowner has bulldozed the path into a hideous Land Rover track. The proliferation of such new tracks into remote enclaves was to be a sad feature of the journey.

At the derelict hamlet of Carnach I left the main valley. A viciously steep pull brought me gasping to the wide-bottomed Gleann Gaorsaic, about 300 metres higher and cloaked in soft snow. Ahead was a stunning prospect: the white crags of Beinn Fhada vaguely illuminated by a milky sun, and to my left the long, wandering ridges belonging to the crown of Sgurr nan Ceathreamhnan. It was another day of utter quiet and stillness, the cold, it seemed, silencing even the cry of moorland birds.

In summer a good path would ease you across the initial miles of bog, but today it lay completely buried. Almost immediately I floundered in drifts to my knees. With the effort I sweated profusely. I would slump down for frequent rests only to be consumed by shivering as the perspiration chilled rapidly. The snow gave a lesson in pacing. My usual two-mile-an-hour gait was no longer possible, and all attempts at haste were deeply tiring. Instead, I made each footfall slow and deliberate, moving with a kind of jerky rhythm, swift enough to stay warm but slow enough to stave off exhaustion.

Of course it made for ludicrously slow progress, crawling speed really, and it seemed an age before I turned the corner into Gleann Gniomhaidh and dropped gently towards Glen Affric. All day I had grappled mentally with my impassive companion, Beinn Fada. For hours this great peak loomed square ahead, then to my right; then, at the last, she forced me out on a weary three-mile detour round her eastern arm. I wondered whether she laughed with contempt at my desultory movements or allowed a certain admiration at my perseverance.

Glen Affric, seven miles from the nearest road, usually offers a choice of accommodation. One establishment has flush toilets, hot showers, a fully-equipped kitchen, wind-powered electricity, piles of dry kindling for the stove and clean wood panelling that insulates you from the whine of the elements. This, of course, is the refurbished Alltbeithe, an official youth hostel. The other is a basic stone shieling with a leaky roof. Beneath a thicket of spiders' webs are bare boards for a bed, a table of corrugated iron and cold rocks you might use to sit on. There is a fireplace, but it is likely piled high with ash, and there is certainly never any wood to hand.

Of the two, the bothy sits more comfortably on its mountain perch. The bare interior mirrors empty flanks which tumble down on both sides, and the neighbouring ruins and lazy beds add a layer of forgotten history to its location on a high watershed. Stalwarts from the Corriemulzie Club oversaw its renovation in memory of two climbing friends, both tragically killed in 1966. In more than a decade of visits to Affric I have always preferred the leaky roof to the comforts of the hostel.

4

Wandering Ridges

I ONCE planned an itinerary for a trip across the Indian subcontinent and now reflect on how easy it all was: 'From Karachi fly to Lahore; train to India and a day in Delhi; down by rail to Bombay, a few days there; then east across to Calcutta and Dacca….' I knew exactly where I would be in a fortnight, in three weeks. I could have planned it to the detail of a school timetable.

The modern motorised traveller and the walker, particularly the mountain walker, inhabit different worlds. One is carried by the miles, the other must make them. One can hold to a rigid schedule, the other—at the mercy of changing weather and morale—must be ready to chop and prune an objective a dozen times a day. My own plans, being loosely constructed, were easily pulled down.

Next day, half-blinking when pushing open the door of my Glen Affric bothy, I saw nothing beyond high mountains which enclosed and pushed in from all sides, white slopes leading up to crests and cliffs. In December the sun struggles to rise above the southern wall of the Five Sisters Ridge, and this morning there was a strange pall over the mountains, something almost oppressive in their bleakness. Venturing outside, the prospect of a long and demanding day was deeply unappealing, and so with plenty of grub, I decided on a rest day, my first since Shenavall.

It was hardly a rest. I cleaned the bothy, buried a mountain of ash and fashioned a stone armchair by manoeuvring large boulders from a nearby ruin. I ploughed miles through snow to gather wood, hauling back wet, weighty loads that would surely require either a miracle or a gallon of petrol to ignite. With the weather remaining calm and cold, by early afternoon I had come to regret my decision to stay low. I took a wander down to Alltbeithe.

A confusion of bootprints led to the wooden building. Surely it would be securely locked, closed for the winter? The door needed quite a wrench. Behind, in the porch, a young man with a goatee beard sat shivering in a thin, green sleeping bag, like an oversized caterpillar. A Swiss student. Having seen the youth hostel's red triangle on his road map, he had stumbled the 30 miles from Cannich over two arduous days.

'I have two nights in my tent and I nearly die, freezing, freezing,' he said,

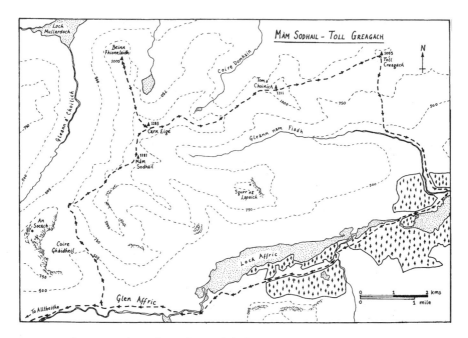

wrapping his arms about his sides and shaking. 'I never come back here. Never.'

He appeared intimidated by the sheer emptiness of the winter mountains, and now he seemed helpless, like a child.

I listened to his grievances with sympathy, then asked whether the hostel was open.

'Of course,' he replied, surprised at my question.

'Then why don't you go in?'

Timidly he pointed to a sign on the inside door which informed members that the hostel was closed between 10 a.m. and 5 p.m., but, 'DURING INCLEMENT WEATHER MEMBERS ARE PERMITTED TO WAIT IN THE PORCH'.

Tempted, I took a peek around the carpeted inner sanctum. Here was real comfort, all the more impressive when compared to the poverty of the bothy. Remnants of breakfast and a still-warm stove confirmed its occupancy although I somehow doubted the visitors were the usual card-carrying members of the Association. Striding back to the bothy I felt I should have offered better hospitality to my Swiss friend, but my fire that evening was a disaster, however much I fanned and cajoled it. And by then he would doubtless have been safe and warm in front of the coal burner, dreaming of summer days and green alpine meadows.

Having lived all my formative years in London, a place where 'extreme' weather amounted to a few inches of snow or the minor inconvenience of a flash flood, it is still a shock in the mountains to be woken by the wind shrieking across the roof and the clatter of rain. Outside, the hills were awash. With one swipe of a south-westerly gale winter had vanished. Every hillside was alive with wriggling torrents, snow-melt combining with rain which fell from blankets of grey clouds to transform the world into a sodden and despairing place. I was not unduly worried. Since the Fannichs I had been waiting for the next big storm, and better this Atlantic depression than a northerly blizzard any day.

I did nothing beyond lying inert in my sleeping bag all day. It was enforced idleness. Conditions outside were so atrocious that only a madman would have ventured into them; so I had no guilty feelings. The hours passed happily, even blissfully; eating, reading, thinking great and idle thoughts. I became so completely immersed in my new novel—by Shusaku Endo—that the sounds of storm no longer registered, the words wrapping themselves around me like a sound-proof box. And later, with little external to focus on, my mind turned inwards, unlocking a repository of recent memories. There was no effort in this. I worked lucidly along the unbroken chain of days and events stretching right back to the breakers at Sandwood, each day carefully recalled, the little incidents and details, my recollections so vivid I wondered why I even bothered keeping a diary. Only a single month had passed but it felt like an age; the hours had come to resemble days, and the days had seemed like weeks. Time had become elastic.

Some plastic sheeting had been placed on the supporting cross-beams, presumably to catch the leaks, but in half a dozen places there were spreading pools where I lay on the rafters. Fresh leaks developed during the afternoon, forcing me on a couple of migratory movements to the dwindling dry spots. By 3.30 p.m. light had drained sufficiently from the day to warrant lighting a candle. I did not bother with a fire: my gear was still dry and I felt little inclination to struggle with wet logs while so warm and contented.

The gale raged all night and all the next day, reducing the snow to a few muddy streaks on the higher slopes. With no river fordable, I grimly donned waterproofs, braved the elements, and had a go at Beinn Fhada, a huge, multi-faceted mountain which rose directly behind the bothy. Approached from Glen Affric, Fhada has a fine symmetrical profile like a pointed gable, but, seen broad-sided, there are many miles of ridge, some narrow, and there is a table-top summit. I simply crept up the east ridge into a wind-driven cloud mass and fought my way terrier-like to the cairn. A trembling expanse of water had formed in Glen Gaorsaic, the three previously frozen lochans having flooded and now merged like an incoming tide.

Back at the bothy I had what at first seemed like an hallucination. Dripping and a little shell-shocked I found myself staring blankly through the window. A tall figure dressed in shiny, black oilskins went by, a man with no rucksack, head hunched low but casting a sideways glance at me. His expression was one of utter grimness.

There was a third morning of rain and gales, the same driving sheets of water as if late for an appointment at Cannich, the same wind—though its apparent gustiness seemed to offer the smallest promise of respite. Once again my scheduled big days on the Mam Soul and Five Sisters ridges were in tatters. I desperately needed some half-decent weather. These gales could go on indefinitely, forever trapping me at glen level. And, food-wise, I was running out of time.

There were voices downstairs. Two men were sheltering from the rain in pools of water, one of whom I recognised as the tall, dark figure from yesterday. Graham and Bob had been working on a footpath in Glen Lichd and were staying at Alltbeithe. Enthused at just talking to another human, I bantered with red-haired Graham, while Bob reticently puffed on a roll-up. They kindly left me some fence posts for the fire and invited me down to Alltbeithe that evening. 'Give you an early start for Mam Soul,' they said. But first was the small matter of Sgurr nan Ceathreamhnan.

For any first-time visitor to this lonely glen, Sgurr nan Ceathreamhnan (1,151m), 'Peak of the Quarters', is unmistakably the most striking among the cluster of mountains, having a shapeliness unusual for a high peak. In certain light an imaginative mind might see her long, flowing ridges—five in all—as folds in a veil, and the twin-topped summit a crown speckled with schist and quartz. For all that Ceathreamhnan is relatively little-climbed, guarded by rough miles and her more accessible neighbours.

Beyond the clichés of guidebooks, the accolades we heap on certain mountains tend to be subjective and personal. Mountains awaken our memories and give shape to our emotions. We love them for their associations, whether as our last Munro, our first innocent climb, or for that display of flickering aurora which we will never see again. Some of us have even put plaques and prayers by cairns, left crosses and scattered ashes.

My own memories of this peak are forever coloured by a visit one winter when I stumbled upon a series of remarkably clear days, quite unmatched before or since. A week of bitterly cold nights had stilled the glens, while the peaks and ridges were heaped with untrodden snow. One afternoon I climbed Ceathreamhnan, lingered at the summit through a flaming sunset, and descended by moonlight. For a few hours that day—or so it seemed then—I had briefly stepped into another world.

The promised break in the weather seemed to have arrived when, by afternoon, the rain relented. A damp chilly wind and patches of blue heralded the change, and already I was imagining views of cloud shadows chasing across clean, rain-rinsed hills. I strode across the watershed for Ceathreamhnan with renewed vigour. But another shower rolled in and drowned my optimism with sheets of icy water. Obdurately, I drilled my legs up a snow-splattered ridge, then, for ease of navigation, latched onto a line of rusting iron stakes—an old boundary fence. At least I was on familiar ground. These stakes would lead conveniently to my first summit, and from there a short linking ridge would put me on Ceathreamhnan, as easy as that. I drifted into an uphill rhythm, hands in pockets, daydreaming, my head full of pleasant thoughts: the fire to come, a steaming shower, the company that awaited at Alltbeithe, and my big plans for tomorrow.

I went over the first top, which was rather featureless, and pushed on for the linking ridge without stopping. Lashed by rain, I was still happily dreaming of that hot shower when a sense of unease began to gnaw at me. The ridge seemed odd. It was broad when I remembered it as narrow, and it dropped endlessly. The map confirmed my error: I was moving north when I should have been heading east. I looked at my watch in horror. It would be completely dark in under an hour, but to descend any further was madness. Bailing out here would leave eight tortuous miles home, and still with this mountain to climb. Frantically I scurried back up the ridge, found the true summit, and charged down like a demon, chasing the last shreds of dusk until I dropped below the cloud and spied the meandering river at Alltbeithe. The last miles were both dark and deluged, but no matter. At the bothy I packed two days' food, bolted down a hot chocolate and left to seek the company and warmth of the hostel.

Drenching rain and a waxing moon alternated, the latter painting the flank of Ceathreamhnan a dull silver and casting a faint shadow of a hurrying figure. A wall of heat greeted my entry. Rock music streamed from one of the rooms.

'The shower's that way,' was Bob's greeting, having smelt me before I had even stepped inside. Later, a bottle of red wine unearthed from my cache went well with a huge bowl of his pasta. Bob, an ornithologist, was curious about my journey.

'So you've walked the entire way from Sandwood Bay.'

I nodded.

'When do you finish?'

'In about three or four months, at Glencoe.'

'Glencoe in four months! You could walk there in ten days.'

'I could, but I've a few mountains to climb on the way.'

He now looked at me suspiciously.

'Are you doing the Munros or something?'

'In winter! You must be joking,' I laughed, ' No, I'm hoping to get up the thousand-metre peaks, at least, as many as I can.'

I explained my strategy.

He was now listening with a kind of weariness. He had heard this all before.

'Look,' he said, 'why climb *those* particular peaks. Isn't this all a bit contrived, a dangerous stunt? Why not enjoy the mountains without a schedule?'

I gave him some spiel about every trip needing the discipline of a target or challenge, something achievable, albeit at a stretch and some personal risk. But I could see he was unimpressed. He persisted with his questioning and was now quite animated.

'But why *every* 1,000-metre hill, and why in God's name in winter?'

Why indeed? I could have mentioned that unforgettable evening not a week ago on An Riabhachan, the colour and light of that wild snowy camp; the satisfaction that comes from a long and fruitful day; the rhythm of a climb and thrill of a running descent; or the sense of journeying that carries you ever onwards, at times effortlessely. The sheer joy of it. I could have mentioned a thousand things, but we were two Englishmen, poles apart, and my words would have sounded crass and pretentious.

'It beats teaching kids,' I said.

§ § §

A friend of mine plans mountain days as if they were military campaigns. After poring over maps and half a dozen guidebooks he would calculate heights, times, distances. Every item carried was weighed to the last gram. By comparison I lost any love of detailed logistics the day I lost my innocence as a hill-walker—when just eighteen, on the first day of my Pennine Way trek. I remember it well. A fine hot morning and I had estimated—as many do—that I would traverse Kinder Scout and be at Snake Pass by lunchtime. I got there by nightfall, just. In-between were ten scorching hours of lost bearings, bogs, blisters and mild sunstroke. Half-crazed with the effort, I had discarded my water and dumped spare clothes to save weight, then later drunk like a thirsty beast from muddy pools to stave off dehydration. And I pleaded with every soul I met: 'Pennine Way? Have you seen the Pennine Way path?'

A huge day was now in prospect: five high and remote Munros. I made no plans. When setting out at daybreak I knew only that for me to be back at Alltbeithe in twelve hours, I would have to rush every mile. The Land Rover track which links the hostel to the outside world eased me along the early miles. I exchanged its comforts for a fine stalkers' path leading me into the wild basin of Coire Ghaidheil. At over 600 metres I saw bleached roots from an extinct forest, testifying to a warmer, drier climate of the recent past. The grey light lingered into mid-morning and a blustery wind carried with it blankets of cloud that smothered the peaks. The day promised little save rain and unpleasantness. At the bealach, and finding no shelter, a cold wind took merciless advantage when I removed my jacket to pull on another thermal layer.

Just down from Mam Sodhail (1,181m), and growing from the scree, are the ghostly remnants of a deer watchers' bothy which would have been occupied all summer. It is an incongruous structure fast disintegrating under the action of frost and wind, and a reminder of the days, not a century ago, when wealthy lairds could indulge their whims at ridiculously little cost.

Once over Carn Eighe (1,183m), the highest point of the north-west Highlands, I dropped from the cloud base to take in Beinn Fhionnlaidh. The view north was of unrelenting wetness, the air condensing before my eyes so that it was like look-ing through a dirty window. If Fhionnlaidh had not attained the magical 3,000-foot mark I fancy she would be little climbed. She is situated out on a northerly limb, and will add two hours to any schedule. On a dour day I found the summit a delightful grassy protuberance, a green splash amid the naked bones of ridges and corrie backwalls. And there was a dramatic view of Loch Mullardoch, wind-scoured and dark, and, I imagined, full of unseen creatures.

Clambering back up Carn Eighe, and enveloped once again by mist and drizzle, I moved with an even greater sense of urgency. I pushed east to where the ridge narrows in places to a knife-edge and undulates like a roller-coaster the entire way to Tom a' Choinich. A sudden cloud window offered a glimpse into the lost world of Coire Domhain: a primitive place, without pattern or order, its bulging, skull-shaped rocks breaking through a skin of peat and heather and forcing a white burn on a drunken path to the loch far below. It seemed the epitome of wildness.

Throughout the day it had grown steadily windier and colder, and now as I approached my fifth and last Munro, Toll Creagach, snow came across the ridge in wild flurries. In my haste on this final section I veered too far south and wasted valuable minutes of light regaining the main crest. It was a little after three o' clock when I reached the summit, which was seven hours from the hostel.

I was now able to relax a little and took immense pleasure in the descent, so glad to be leaving the mist and cold behind. Coming off the last slopes was a revelation. Having never been this way before I found myself at the bottom of a hidden mountain amphitheatre, a secret, out-of-the-way glen. The map suggested nothing of its beauty, and having been blinded by the day's haste, at last I was made to pause and wonder. On a darkening afternoon here was a profusion of autumnal colour that no labour of words could adequately describe. Here was the *genius loci*, and both place and moment seemed heaped with significance.

Close to the road I passed three elderly walkers and a dog.

'Been up on the tops?' one of them asked, his face wreathed in smiles.

'All day,' I replied.

'Well, you're down now, and finished just before dark, good timing,' he said.

'Finished! I wish I were. I've still thirteen miles to walk.'

They looked aghast.

For much of the way a waxing moon added interest, flitting from behind fast-moving clouds, illuminating the path ahead. The weather, though, broke again long before I reached the hostel, and for what seemed like hours I walked hunched up, pummelled by a cold rain. Whenever I raised my head, the silvery darts caught in my beam had a dizzying effect. My face streamed, the water seeping inside to saturate my fleece and thermals. Arriving back around eight, I was beyond the point of caring much about these things in any case. It could rain all night, and probably did.

The interminable flanks of Mullach Fraoch-choire (1,102m), which had stared down at me for some days, were finally tackled. Joints were like rusty hinges, limbs stiff and sore, lethargic from a fitful night's sleep and gross overwork. Hamish Brown claims to have read his way up these slopes. I measured my gain on the flanks of Ciste Dubh opposite. It is a steep, brutal climb, so steep that in only twenty minutes you gaze down as if you were a bird soaring over the wastes of the Affric basin. Overnight snow had given yesterday's mountains skull caps, but this was my last view as another shower swept in from the west. There were other peaks on this range, but they could be climbed later from the Cluanie Inn. Just now I was deeply tired. I retreated wearily to the bothy for an afternoon in front of the fire.

After a long and dreamless sleep the thought of tackling the spectacular Five Sisters Ridge should have rekindled my enthusiasm, but from my Affric base these two far-flung peaks shrouded in a drizzly mist promised only a mammoth twenty-mile effort and no views. It took a couple of brisk miles along Glen Lichd to shake off any lingering sluggishness. Glen Lichd must surely surpass even Glencoe in terms of grandeur. At times it is more like a giant gorge, its sheer size intimidating, big enough to make the world's greatest monuments—pyramids, cathedrals and skyscrapers—shrink by comparison.

The path skirts a series of truncated spurs, then twists and drops alarmingly. Immediately ahead, and always in the frame, rose my target this morning, the east ridge of Sgurr Fhuaran, which loomed ever higher as I was sucked further into the bowels of the glen. All about, the mountains grew more huge and seemed more harsh, while I began to feel increasingly more apprehensive.

A couple of Gore-Tex clad shepherds with dogs ambled into view.

'Seen any sheep?' the older one asked.

They were pleased when I mentioned the old shaggy creature—more wild beast than domestic animal—I had seen by the bothy the day before the storm.

I crossed the River Croe, which swept through a small gorge fringed with birch and alder, then launched myself at the east ridge. Such was the steepness of this first section that I feared a slip here might not be arrested. I moved with utmost care. The ridge levelled out before a final 50 metres of giddy, narrow crest covered in soft snow. It is without doubt the finest way to gain the Five Sisters.

From Sgurr Fhuaran (1,068m), the main ridge plummets steeply then wriggles its way southwards over the sizeable top Sgurr na Carnach and onto my second Munro, Sgurr na Ciste Dubh, 'Peak of the Black Chest'. Leaving my sack at the small bealach, I went up with only camera, map and compass. I had felt cheated at the lack of views all week, but particularly from this ridge which I knew so well from previous traverses, my first on a blistering August day in 1982. Then, of the seemingly dozens of mountains, I could identify only Liathach and Ben Nevis, the rest unknown and unclimbed.

Backtracking, I followed my prints down but could find no sign of my sack. A frustrating half-hour was spent searching, made all the worse by my impatience to be down and away from this high, exposed ridge. It was maddening. I cursed loudly and vowed never again to indulge in such stupidity. Had an unseen walker removed it, thinking the owner was lost or injured? It was utterly implausible but after another thirty minutes of fruitless searching I began to believe it. Then I realised the true bealach was a little lower. I found my sack about twenty metres away, exactly where I had left it. I dropped into the abyss of Choire Dhomdain in a frantic, half-controlled descent, and was back at the bothy by dusk.

It would have been easy to rest up here for a fifth night, but at some time this evening I was expected to make a phone call home. After strong coffee and a hunk of fruitcake, I left in the dark for Cluanie. Unaccustomed to the weight of a full rucksack, and with a dim headtorch, I stumbled through a maze of watery ditches for a mile before locating the path. It was in a glutinous, near useless state, as wet as I could remember it. A mile before the road the clouds lifted to show moonlight falling on the South Kintail Ridge, gleaming brightly on the snows. I was now moving more easily, buoyed on by that sense of well-being which always takes hold as you come to the end of a long day. Finally, a fortnight and a day after I'd left Strathcarron, the orange lights of the Cluanie Inn came into view. It only took an hour to forget all about walking and mountains. The soft, red carpet and white-rippled wallpaper, the large mirrors and brass-coloured taps, the all-pervading odour of cleanliness; it all helped to trick the mind into thinking the wilderness was gone—at least for a while.

Anyone lucky enough to experience a day in the north-west Highlands with fresh snowfall, calm, clear conditions and the lingering colours of autumn, will understand when I say that for the promise of such days we will suffer much. Next morning the winter sun returned with such brilliance that it dispelled the last doubts I had about this journey. And it made a nonsense of the forecast.

The two Munros on the eastern extremity of the Kintail ridge—Aonach Meadhoin and Sgurr a' Bhealaich Dheirg—were a simple matter of a few sunny hours in the cold, still air. I left late morning and returned mid-afternoon. On Aonach Meadhoin I might have pointed my camera in any direction and been rewarded with a treasured slide. Oddly, most distant horizons lay wrapped in cloud, yet here I was bathed in sunshine and blue shadows. South and west, like a crumpled blanket, were the mountains to come: the South Kintail Ridge just opposite, the Saddle, the peaks of Knoydart; and the snowy A' Chràlaig range for tomorrow.

I continued along a ridge of unmarked snow, so dry and powdery it appeared like china dust; then a short, effortless climb to Sgurr a' Bhealaich Dheirg, 'Peak of the Red Pass', a favourite mountain of mine. Its actual summit is out from the main ridge and needed an awkward fumble across slabby boulders to reach, mindful of the severe drops on either side.

A last nostalgic look at yesterday's hills: prominent among the jumble were Fhada, Ceathreamhnan, Mam Sodhail, all radiant in sunshine. I dropped down in a mood of deep contentment and returned by way of the old military road, the cloud and deluge of Affric consigned now to a distant memory.

With staff outnumbering residents the Cluanie had a friendly, convivial atmosphere. I was treated with great hospitality. All manner of facility was on offer, much of it way beyond my simple needs. After a fortnight of basic living, the soft beds, bath, bar, and good food seemed to me a wonder of sophistication and comfort. The sauna, sunbed and jacuzzi I left for more imaginative guests. Last summer's warden at Alltbeithe, I was told, regularly exchanged the 15-mile walk for the pleasures of a jacuzzi and a little pampering in the sun lounge.

Three Munros were required if I was to set the seal on this area and be free to head west to Knoydart. But I had a map problem. While A' Chràlaig towered almost directly above the Inn, two other peaks, Sgurr nan Conbhairean and Sàil Chaorainn, lay to the east, away from the road and on the next Ordnance Survey sheet. And that particular map—I remembered now—lay buried in a food cache somewhere in the wilds of Knoydart. Of the two peaks, I had studied Conbhairean yesterday so could negotiate her western flanks, but Sàil Chaorainn had been completely hidden. Nobody at the Inn could help so I set out rather over-dependent on compass, altimeter and whatever details I could dredge up from the memory of an August day some eleven years ago.

It always seemed to me that most days were a miracle of achievement, and however fit and confident I became in the months ahead, this conviction persisted so that it became the common strand of the journey. Every morning when setting out alone to climb a group of hills I tended to be plagued by the same negative thoughts: they were just too huge or remote, conditions were too windy, I was too tired. My reason absolutely denied I would get very far. Then somehow, after a couple of hard hours, almost disbelievingly, I would arrive at the summit, perspiring and warm. I would find the wind was quite tolerable and between the spindrift and clouds the views were magic. There had been a complete transformation in my mood since morning. Perhaps this is why the business of climbing is so pleasurable and so addictive.

On this morning as I toiled above the snowline, helped for a while by a strong backing wind, the weather rapidly turned sour: biting spindrift which wizened my face, and a perishing cold. But there were also blasts of sunshine, blinding white on the massed mountains to the north, and roving cloud shadows across the steep sided glens. From A' Chràlaig I dropped east, giving a wide birth to the left edge where cornices were developing, and, despite raging snow showers, had no difficulty locating Sgurr nan Conbhairean. The summit area was a prevailing white-out.

As anticipated, the east face was broken into cliffs, and I assumed it was now merely a case of dropping down and trailing north to where I knew Sàil Chaorainn lay. However hard I tried I could remember next to nothing about this peak which lay beyond the bounds of my map. I soon discovered why. As a mountain it is instantly forgettable, its only feature a cave low down in the eastern corrie where Charles Edward Stuart, on the run after defeat at Culloden, spent a miserable week hiding from the redcoats. Contemporary Jacobite groups, I am told, have been known to spend a night or two in the cave. On that wild afternoon it would have been my absolute last choice of residence.

I turned around and began the long trek back to Cluanie, wondering who would be the first to emulate the pioneering spirit and complete the Munros without using maps.

5

Knoydart

SOME DAYS, during the empty hours of a trek or misty ascent, my past would come clambering back into focus, like a reverie.

They were quite mad, every one of them—not a group you could easily forget. On Thursday mornings I would hear them coming along the corridor: a collection of high-pitched voices and discordant chatter, a scream or two. Why were they, I wondered, always released early from Maths, a full two minutes before the bell? And why, despite this 'special needs' group only numbering fourteen, did they always manage a scrum on entering my room, as if the corridor was suddenly full of poisonous gas? While their birth certificates confirmed their ages as young adolescents they were a medley of dimensions, from an adult in school uniform with the physique of a coal miner, to a half-pint infant straight from reception class. Their facial characteristics, it seemed, covered the gamut of human emotion, from a set-in-stone grin—maintained even at the height of a morbid video on earthquake victims—to profound puzzlement, or thinly-disguised cunning.

My first lesson was a nightmare. Giving each an outline map of the world, an atlas, glue and some coloured pencils, I set a task: 'Using your atlas, label the world's ten longest rivers.' Something easy to get them off the mark, I thought. Nothing prepared me for their reaction. Some began colouring the sea green or stuck their map in upside down, others sat looking puzzled and vacant, one started doing his Maths homework. None could manage an atlas. I was already counting the days to summer.

That first term is forever engraved on my memory, good and bad. When somebody had scribbled 'CAWTHORNE IS A BASTARD' in the back of a school text book, the Deputy Head reassured me.

'Don't worry. That means you've almost made it as a teacher.'

'How do I know when I have made it?'

'When they write *Mr* Cawthorne is a bastard.'

⸘ ⸘ ⸘

I exchanged a centrally-heated room for a moonlit night under nylon, walking the ten miles to Glen Quoich refreshed and rejuvenated, and fitter than I had felt

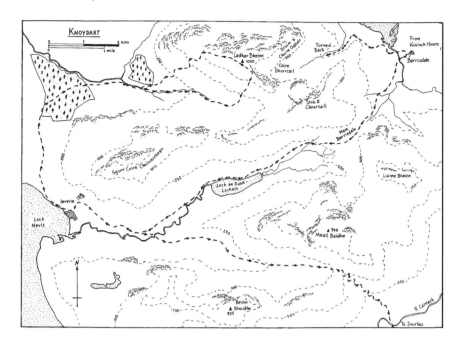

in years. Despite my longest continuous mountain walk for more than a decade, I was never more at ease in body and mind. The malaise—predicted by some—had not set in. Instead, the journey had become increasingly an intoxicating and addictive experience. A premature ending was unthinkable.

At Glen Affric I had suffered an especially anxious dream about finishing my journey prematurely and being back at work. I remember waking up with intense relief at the reality of another three months of winter stretching ahead of me. Any future is unknowable but mine seemed limitless. I could visualise the route—knowing most of it well—but could not see the shape of individual days, whether sunny, stormbound or flooded. Nor could I imagine walking another thousand miles, climbing another hundred peaks. Glencoe, three hours away by car, was in my mind as a vague place I would never likely reach.

While I was always reluctant to cement any section into a slavish schedule, on this occasion I had no choice but to commit myself to a rendezvous with my brother, Jon, in nine days at a location a little beyond the Great Glen. On paper, the intervening 140 miles and ten 1,000-metre peaks seemed straightforward enough, but it was now mid-December with the Winter Solstice, typically a wet and stormy time, approaching. And of course there would be no help *en route*: no shops, accommodation or phones.

Benign conditions helped me along the Cluanie Ridge the next day. This ridge is custom-made for Munro-baggers. In less than seven miles it never climbs higher than 1,030 metres, nor drops lower than 700, and in a few unhurried hours you can notch up seven Munros. Many, perhaps guilty at such an easy haul, will extend their day westward to tackle Sgurr na Sgine and the Saddle, more challenging fare.

Many years ago while climbing Gleouraich, a mountain to the south, we caught a sunlit glimpse of the verdant flanks of the Cluanie Ridge through a window in the mist. Our eyes fell on the incredible zig-zags of a stalkers' path which had etched a route up to the narrow crest. We dubbed it 'Stairway to Heaven' and wondered whether we might ever find the necessity to climb it.

This morning it carried me upwards from Glen Quoich into a thick, seething mist, which, on the crest, billowed up from the northern corries like steam from a cooling tower. The absence of wind made it eerie and silent. I moved eastwards to take in Aonach air Chrith, then retraced my steps and bounded seawards over thawing snow to Sgurr an Doire Leathain and Sgurr an Lochain. With no visibility beyond a few metres I was pleased to be dropping back into the depths of the glen. Passing a boarded-up lodge, I cast about for my tent. For a while I could not make it out, the green fabric in perfect camouflage with the swards of the river bank, a pin-prick beneath the mighty face of Gleouraich.

A chilly east wind picked up during the night, bringing with it a clear moon-filled sky and, by morning, a touch of frost. My vestibule framed perfectly the bulk of Sgurr a' Mhaoraich, which glowed the colour of old papyrus in the early light.

Some cloud had filtered in an hour later when I set out to tackle Gleouraich. Her narrow north ridge gave a delightful scramble, the rocks cold to the touch, still glazed in ice crystals. The route had a lonely, pioneer feel to it: no crampon scratches or boot-polished slabs, barely any evidence to suggest curious walkers ever stray onto this side of the mountain. On the summit ridge I joined a serious-looking path which snaked up from the more accessible south side and Loch Quoich road.

I galloped down and after a second breakfast made westwards for Sgurr a' Mhaoraich. A golden eagle glided in the blue air high above, wheeling downwards in a giant swoop, then climbing again until it vanished behind a summit ridge. I climbed for a while in the deep shade of a corrie, the east wind now stronger and bitterly cold whenever I stopped. Emerging at the high bealach I shivered hopelessly while pulling on extra layers: balaclava, mittens, another mid-layer garment. Then, leaving my sack, I clambered the final half mile to the summit.

Strangely, there was less wind here. I marvelled at the view. Northwards, the high tops were soft and pink in the late afternoon sun, while behind was a panorama of unrelenting ruggedness: the mountainlands of Knoydart and Dessary. The forces of Creation must have gone into a blind fury as the land here seemed without pattern or order, all cruel twists and contortions, beauty of an agonising kind. If mountains could talk, here they would have screamed, and even now, during the absolute silence of some days, you fancy an ear laid to the ground might yet hear the last painful rending of strata and folds settling deep within the crust.

As on a hundred other descents, tiring limbs, a heavy pack and dimming twilight all conspired to make the way down, through rock bands and wet grass, a tricky one. Another hour of struggle and I found myself splashing through the black liquid of a river, and felt the pleasing solidity of boots on tarmac. A bumpy pitch was found on the coast path a little beyond the hamlet of Kinloch Hourn. Happiness, I concluded, was a full day with great views, the sound of a restless sea and the untouched contents of a food cache stuffed with all manner of goodies.

Knoydart lay only seven miles west, but first I had the business of climbing the Saddle to the north, my final peak of the Glen Shiel switchback. With the moon dropping from the sky—it seemed—I passed Kinloch Hourn lodge, stooped beneath an arch of rhododendron bushes, then headed up a path to a line of electricity pylons whose cables hung like silk from monstrous spiders. It was my second morning of empty skies.

An unfamiliar view of Knoydart emerged through a gap in the hills, then, from an interconnected maze of paths, I chose one which carried me painlessly across the acres of brick-red moorland. It tipped me abruptly by a crystalline burn in the cauldron of Coire Mhalagoin where a cold, gusty wind came down from the tops. Bouldery slopes climbed to grey-blue screes and crags, then a wild sweep of summits. A magical setting.

About midway up, and while stopping in the lee of a boulder to pull on another layer, my sack took a tumble. Involuntarily I swung round to grab it but tripped and landed spreadeagled, screaming as my knee struck something sharp. Having calmed down I retrieved my sack, nursed my throbbing knee and prayed it was only bruised—a damaged ligament here would surely spell the end of my walk. I hobbled up the remainder of the climb. A glorious sun-speckled vista awaited: the Skye Cuillins completely clear, cloud shadows racing each other along the Five Sisters Ridge, everything sharp-edged, as if cut from cardboard.

I was busy shovelling chunks of tuna into my mouth and sheltering from the icy wind when a strange thing happened. A red, woolly hat poked above the nearby crest and materialised into a solitary walker, a wiry-faced man in his late forties wrapped in a turquoise Gore-Tex jacket. I was so used to the loneliness of my days I had given up utterly the expectation of meeting anyone before the Christmas holidays. Of course, I had met hoteliers, village storekeepers, estate workers, shepherds, but only twice since Sandwood had I chatted to complete strangers on a mountain. He was an amicable fellow, and we photographed each other and waxed lyrical about the needle-sharp conditions. He had climbed Lochnagar the previous day, a mountain I hoped to reach by February.

The coastal path from Kinloch Hourn to Barisdale Bay is, by general consent, one of the finest in Britain. For seven miles it weaves through relict Caledonian pine, riding high above rocky coves and tiny bays. Climb a shoulder or two, and on a clear summer's evening you march towards the great red disc of the sinking sun. But it is not much fun in complete darkness and with a gusty wind. I fumbled along hoping the next rise was the last, that the path would soon level out and become the track that carries you the final easy mile to the estate bothy.

The place appeared to be empty. I settled into the front room and waited patiently for the gas flame to work on a pan of water. From another room the scraping of heavy boots announced the arrival of a garrulous chap, Gary from Helensburgh, muffled in a thick, down jacket. He laughed as he pointed to a sack of coal on the floor, and told of some lads from Liverpool. They had arrived late and tired with much coal and kindling, but found the door bolted and were forced to bivouac. In the morning they tried the door again; another good pull and this time it opened. But their joy was short-lived: the old fireplace had been bricked over, a 'Fire Hazard', the sign said.

Despite my fatigue, throughout the long night I was dimly aware of the chaos outside. By first light there was a roll-call of disturbing sounds: a padlock being beaten against some wooden gates, a trailer lifted then dropped, something gnawing at a stone wall. There was a sudden rush as a gust swept across the roof, then silence. Gary was pleased to be leaving. After two plates of sludgy porridge with the last of the sugar I made off in the opposite direction, bound for Ladhar Bheinn.

Both the beauty of Barrisdale Bay and the prize of the Ladhar Bheinn have made this area a magnet. Stepping outside, I recalled the previous spring when I last passed by: a John Muir Trust work party had just returned from the hill, Duke of Edinburgh groups were milling around their bright orange tents, others filled the bothy to overflowing; enough young people, I reckoned, for a mini rock festival.

It is not difficult to see why people come. Ladhar Bheinn vies with An Teallach and Liathach in terms of 'pulling power', and is one of the finest peaks of all. A large, intricate mountain, her prominent features are the striking bowl of Coire Dhorrcail and a complex system of ridges converging near the summit. She is a thousand metres straight from the seashore. But perhaps even more appealing is the dramatic proximity to the Atlantic Ocean, the views across to the Hebrides, or east along the fjord-like Loch Hourn, with echoes of Norway or New Zealand, scenery which has no equal in Scotland.

Like most people I approached Ladhar Bheinn from the north, taking the stalkers' path round into Coire Dhorrcail. From here the knife-edge of Druim a' Choire Odhair climbs steeply to the main summit at 1,020 metres, both an aesthetic and challenging route. But, out on a limb in the west and facing the wrath of the Atlantic, Ladhar Bheinn is also a wild mountain.

I struggled just to reach the base of the mountain. The earth quivered before the storm, the air full of wind-blown grass, like confetti; birch trees buckled and swayed, and sudden, violent gusts pushed me back and off-balance. Worst of all was the sheer noise, a continuous whooping which dulled my senses to an extent that I seemed immersed in a cerebral fog.

At about the 300-metre level, as I rounded into the corrie, conditions worsened.

The wind, now funnelling down from the ring of high cliffs, again knocked me sideways, and this time I went over and tumbled a few metres downslope. From above came a disturbing *cra-ack*. A branch had been near-wrenched from the main trunk, and now hung loosely like a piece of broken guttering. I heeded the warning. If my movements were being impeded in the shelter of a corrie, then attempting an exposed narrow ridge at 1,000 metres would be lunacy. Still shaking from the fall, I turned and made back for Barrisdale.

It was strange to be retreating when there were pockets of clear sky and streaks of sunshine on Beinn Sgritheall opposite, and any photograph would have rendered it a tranquil scene. The mile back into the teeth required an hour of effort. Exhausted, I slumped in the nearest chair, but quickly grew cold. I climbed into my sleeping bag and rather worried about my failing schedule and dwindling food—now only packets of soup and a couple of tins of fish remained. The days lost would put enormous pressure on my rendezvous in four days' time. Thinking ahead, I hardly dared consider how I would cope with a similar situation in the middle of the Cairngorms. I took solace in the bothy log book, but much of it read like Captain Scott's diary: a litany of storms and epics. With no fire, no company, and little to eat, the bothy had become a cold and dispiriting place.

All night and subsequent morning the gale continued in a metronome of clanging metal and squeaking doors, like a soundbox of discordant noises. The trailer though was strangely silent, and peering through the window I saw that it had been flipped onto its side. Ladhar Bheinn, I decided, was still stormbound, and all thoughts turned to the matter of food. Already, after a breakfast of weak soup, I had that gnawing feeling in the pit of my stomach. Being of a slim build I have few bodily reserves, and without continued sustenance soon become weak and dizzy. In the past I have often underestimated my appetite and finished trips by surviving on half rations for days on end. In East Africa I once lost a stone and a half in a week.

Inverie is a tiny, landlocked village on the western fringe of the Knoydart peninsula. It promised a phone, accommodation and, more importantly, a store. It was only a seven-mile walk, up and over the Mam Barrisdale pass.

The wind, while having moderated a touch, still harried me high on the pass. An uprooted tree blocked the Land Rover track leading down to the village. Having secured a bed at the salubrious Torrie shieling I went down to the shop and deserted waterfront. Half the population of fifty-four, including my friendly host Roger, were attending a Christmas concert and church service at the local primary school.

Later, after a gargantuan meal I was able to relax in front of the huge wood burner and watched as Roger piled more logs onto the fire.

'Did you catch tomorrow's forecast?' I asked.

'Staying dry, I think. Then he added, as an afterthought: 'Weather's gone to pot.'

An autumnal, snowless view from Ruadh-stac Mòr, Beinn Eighe, to the wastes of the Flowerdale and Shieldaig Forest. Liathach, unseen and a few miles west, would also be climbed on this short November day.

'Nest of Fannich' as it was in 1984. Now, sadly, a ruin.

Overleaf: *'Peak of the Feinn' or Sgorr nam Fiannaidh, Glencoe, taken during our non-stop trek over the Munros in 1986. Images like this one would haunt me until I committed myself to another journey.*

Leaving the sanctuary of Strathcarron to go east and begin the sixteen-day trek to Glen Shiel: 'a melancholy view of wild, bare mountains with vaguely familiar names'.

From Sgurr na Lapaich on the last day of November looking north-west to Lurg Mhòr and the distant Torridon Hills.

Top: *Evening sunshine on Mullach Fraoch-choire and A' Chràlaig.*
Above: *A' Chràlaig summit. Snow clouds gather ominously over the Affric Hills on a squally day in December.*

Overleaf: *Maolie Lunndaidh and Sgurr a' Chaorachain from Loch Mòr.*

Chasing shadows on the Mamore ridge with Ben Nevis and the Aonachs behind.

Gavin traversing Binnein Mòr, while Schiehallion and the Ben Lawers range are prominent on the skyline about f
miles to the east.

In the morning I tried phoning half a dozen people but only got answering machines; it was 8 a.m., and I guessed everyone had either left for work or was sleeping off pre-Christmas hangovers.

Climbing Ladhar Bheinn from the south is a kind of blasphemy. The route must have been the invention of a dull-witted peak-bagger for, aesthetically, there is nothing to recommend it. The approaches are long and wearisome, and the climb itself, up a uniform flank, is a poor relation to routes that trace her northern corries and ridges. Some reward was the Hebridean view west: the Isle of Rum poking above a line of near hills; Eigg emerging like a submarine floating on a glassy sea that mirrored lines of streaky cloud. Closer were sunless hills, coloured earth-brown and shades of muted green, dotted with lichen-splashed boulders. Being icy and hard-frozen, the final ridge was lethal. I found the summit wrapped in cloud and under a covering of recent snow. There is a magnetic variation here but I merely retraced my footprints and was back at Inverie by early afternoon.

Leaving this self-contained and friendly community, I now set out on an easterly course along the grain of the land that would ultimately lead to the Eastern Grampians. A fine path took me up Gleann Meadail through a tight knot of mountains and towards a high pass. I quickened my pace, keen to make the col before nightfall. Ahead, and to my left, the high crags of Meall Buidhe were momentarily stained as if with purple dye, while behind sunset colours were ranged across Inverie Bay. The path climbed without a single sharp bend, lifting me high above the glen and into a thickening gloom. A final lung-bursting effort, and I could see the dimmest outlines of tomorrow's mountains, implacable and brooding.

The mini hairpins of the descent were tricky to follow in the half-light and I stumbled along until the darkness forced the use of a headtorch. Although day after day, for weeks, I walked into the dark of late afternoon and evening, I never really got used to it, certainly never enjoyed it. Often the day seemed to disintegrate into a frenetic and traumatic experience. And it was endless. Time dragged, and the more I yearned for the walking to stop, the longer it lasted.

I decided to walk without the headtorch for as long as possible, making use of the ambient light from a half-moon, or the last glimmer of twilight, for, once switched on, my range of vision would suddenly be limited to that narrow arc of my beam. All around and pressing in was a claustrophobic blackness. I could avoid that patch of ice or slime-covered rock, but could not see beyond the dark wall ahead, and, on difficult, trackless ground, I wove a hopeless, drunken path, adding an hour or more to the day's schedule.

With some difficulty I located and crossed the bridge spanning the River Carnoch. While I appeared to inject more pace into my walking, being keener than ever to finish, in reality, I slowed. I could not see my target—the headland that poked into the mouth of Loch Nevis—so I traced a meandering line across the salt marsh at its base. It had been dark for a full two hours when I rounded the last stretch of slippery coastline and bore down on the faintest outline of a building: Sourlies cottage.

Two hundred years ago there was a thriving community here. Then came the Clearances:

> All was silence and desolation. Blackened and roofless huts, still enveloped in smoke—articles of furniture cast away, as if of no value to the houseless—and a few domestic fowls, scraping for food among the hills of ashes, were the only objects that told us of man. A few days had sufficed to change a countryside, teeming with the cheeriest sounds of rural life, into a desert. (Eye-witness account of Strathbora Clearances, 1821)

Now it is one of the loneliest places in Britain.

Sleep was a deep oblivion. The first sounds in the dark of early morning—the Saturday before Christmas—were a steady rain on the corrugated plastic skylight, and the faint roar of a waterfall across the bay. From the glow of two flickering candles I began the ritual of breakfast. All I could possibly need was at arms reach: stove, matches, a pan brim-full with water, porridge, sugar, tinned milk, a packet of biscuits which I eyed hungrily, and today's map to mull over—better than any room service in any hotel.

Sourlies, with its fish nets fashioned into hammocks, its plastic crates full of driftwood, and its odour of salty dampness, resonates with images of the sea from Cornwall to Cape Wrath. Two rickety wooden tables, half a dozen steel-framed chairs, and some rough-hewn bunks complete the furnishings. A single skylight and tiny west-facing window reluctantly let in the day, and at nine it was still gloomy when I pushed open the door to brave the damp and drizzle, and make off up the path.

Sgurr na Ciche is a peak from a child's imagination, poking freshly snow-covered through the mist like a monstrous stalagmite. My planned route lay eastwards from Sgurr na Ciche, over Garbh Chioch Mhor, then along a particularly rough section of ridge to Glen Kingie for the night. But now burdened with the extra weight of a cache, I just could not conceive of hauling this load over undulations of ridge through fresh snow. As I had done since Cluanie, every time my rucksack straps dug painfully into my shoulders, I went through the items I would post home at Invergarry, one by one, like an incantation—maps, books, exposed film, a tripod I had never used, clothes I could do without—and this cheered me no end.

By leaving my tiny bivvy tent on a knoll at 750 metres and filling it with the bulk of my gear I was free to enjoy the mountains unburdened. I scrambled up a fine water-filled gully to a miniature col, then cautiously kicked steps up steep snow to the pointed summit. A thawing mist crept in to cheat me of a view. The snow gave a friendly appearance, moulding everything in a uniform white, but it concealed treacherous patches of blue water-ice and demanded utmost care. It was both mentally exhausting and utterly absorbing.

Navigation was considerably easier now for I knew the old boundary fence would lead straight to Garbh Chioch Mhor (1,013m), but I had forgotten about the bellies of slimy rock, now snow-covered, and numerous outcrops that forced detour after detour. The short winter days had made speed a preoccupation but there could be no safe rushing in such terrain. Having found the summit I went downhill at a snail's pace, employing caution until I was free of the ice and could move with some abandon over the wet grass.

Layers of mist gave upper Glen Dessary a 'lost world' feel but once in the lap of the valley all sense of remoteness was gone, the wilderness here undermined by the intrusive presence of man-made forestry. Hamish Brown walking the Munros in 1974 first noticed the creeping tentacles of afforestation into this wild region, calling it 'an act of vandalism'. Today the vandalism is complete and irreparable: the myriad browns and yellows of deer grass have vanished beneath a carpet of evergreen, like a fine antique floor hidden under a cheap rug.

Tricky conditions high on the ridge had soaked up a considerable portion of daylight, and I now found myself approaching Glen Dessary farm with only about thirty minutes of light remaining. Yet another night march was in prospect, the heavy cloud cover promising to curtail even further the short twilight. But I was not unduly concerned. There was not far to go, a little over three miles to a bothy according to the map, and all of it on a path. The reality was somewhat different.

At first I went smoothly uphill to a long, boggy watershed. Light drained rapidly from the afternoon, the drizzle thickened, but I could see ahead the line of the path. It crossed a burn, then dipped sharply into the murk of Glen Kingie. It was windless and perfectly quiet as I adjusted my waistbelt and hastened my stride a little. Soon, I thought, I should be in a dry place; I could remove this irksome weight, stop this endless movement and just be still for at least the next twelve hours. A fine thought and it spurred me on. But the path, no longer maintained by the estate, became thin and vague, then seemed to vanish altogether. Frequently I went astray, now in trackless deer grass by a river or in the middle of a quaking bog. Wet, tired and increasingly irritated, I ploughed on regardless for another hour, finding and following a largish burn downstream until my torchlight caught the dull sheen of a corrugated roof. It was the bothy, and I let out a cry of relief.

It was difficult to relax. The last hour had brought me all the stress and hassle of a bad day at school. I swore loudly when my meal, so meticulously prepared, tipped onto the dirty, wooden floor. Shaking with frustration, I diligently scooped it back into the pan and placed it once more onto the cooker. But my action was clumsy and again it slipped off, this time spreading itself even further across the floor. I grabbed the broom, swept the lumpy yellow liquid onto a shovel and flung it outside. Plain egg noodles and a double helping of sugary oats would suffice instead. Later, I dreamt of greasy take-aways, of tikka masalas and my favourite Birmingham balti houses.

On the morning of the Winter Solstice next day, I stood on the summit of Sgurr Mòr with a glowing sense of completion. This was my last peak north of the Great Glen. I had raced a band of mist to the ridge hoping to snatch a last look at these vast landscapes. Most imposing of all was Sgurr na Ciche in its perfect symmetry: a pale, sunless crest slicing through the languishing Isle of Eigg beyond. Everywhere was rough-hewn: steely slabs and rakes; only the distant Loch Hourn had any softness, a pool of sunlight and a splash of green rhododendron shrub. If I saw the hills of Shiel, Quoich and Dessary again this winter they would only appear as distant lumps on a western skyline.

Lunching back at the bothy, any elation at completing the mountains was tempered with the need to cover a good distance before nightfall. I harboured great intentions of walking long into evening but, in the event, found I had no stomach for it. It was barely dark when at a bend in the track among anonymous forestry, I pulled up by a moss-covered clearing. I went no further. By pushing on too hard there was a danger I would undermine the enthusiasm and balance that had carried me thus far. The pegs refused to bite the gravel so I lay small boulders at tent corners. I prepared a meal and thought mainly of tomorrow, and whether I had the strength and motivation to pull off a twelve- or thirteen-hour day.

After a frosty night came the time to pull on two pairs of icy, wet socks, the inner pair worn and frayed at the heels. It was still gloomy at 9 a.m. when I dropped steeply to Glen Garry and entered a freezing mist. To make this rendezvous I had no choice but to squeeze two days into one. By evening I needed to reach a remote bothy beyond the Great Glen on the northern slopes of the Creag Meagaidh, a distance of perhaps twenty-four miles, and I was unsure about the route, some of it trackless, all of it unfamiliar.

A few boggy miles led to the hamlet of Garrygualach, which had an air of neglect. Very recently people had made an effort here: there were tiny one-room bungalows like houses for dwarves; a garden with its glasshouse and scented herbs; a partially-built wall; but it was as if the residents had suddenly fled, leaving tasks half-done. A couple of miles further on at Greenfield I passed the first inhabited houses since Dessary. Beyond the parked cars were tidy gardens and stacked firewood. Thick smoke piled from a chimney. I heard a radio and someone rooting about inside a tool shed, but no one noticed the lone walker, ill-shaven with muddied gaiters, hurrying past and heading east.

As I entered a large area of forest the track split. My map indicated the left fork. But after twenty minutes or so this ended abruptly in a confusion of felled trees. Quite obviously I was off-route (I later discovered my map was out of date). Not wanting to turn back I pushed on, though with increasing difficulty, boots slipping on greasy logs and caught by protruding stumps. Forestry vehicles had flattened a track of sorts but even this soon vanished, and then I was stooping low, half crawling really, eyes closed, through a dense thicket of branches. Progress was hampered, and inevitably I grew frustrated. From somewhere came the roar of a waterfall. In ten minutes the trees opened to a fantastic gorge and the Allt Ladaidh thundering its way to Loch Garry. I marvelled. Untouched for decades by humans or grazing animals, here was an exotic livery of wildflowers and woodland clinging to mossy walls. Some trees had toppled to bridge the falls, others lay strewn along its bed. Looking skywards, the sunlight was filtered by the mist and forest canopy into delicate shafts, as if through stained glass.

A skeleton of a path traced up the gorge, back to the main track, then a few easy miles to Invergarry. Hauling a pack, I could not have moved faster in stiff-soled boots and almost broke into a jog on the long decline to the Garry. That the post office was closed for lunch confirmed my suspicion that everything appeared to be conspiring against my plans. But I could wait. Posting home over two kilos from my sack cheered me no end, even if I replaced much of it with carbohydrate goodies from the shop.

A cycle route in the trees above the Caledonian Canal enabled me to avoid the few miles of main road. I crossed Laggan Bridge and the Great Glen, and in doing so put the north-west Highlands behind me. But I hardly gave it a thought. It was 3.30 p.m. and it would be dark in about an hour; twelve miles and a high pass still stretched out ahead. Little else mattered.

There is no route over the hills from Laggan to Glen Roy. The mature ranks of conifers are an apparently impenetrable barrier and you would need a machete or chainsaw to make any headway. However, from South Laggan the map indicates several tracks taking you up the steep hillside far into the woodland, and from there I hoped it might just be possible to negotiate a stream bed to open moorland beyond.

Darkness came early among the dense ranks, and from the highest point of the track I peered into the murk of the forest. A frothy brown stream emerged from the dead undergrowth—my route. To reach it I scaled a four-metre-high fence. I dropped immediately into an alien world of wet, greasy darkness. It was impossible to walk up the burn; instead, I hugged its steep banks, teetering on slimy boulders above a plunge pool, negotiating one impasse with a belly-crawl over a sludge of needles, and another by hauling at tangles of roots. Everything was loose and wet and crumbly, the moss-covered banks offered no footholds, clumps of heather came away in my hand.

Somehow I relished the struggle, the fighting and crawling, the body charge through a dense thicket, the momentum of it all, as if something indefinable pulled me on. Every little victory—scaling the high fence, the mad scramble up a slippery bank, bursting through to open moorland—gave a buzz of excitement and drove away my fatigue, propelling my legs upwards. It was a wild and primitive performance.

The moorland was comparatively easy. I stopped to compose myself and set my compass. A bearing led south-east into the depths of Glen Turret, but I hugged the burn too closely and stumbled on steep ledges above a waterfall, knocking stones into the abyss. I backtracked out. To my right in the distance were the orange lights of Brae Roy Lodge and the barking of excited dogs. At last I was on familiar ground, and then a rough track. Another couple of hours and it took me towards a light at the remote headwaters of the River Roy.

6

Creag Meagaidh Christmas

INSIDE THE bothy, and, despite its thick walls, the continual babbling from a fast-flowing burn not a few metres to the east of the building could be heard. A few years ago this unstable bend in the river had seemed certain to erase the bothy from the landscape. But in a single weekend a prodigious group of volunteers, working like demons, shored up the riverbank with a meshed wall of boulders and delayed nature's advance for at least another decade. Somebody had left a poetic account of the heroic work party and their exceptional labour, and it read, I fancied, like an Ossianic tale of daring and triumph.

There were also some notes on the building's history. An 1881 census mentioned eight people living here, half of whom were given as 'scholars'. Reading all this I was reminded of the layers of human history underpinning these high, remote dwellings. Many were originally built as summer shielings, when the Highlands were threaded with clan-based communities, and date from the eighteenth century. In summer the cattle were herded away from the exhausted straths and fattened on the sweet grass by the shielings ready for the autumn markets. After the frugality of winter it was a happy time for the families, the men tending the herds, the women making cheese and butter and spinning wool. With the coming of the 'great sheep' the cattle economy was undermined. The people left, or were evicted. The land became empty and the high shielings fell into ruin, mute and eyeless, as much part of today's landscape as the skeletal remnants of forests found among the peat. A handful under the auspices of the Mountain Bothies Association have been restored to use, and, though basic, retain something of their former existence.

I caught a profile of Jon peering out through the small skylight, his breath condensing on the dirty glass. He wore a puzzled expression.

'What's the weather doing?' I asked.

'Hard to say. It looks pretty cloudy.'

'Is it raining?'

'Umm… no.'

'Good.'

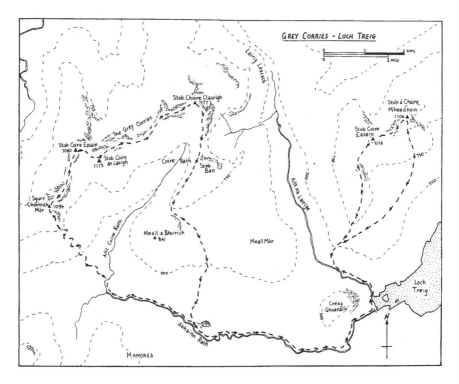

I roused myself, poured a mug of oats into a pan of cold water, lit the gas, and patiently nurtured the mixture into a steaming mush. With great relish I tucked into the mountain of porridge, now smeared in brown sugar and surrounded by a moat of condensed milk. Jon looked over and screwed up his face.

'Looks foul.'

'Delicious,' I said, my mouth full, 'especially if you're as hungry as I am.'

'Hungry!' Jon looked bemused. 'What about that huge meal I made you last night?'

'That was last night. This is morning.'

Jon smiled.

'Do you remember when you turned up last night?'

I nodded, still eating.

'Well, you looked a little crazy, like a man possessed. You had this manic grin across your face and your hair was all matted. You gave me a bit of a shock.'

'You did seem a little taken aback,' I said.

'I hardly recognised my own brother.'

'Can't say you looked all that familiar yourself,' I added, eyeing his shop-fresh fleece and shiny new gaiters. 'You look as if you've jumped straight from some glossy catalogue.'

Jon laughed and threw me a luxurious new pair of padded socks.

'Put these on and let's get going.'

We didn't get far. While Jon had all the energy of an unleashed bloodhound, my first wobbly steps were those of an ageing, decrepit thing. I could barely function. My joints were stiff, my legs achy and leaden, and my right thigh in particular tingled and felt oddly sensitive. I needed a good rest; Creag Meagaidh could wait.

Jon scampered up a nearby hill while I searched for fuel, stuffing my sack with peat blocks someone had dug during the summer and left on the moor to dry. Then, rather rashly, I grappled with a monstrous rotting trunk, momentarily forgetting how a simple back strain would scupper the entire journey. I left it for future gangrels and carted back more manageable pieces.

According to guidebooks the mountains which comprise the Creag Meagaidh massif are sensibly tackled from the south. The approaches are relatively short, the Munro peaks forming a convenient line and, if walking west, you finish overlooking the A86. A nice, tidy round, and on any fine February weekend the car park at Aberarder is busy with climbers, walkers and ski-tourers. No mention is made of the northern approaches we intended to follow. Logistically, they make little sense. There are no paths and you must pick your way across long and arduous miles of moorland, most likely meeting no one.

As I was unsure about Jon's level of fitness we set out with the modest intention of climbing only a couple of peaks.

'Which ones?' Jon wanted to know.

'Stob Poite Coire Ardair and Carn Liath.'

'Where?'

I pointed ahead to a bleak, snowy profile half obscured by a cloud bank.

'What about that monster on the right?'

'That's Creag Meagaidh, and I'm saving it for Christmas.'

Jon is no serious hillman. Prior to this trip he had climbed a mere half-dozen Munros, although to be fair, these hills were cherry-picked from Knoydart, Affric, Glencoe and the Cairngorms, and climbed as part of multi-day treks. What he lacks in experience seems compensated for by raw enthusiasm. This was not always the case. Some years ago I had managed to persuade him to forego his usual ski holiday for a February week in the Highlands. He very nearly regretted it. An attempt to ski the Larig Ghru through the Cairngorms ended prematurely in a grim snow-bound bivvy. Through the all-night blizzard, wrapped in cold, clammy sleeping bags, we sang, whistled and howled away the long hours till dawn. 'Never again,' he said afterwards, convalescing in an Aviemore fleshpot. But two days later we broke a fresh trail to the top of Glencoe on a windless, cloudless afternoon. 'Is this the best day of my life?' he said, and was hooked.

Embracing a raw and windy morning, we stole away from the watershed. The stiff breeze strengthened as we covered the moorland miles, climbed into a shallow corrie, then up a snowy shoulder to face a violent hail shower. Jon toiled some

Council of war midway up Carn Liath as conditions rapidly turn sour. Jon drove four hundred miles to join me for a few days before Christmas.

way behind, working off an excess of Christmas partying. I waited. There was no shelter so I crouched low in a foetal position, back to the wind, ice pellets rattling by. In ten minutes Jon's rocking shape appeared, snow and ice whipping his face. He looked shell-shocked.

'And you do this every day. You're a bloody maniac.'

'It's not always this grim.' I shouted.

Jon looked at me disbelievingly.

'So where's this Stob Poite thing or whatever it's called?'

'Behind me, about a mile away.' I turned and got a face full of stinging hail. 'But let's forget it and go with the wind to Carn Liath.'

The wind, which was barely tolerable, bounced us along the ridge, eastwards and over a number of confusing minor tops. We stopped often to confirm our wavering position. Spindrift and falling snow mingled thickly. On Carn Liath the wind had scoured the screes clean of snow, turned our jackets into the texture of cardboard, and frost-feathered Jon's face. We touched the cairn and fled. Darkness overtook us during a descent of seven trackless miles in falling snow and sleet, then drenching rain. A day's rest had fully recharged my batteries but Jon, bashed about on the ridge, now flagged alarmingly, so the last miles must have seemed endless. His enjoyment was more in retrospect when, later, we celebrated Christmas Eve with a huge meal in front of a blazing fire.

Jon left early on Christmas morning. Watching him go I did not envy his long drive to the West Midlands. I was unlikely to see him again this trip. He had opted for the guaranteed pleasures of a ski holiday in February rather than meet up again for more punishment.

'Good luck on Creag Meagaidh,' he had said on departure. Overnight snow covered the hills. Winter was creeping down the mountainsides.

Creag Meagaidh has always been a special place, so it was no surprise when in 1975 a large chunk of it was designated as an SSSI (Site of Special Scientific Interest) for 'its diversity of natural habitats from lochside to summit plateau'. Unfortunately, in 1985, the land—in private ownership—was sold cheaply to a private forestry company, Fountains Forestry. They immediately proposed to plough and plant an extensive area with Sitka spruce. A public outcry ensued and the name 'Creag Meagaidh', previously an obscure corner of the Highlands, was thrust into the nation's consciousness. A fierce, highly co-ordinated campaign led by an alliance of conservation groups eventually resulted in Fountains selling the land to the Government (though at a 50% profit). The area became a National Nature Reserve managed by Scottish National Heritage, whose simple aims were 'to promote naturalness'.

During fifteen years under their stewardship the land has witnessed a quiet ecological miracle. I went there recently at the height of summer and was astounded. By the removal of most of the deer and sheep the natural woodlands have flourished, tree regeneration increasing ten-fold. Plant communities have blossomed and previously scarce animals returned. It is a comforting thought at the turn of the millennium that there are a few energetic people working to reverse the decline of centuries and reinventing the richness that was once to be found throughout the Highlands.

The headwaters of the River Roy, which disperse like so many blood vessels, led me onto the unbroken snow of Stob Poite Coire Ardair. From the summit, through a veil of racing cloud, I was given a tantalising glimpse of Coire Ardair: snow-blasted buttresses much broken with ramps and terraces; to me austere and menacing, but to the dedicated ice climber one of Scotland's finest winter playgrounds. The clouds lifted marginally as I gained the rim of the Creag Meagaidh plateau. From the innumerable snowy peaks I recognised a distant Sgurr nan Conbhairean—which I had climbed in similar conditions a fortnight before,—while below were inky glens and dark swathes of plantations. There is a spacious, Cairngorm-like feel to this mountain. The ceiling of smoky-blue clouds hovering just overhead gave an exaggerated sense of elevation, and breaking trail for a mile or so into a bracing headwind and across a fresh mantle of snow was an uncontained joy.

The plateau area suddenly seemed busy. I waved to three people plodding north, then, just ahead, spotted two more leaving the summit and moving west. That made nine people seen on 44 peaks in six weeks. Beyond these black dots was a horizon thickening to sombre grey, though eastwards held a strange yellow glow like an Arctic twilight. I had hoped to continue on to Beinn a' Chaorainn but conditions were once again turning sour. With an ice-axe I dropped steeply to Lochan Uaine, around Loch Roy, negotiating the deep drifts with care as the cloak of snow here concealed many boulders and snares of loose scree. The weather deteriorated rapidly, snow clouds tumbled down behind me, and it was sleeting heavily on reaching the bothy.

After a substantial meal, I ate the last of the cake, drained the last of the Drambuie, and, before a sweltering fire, pondered the wild days that were surely just ahead: Ben Nevis, the Aonachs, the Grey Corries, the Mamores, then east to Ben Alder. I turned in with the strong feeling that the real battles were yet to begin.

In summer I would have saved a day by going over Creag Meagaidh with a full pack, polished off the remaining peak and dropped to Glen Spean ready for the next section. But hauling a 20-kilo load over snow-bound hills was never going to be a realistic option. I did manage it on a few occasions, but the extreme effort put paid to any vestige of enjoyment. The pleasure of climbing is to move fast and unhindered. The portage of overnight gear and food I left for the gentle through routes linking mountain areas, or for the graded trails over high passes.

So with a Munro still to climb and a full pack once again, I toiled up rough moorland towards the Burn of Agie and cast about for a place to cross. Filled with overnight rain it tumbled over a succession of minor waterfalls, through a shallow gorge and presented few breach points. My first attempt was abandoned midstream. After a precarious leap, my boot soles slithered off a boulder and I narrowly avoided a freezing bath in a plunge pool. Detouring downstream for thirty minutes I lurched across a line of stepping stones then got into serious difficulties scrambling up the near-vertical far bank. Reaching the point of no return, I yanked on tree roots and heaved myself clear, cursing and gasping at the drama of it all.

The climb up a misty Beinn a' Chaorainn was less eventful. The ridge had been scoured clear of snow and delicate cornices were forming over the east face. Once down I collected my sack and latched onto a fine path for three miles, leading through a dreary fringe of plantations and finally the Glen Spean road. All progress today seemed to demand more than the usual effort; my movements were lacklustre and disjointed, my left ankle and foot swollen and my right thigh in particular some-times erupting into painful spasms. I sensed I had not fully recovered from the exhausting trek of last week. And there could be no respite tomorrow as I was committed to another rendezvous, and a further fifteen-mile haul.

At Achluachrach Independent Hostel I hoped to find a bed, a shower and some food. Gavin Hogg, the proprietor, ably satisfied the first two needs, and room-mate Andy kindly offered to share his provisions. The hostel was filled to the rafters with a climbing club just arrived from York. It was a bewildering experience. I had not been with this many people since Kinlochewe Hotel Bar. The small kitchen and eating area was total chaos with fifteen excited people trying to cook, eat, wash up and talk simultaneously. They moved around like busy waiters clutching plates of steaming pasta and mugs of tea. The animated banter was of the weather and prevailing snow conditions: 'Who's got tomorrow's forecast?' 'Any ice on the Ben?' Plans were being hatched, maps and guidebooks mulled over, routes discussed.

Everyone's enthusiasm had paled a little by morning. Early glances outside revealed freshly-whitened mountains half-blotted out by clouds, from which fell a steady rain. 'What are we doing today then?' was the question on most people's lips; but the question, once uttered, was left to hang in the air like a discarded balloon, nobody willing to grasp it and make a decision.

Fresh from their offices and classrooms, the climbers could not have found the hills that morning particularly inviting. Somehow in the excitement of planning and expectation we become blinded to the reality of a West Highland winter. The January minima for Fort William are no lower than those for London, while precipitation is four times greater and gales five times as likely. There is a mythology peddled by those with a commercial interest in winter, and our shelves are stacked with lavish photo books depicting ridges heaped in pristine snow set against flawless skies. We remember the extraordinary tales of W. H. Murray, of the Aonach Eagach by moonlight, of untrespassed snows and rosy dawns, but we forget just how wet and nasty the weather is likely to be. Since leaving Sandwood I could count my 'dry and sunny' days on a single hand.

They were still debating when I crossed the bridge over the Spean and moved west along the south bank of the river. The track was a quagmire of animal excrement. Three sheepdogs in a Land Rover howled and barked hysterically as I scaled a locked farm gate at Monessie. Rain fell intermittently, and for brief minutes the sun, like an invisible artist, came through to ignite lines of fiery bracken and splash vivid greens on the sheep pastures.

Further on, at Corriechoille, I hid my sack and detoured two miles to Spean Bridge to reprovision—I was not due to pass another store until Braemar in the Cairngorms, very likely a month from now. Somehow I contrived to cram a week's groceries into an already full sack, wondering how I would ever haul it another ten miles over a high pass. But once a little uphill rhythm was achieved the weight became more bearable, and the stops less frequent. And as the afternoon wore on and the scenery turned wilder, the burden seem to lessen.

Scotland's highest mountains loomed to my right, growing steeply from bottle-green forests to white flanks and banks of cloud. This range, from Fort William to Loch Treig, forms a near-impenetrable barrier, breached only by a single pass, the Lairig Leacach, which I followed now, and which took me eventually to Glen Nevis and my base in the heart of the mountains.

I encountered six people, all smiling from within rain-soaked waterproofs and stopping for an idle chat. At Lairig bothy a lad from Dundee with long hair and a goatee beard insisted on making tea but, with one eye on the weather, I left as steam hissed from his pan. I bent low on the taxing climb to the pass, the cold wind now blowing snow into my face. A wild night was gathering here and I was glad to be on the final leg to the bothy. There was no sign of Gavin Davidge, a pal from the West Midlands.

No sooner had I eased the load from my shoulders when two young German lads, looking demoralised, came through the open door.

'We stay here tonight?'

'No problem. It's an open bothy, anyone can stay.'

In minutes they had turned the main room into a refugee camp, their gear strewn over a substantial portion of floor, outer clothing dripping from a line and pooling onto the wooden boards. I left them happily absorbed on their hands and knees, heads in the hearth, a couple of human bellows puffing at a smoky fire.

Unburdened, I jogged down to the river. I had seen a solitary light from afar and guessed it to be Gavin. He carried a tonnage of food, a rope and a grim long-range forecast. He also brought news of home, of friends unseen for months, and filled me with the normality of life I had so recently known but which now seemed worlds away. Gavin's arrival guaranteed company through to the New Year.

Next morning's sleet and rain inspired little beyond a discussion of our climbing strategy for the coming days. The mountain chains which array themselves in switchback ridges either side of the water of Nevis—Ben Nevis, the Aonachs, the Grey Corries, the Mamores—presented the toughest hurdle of the journey thus far. In certain icy conditions the difficulties of a Carn Mòr Dearg arête or the needle-edge 'Devil's Ridge' were technical as well as physical. By using the bothy as a base, the fifteen peaks arranged themselves into five challenging days. Although we were well-provisioned, a week of wild weather would have our plans in tatters—and here were some of the stormiest hills in the country.

The Germans, Thomas and Tobias, were a little reticent at first but good-natured. From Bavaria, they were fresh out of National Service—which explained their US Marine-style crops, black ankle boots and khaki jackets. Having survived a wretched wet night when their tent collapsed, just getting here had been adventure enough for them. I asked about their plans.

'We dry our boots first, then maybe we try for Rannoch Moor,' Thomas said.

'You mean Rannoch railway station?'

'No, the moor I think.'

He unfolded an old map showing the whole of Scotland. It had tiny scale and was covered in strange blue circles.

'Isn't that a military map?'

'Of course, but it is still okay?'

'It doesn't even show Glen Nevis.'

'But here is Rannoch Moor,' he said, pointing to a brown splodge in the middle of the map. It was indeed clearly labelled.

'Why, the moor, it's just a massive bog' (I spread my arms wide), 'no paths, no bothies, nothing to see, and very wet.'

Thomas looked disappointed.

'Very wet?' he repeated.

Both myself and Gavin nodded solemnly.

During the long evening the wind abated and we noticed huge pockets of clear sky littered with pin-pricks of stars. At dawn our wildest hopes were realised. As we stepped out with bare feet onto frozen ground, already yellow light fed down from summit ridges, casting long shadows on the snow, and the sky was a fresh-painted ceiling of blue. Our condensed breath rose vertically and we spoke in lowered tones, almost whispering, as if a loud word might undo what morning had spun.

The Germans, encouraged by the weather, decided to linger a few nights. They asked where they might buy groceries and whisky.

'Kinlochleven. It's a 15-mile round trip, about 25km.'

Then, watching us pack our hill gear, they asked: 'Can we get there by going over a mountain?'

Gavin looked at me. They were obviously ill-equipped to be on the ridges—no ice-axes or crampons—but we could see they would go anyway.

'Follow our steps up Sgurr Eilde Mòr,' I replied, gesturing to a white peak across the river, 'then it's southwest to the path and Kinlochleven. And watch for the south ridge, it's pretty steep.'

Gavin lent them his spare map and compass, and we began working the long, heathery slopes to the snowline. There was not a breath of wind. The muddy pools among the bogs were skinned with ice. Sandpipers swooped and dived at our approach and a few pale-rumped deer skipped away. A playful shout turned us around. The Germans, stark naked, were splashing each other with childish abandon in the Abhainn Rath.

'Crazy loons,' Gavin mumbled, 'Reckon they'll ever make it?'

'Not a chance if they come this way.'

My opinion was confirmed when we reached the snow, for it was soft and arduous and we were soon gasping with the effort.

A vast panorama unfurled. From unbroken snow at the summit we gazed silently in all directions, at a loss for words. Across the moors and straths the low sun sought out the lingering hues of autumn, browns and burnt reds, then snow like a tidemark. A slight haze denied us the Cairngorms, but most of the southern and western Highlands lay in view. In an arc across the brown expanse of Rannoch I pointed out the cone of Schiehallion, Ben Lawers, the whale-back of Ben Alder, the Beinn Dòrain Hills and Glencoe's Aonach Eagach, like jumbled newsprint, all slashed with black lines.

'What's that huge one nosing above everything else?', Gavin asked.

'Bidean nam Bian. Journey's end.'

Across the glen, impassive and benign, hunched Ben Nevis and her acolytes, and I wondered whether I had blown my best chance of tackling the notorious arête in such fine conditions.

We exercised extreme caution negotiating the south ridge, for the unconsolidated snow hid many sharp rocks and loose scree. The climb up Sgurr Eilde Beag was equally steep, particularly the final metres where we overcame a small cornice. Casting back we noticed a pair of tiny figures staggering in line to the summit—surely the Germans.

Other groups of walkers could be seen on the ridge, tiny black dashes, some moving with painstaking slowness, others gathered motionless on summits. Breaking a fresh trail we contoured beneath a nameless top, heading for Na Gruagaichean. As I approached, a couple of buzzards sprang to life, circling high overhead and fading to specks in an immensity of sky.

The weather was turning. In the last hour a film of high cloud had begun to filter the sun, and now encroached from the south like swarms of locusts, obscuring the peaks of Glencoe and spilling into the deep slash of Loch Leven. We made with all haste for Binnein Mòr, reaching it as drifting cloud enfolded us in a thick fog. A dash down the knee-deep windslab on the steep east ridge, and we were safe in the bowels of the glen by last light.

With the cloud cover night came on early, and we fumbled across the wastes of Coire Bhinnein before reaching the good path along the glen. As darkness filled the valley we became aware of a light floating in the gloom across the river about a mile away. For a while it moved eastwards towards the bothy, then it changed direction and began making height in Coire Rath opposite—strange, because only snow-bound cliffs and a high ridge awaited.

But as we turned right the light followed, and it now gained ground until I felt we were being stalked. Was this some military crank on a night exercise? Gavin was tiring so I pushed on ahead to start the fire. The bothy was empty. I lit some candles, boiled some water, and was about to put a match to kindling when a weary Gavin shambled up.

'You still being followed?'

'Kind of. He, or whatever *it* is, crossed the river again and now seems to be exploring the ruin.'

'Strange behaviour.'

Ten minutes later the door was flung open. A bearded figure clumped in breathing heavily. Paul Winters.

Two weeks ago I had sent Paul a date and a six-figure reference while at the Cluanie but was unsure whether he would show. He now claimed I had given him the map reference for the derelict lodge on the far bank—which I probably had, now I think about it. We settled before a good fire and took bets on when the

Germans would arrive. Gavin reckoned ten, I suggested nine, so it was a surprise when they shuffled in a little before eight. Thomas shivered uncontrollably and hugged the fire, Tobias crawled straight into his sleeping bag with a nosebleed and a bottle of whisky.

Next morning the lapping of rain on the corrugated roof inspired no one as a depression moved across Lochaber. A partial thaw had filled the burns and the hills were hidden in blankets of cloud. All day the Germans slept like hibernating creatures, emerging only to grunt a greeting, answer the call of nature or fill another cup with whisky. The three of us sat about the fire recounting past epics. Around midday a slightly eccentric couple popped in, rather wet but incredibly cheerful. They survived on a vegan diet of couscous and porridge, and Schiehallion was their eventual aim.

Some winter days have an intensity which is difficult to explain. It may be the limited hours of daylight, the poor conditions, or the necessity to keep warm, but you move with more purpose and urgency than you do on any jaunt in summer. Under a covering of snow, the mountains are taller, more remote and more menacing than they have ever appeared before.

But on New Year's Eve it was the gleam of light on snow which lured us up to the high ridge of the Grey Corries, like moths to a bright lamp. There were cheerful patches of blue sky, a steady breeze from the south, and, for minutes, the sun bathed us with a faint warmth, threading loops of silver on the meandering Allt Rath.

After weeks of travel I had built up an enviable level of fitness and moved uphill with the ease of a finely-tuned machine. The lethargy I had felt on the walk to Roy Bridge was gone. My friends, on the other hand, were struggling a little, continually at full stretch. Their styles were very different: Paul plodded up in a relentless, methodical gait while Gavin gained height in youthful bursts of speed, but needed frequent rests. In this way we gained Sgurr Choinnich Mor (1,095m).

Underfoot, the rain-soaked snow had frozen hard. The breeze strengthened into a fierce east wind, penetrating and cold, and the entire atmosphere paled. We watched the peaks of the Grey Corries disappear into ominous-looking clouds, and now as we descended the air filled with snow. I have never managed to reconcile myself with just how fast weather deteriorates in the Highlands.

Climbing Stob Coire an Laoigh the snow came horizontally into the face, stinging and blinding. I rooted about for my goggles. This one item of equipment—often overlooked—added immeasurably to the quality of life on that ridge. I peered ahead into the teeth of the blizzard with complete impunity, keeping a wary eye on the precipitous slopes to my left. By contrast my friends suffered, defending their vision with mittened hands, and in the whirling drift their movements were ghostlike and wavering.

It was odd then that I should be the one to slip. Descending a minor top as the ridge twisted northwards, I happened to glance back at the others. Taking my eye from the treacherous verglas, I stumbled and fell onto some nasty blocks. A spasm of pain came from deep inside my right thigh. Limping to the next col a little shaken, my mind entertained all manner of gloomy thoughts of long rests, even treatment—or defeat. I pushed these to the back of my mind and trudged on for our final peak, Stob Choire Claurigh (1,177m) in a complete white-out, the snow on the surface now merging with that falling. There were minutes of fumbling about until we located the buried cairn using the altimeter, then fled into the relative shelter of Coire Rath.

It was snowing hard to the level of the bothy. The Germans had been assiduously collecting fuel but unfortunately their National Service training taught nothing about the need to conserve native woodland. They looked up and grinned while busy sawing and stacking small piles of rowan branches which they had wrenched from a living specimen by the river.

There began the long, unchanging ritual of evening, which tonight, being Hogmanay, would extend into the small hours. Bothy life is not for the idle. To satisfy basic needs, such as food and warmth, involves effort and some degree of skill, but providing warmth is especially demanding. Once the snow has been shaken from cagoules and they hang dripping from the rafters, all efforts are focused on constructing and nurturing a fire so efficient it will readily turn wet stumps and damp peat into searing heat. So, from the far room, comes the staccato sound of wood being smashed and sorted, while a self-appointed expert stoops over the hearth and coaxes a bit of heat from a pile of kindling. It is a task best left to one person. The fire-tender knows when to poke or rearrange, or add, and knows also the weight of expectation resting on his shoulders. If the fire fails, the evening will effectively be dead.

Already Gavin, taking charge of cooking, has reserved a corner of the floor for his kitchen. With two stoves roaring he is surrounded by a wall of tins, food packets, mugs, pans and plates. Soon comes the aroma of coffee and the smell of frying onions. Later, after the third or fourth course and endless brews, port and whisky are passed round. Still hours before midnight and with our tongues loosened, there are rounds of singing, and room for the raconteurs among us. We stare into the fire, which crackles and spits and flares and for a minute gives the light of a hundred candles, painting our stubbly cheeks bright orange, throwing shadows across the back wall like dancing mannequins, haunting and beautiful. We had expected to make space by the fire for more arrivals but nobody came, and at midnight we bellowed our greetings to each other, then outside to the mountains hidden beneath the blanket of night and lightly falling snow.

I wanted a couple of days to rest my leg, which I sensed had been deteriorating since the long walk to Glen Roy; the slip on the Grey Corries merely aggravated any niggling strain or bruised muscle. The weather obliged. Rain, sleet and snow alternated for two days, the peaks wreathed in fast-moving clouds, spawned by a westerly wind frequently touching gale force. With the Germans gone and my friends departing soon after, the bothy was suddenly very empty. I became more aware of the hollow sound of the wind, and the scratching of a rodent. My solitary candle cast a large dark shadow on the ceiling. I turned my thoughts inwards but in the fire that evening I saw all the uncertainties of a long winter stretching out ahead. I longed for a fair day. The next day, 3 January, was quite the worst of the entire journey.

During the London 'hurricane' of 1987 I remember being shaken from sleep by the incessant clamour. I peered through my window with a sense of unreality: a tree I had known for most of my life lay strewn across the road, its thick canopy smothering my neighbour's car. Eddies of domestic rubbish, paper and plastic, were lifted high into the air, and the trees still standing were shaking with such violence I doubted they would survive the night.

That morning in Glen Nevis I had been woken by shaking roof timbers and hailstones rattling the skylight like automatic gun-fire. I opened the door in disbelief: spray whipped up from a brim-full Abhainn Rath was being thrown windward twenty or thirty metres, sheets of rain and sleet blanked out the hills opposite. I went back to bed, but the violence of it was unsettling, denying me even the concentration to read. At the crescendo of each gust I could sense my body tightening. I clenched teeth and hands and subconsciously paused for breath. I was at siege, these four thick walls enclosing the only pocket of calm air and dry ground for many miles around, and I visualised the roof being torn off like that of Cherry-Garrard's hut in the Antarctic. I could barely imagine the shrieking winds and blizzards which, just then, would be tearing across the summits.* Later, to conserve my few candles, I lay in darkness and channelled my thoughts back to that sunny day on the Mamores.

After so much noise it was uncanny to awake and hear nothing: no wind, the tapping of rain gone. Keen to deal with the two Munros above Loch Treig, I packed a day sack and followed the Abhainn Rath eastwards. Someone with no memory would have wondered at the dead sheep and uprooted birch, but, given the morning's calmness, could hardly have guessed at yesterday's chaos.

The path twisted around a bend, northwards, and past a deserted lodge. Here I left it to strike up the long, southerly ridge of Stob Coire Easain. Recent snow gave the appearance of having been violently sprayed onto the rock like white pebble-dash. Wind-scoured ice and deep drifts alternated, then a fine corrie curled around to the summit at 1,115 metres. Reaching the cairn brought with it the sense of patience rewarded and the finest feelings for a week. A sunless, wintry scene unfolded, almost entirely monochrome: grey valleys, dingy flanks climbing to a featureless white, the heavy cloud blanket lingering just above the tops. There was a strange absence of movement. Yesterday, the winds of the world had converged here, today a lit match would have been untroubled. Covering the short distance to my second peak, Stob a' Choire Mheadhoin, I passed a couple of local gentlemen toiling through deep snow. It was a Sunday, and, for most, the last day of a fortnight's holiday spanning Christmas and Hogmanay.

* Gusts on Cairngorm summit were recorded as 148mph that day.

Next morning I left early to walk the fourteen miles to Fort William, determined to bury a nest of worries before they hatched into a complete breakdown of confidence. I sensed my troubled thigh to be improving, but still the pain erupted with an occasional footfall and still the doubts festered. I sought more peace of mind than treatment, knowing full well any medical advice would simply boil down to one word: rest. I was not going to rest but nor did I want to cripple myself through stupidity.

The walk was a gentle and sunny descent to the sea at Loch Linnhe, the easiest going for weeks.

Nevis Watershed

'YOU'VE FALLEN off the mountain?'

The pretty young Asian doctor in casualty had a disarming smile. But she appeared sceptical.

'No, not exactly…' I admitted, and explained that I hadn't actually fallen but rather stumbled, though the problem really started a couple of weeks before that, the stumble merely aggravated… 'I'm just after a diagnosis,' I said finally.

'We only treat emergencies and referrals. You'll have to register with a local doctor.' Another disarming smile.

The surgery she recommended could only manage an appointment the day after tomorrow. The receptionist was surprised I was in such a hurry. 'There's plenty to do in Fort William you know,' she said, as I was leaving.

The town centre was a bewildering assault on the senses. It seemed a foreign, alien place, and I felt a complete stranger, quite out of sorts with the utter normality of this Monday afternoon. I was like someone who had been exiled from his country for a long time, returning starry-eyed at the confusion of people and vehicular noise, almost choking on perfume scent and car exhaust. But most arresting was the complete absence of urgency in people's movements. There was no hurrying, everyone was going about their business in a calm and casual way. People were *idling*. Later, sitting down to the novelty of a cooked meal and losing myself in a newspaper, I felt wonderfully anonymous among the handful of other visitors.

The Backpackers hostel was a friendly if strangely rootless place. Inside, little reminded me of where I was, and I might have gazed from the dormitory to see the backstreets of Nairobi, Cairo or Kathmandu. Not a single Scots accent could be heard among the medley of Americans and Europeans.

As a traveller on foot I was received with a mixture of curiosity and puzzlement.

'You've been walking trails for all that time. Jeez!'

The talk was all Thailand and India, touring Europe, 'staying with friends in London', the merits of this or that guidebook. For most I imagined Scotland was just another country to tick—Edinburgh, Loch Ness, the Skye run. Everyone seemed to be 'doing Scotland on the Haggis Bus', the common denominator.

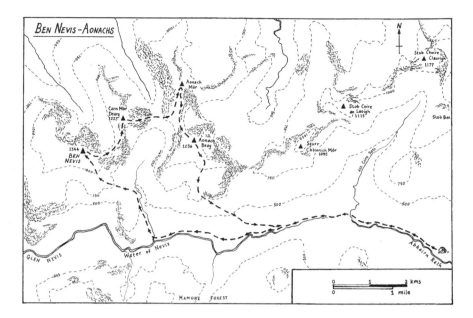

'You've never heard of the Haggis Bus!' The American looked at me in amazement, as if I had not grasped some self-evident truth. I confessed I hadn't, apologising for being so ignorant. I imagined a bus shaped like a sheep's intestines full of bland people with checklists of tourist sites on some cultural orienteering course. It occurred to me that many here indulged in the usual pitfalls and clichés of modern travel; comparing Edinburgh to Venice, Loch Lomond to Lake Geneva, the Highlands to the Alps, exchange rates, prices, places to stay. It was 'comparative' travel, hackneyed territory dredged up from standard guides and superficial visits. An overdose of culture and countries, it seems, leaves us dulled, like an over-long visit to an art gallery, and undermines our capacity to be moved and slightly changed by the places we visit and the people we encounter. I turned in thinking that perhaps real journeys only really exist in the imagination.

On my second morning a few less typical types emerged from the dormitories to plan bold outings and pester me for advice and bits of equipment. The civil rights lawyer collaborated with a Peace Corps worker to tackle Ben Nevis, but I was most interested when two attractive German girls asked about walking through Glen Nevis on an ambitious jaunt to Rannoch Moor and Corrour station. They would pass by the bothy and could leave a note with my equipment—unattended now for two days. I willingly lent them a map, torch and compass.

John Hillaby's classic *Journey through Britain*, describing a thousand-mile walk from Land's End to John O'Groats, was probably the first travel book I ever read and it came to mind as I approached the surgery. Reaching Bristol, Hillaby had been troubled with overworked muscles, and even contemplated ending his walk. The hotel manager put him in the capable hands of his head porter, an ex-boxing coach of some fame. And his prognosis: 'What you need sir, is *exercise*.'

The doctor poked and prodded me in various places and listened with practised nonchalance while I described the symptoms.

'Hmm,' he leaned back with a long sigh, then pulled from the shelf a large tome.

'Reckon you've trapped a nerve, that would explain the spasms and sensitivity. Ah yes, here it is… the sciatic nerve. That's the one.' He read for a minute, closed the book and looked over with a slightly patronising expression.

'You've managed to trap your sciatic nerve. Nothing to worry about, these things right themselves on their own. Don't climb any mountains for a while though…'

Discussion back at the hostel was more animated than usual. Everyone had arrived back early, the German girls defeated by a flooded river and the Americans overwhelmed by 'snow and crazy winds' not halfway up the tourist path. Unbeknown to me, two others, American students, had made an attempt on Sgurr a' Mhaim (1,099m), a mountain of unrelenting steepness. They had a lucky escape, narrowly averting serious injury or worse. Nearing the top, the leader, without crampons or ice-axe, slipped on hard snow and sailed down out of sight. Only a cushion of soft snow lower down saved him from becoming another sad statistic for the Lochaber Rescue Team.

Leaving Fort William on a grey morning, I began an ambitious day which would see me cover the length of Glen Nevis, and take in three Munros to boot. A log-jam of commuter traffic poured into town as I made my way out, passing the visitor centre and youth hostel, beyond the Nevis Falls to where the road becomes single track, then finally just a beaten path. In summer cars and caravans clog this popular run; today hardly a vehicle passed during the six miles to the road head.

At the Steall Falls I stashed a pile of grub, then examined the broken slopes above for a way into the hanging valley of Coire a' Mhail. The falls, deafening and mesmerising, crashed at my feet from an icing of snow. Much of the way was defended by rock bands, but an exploration found a steep, wooded ramp which seemed to offer a line through and give access to the three peaks of the central Mamores. I immediately began climbing.

The ramp, I soon discovered, quickly became a loose, sodden gully of an angle approaching that of a rock climb; handholds were roots and birch branches, and much was crumbly to the touch. Dislodged stones rattled down at my feet. A surge of adrenaline gave a familiar sensation, triggered when the walker strays into the terrain of the climber, and I realised I was way out of my depth. There was a mad, frantic scramble. I hauled myself up, lay on my belly, shaking with delayed shock—if that was the only way up, I thought, this corrie must be seldom visited. Since morning the sky had darkened, and now clouds were spilling low over the mountains. A change in weather seemed imminent.

My peaks, now hidden, encircled the corrie above, forming a well-known and dramatic horseshoe, the 'Ring of Steall'. The climb to Sgurr a' Mhaim, very steep and connected to the main Mamore crest by a slender ridge, begins the traverse. This peak lords over the glen and is often mistaken for Ben Nevis by first-time visitors. Certainly she has a symmetry and beauty lacking in the other, and she is a thrilling climb.

The snow, soft and exhausting lower down, hardened until I attached crampons and reached a lofty summit heaped in frozen drift. There was hardly a breeze and I marvelled at the strange, frozen world I had entered: every rock sheathed in rime and grey ice, the ridge obliterated beneath accumulations of snow. Despite white-out visibility these were the finest winter conditions of the journey.

A sense of exhilaration buoyed me along to the Devil's Ridge—the way becoming like a high wall whose base I couldn't see beyond a cushion of mist. Always narrow, the ridge now converged to the width of a metre, until I was brought to a halt on a white block with airy drops all round. An ominous-looking cornice had formed just below, barring the way. With shaky limbs, I kicked down a tiny gully, manoeuvred myself over a nasty gap and up to relative safety.

Realising it was already mid-afternoon came as a shock, as I had failed to take into account the hours of ascent and negotiation. Without stopping, I hastened over Sgorr an Iubhair and flew along the ridge for Am Bodach (1,032m). Just for a moment the cloud that had encircled me for so long disintegrated. Through a window I caught a smudgy glimpse of Glencoe, and, far below, the dark miles of Loch Leven reminded me that I was still high on a ridge and now in fading light. On Am Bodach I set my compass in a rising wind, my watch now indicating that the sun had already dipped below the horizon. I immediately started down.

In my haste I blundered off-ridge onto an area of dangerous windslab. Large slabs began peeling off around and beneath me, and for a few terrifying moments the entire slope seemed about to collapse. Thrown onto my back, I was carried down as if on a moving carpet, though in seconds had come to a gentle halt. On trembling legs, I picked myself up and traversed endless slopes to be away from the danger zone, slabs continuing to shear off until I found the gentle bowl of the corrie. In the gloom, I sat and pondered the remaining two hundred metres which still separated me from the safety of the valley floor.

An ancient glacier once bulldozed a route down the Nevis valley, excavating a vast trench, one side of which I now sought to descend. There was no question of locating that gully again, which, in any case, would be suicidal in the dark. If I strayed too far left I would end up among outcrops, while progress right was barred by the Steall Falls, whose thunder was a continual ringing in my ears. So I went straight down, hoping to string together a safe line along a labyrinth of ledges and ramps.

My choice of route was a dangerous mistake. Three times I dropped into hopeful gullies, clinging grimly to heather and birchwood, only to find my way barred by an outcrop or sheer drop. Each time I was forced to climb back up, frustrated and exhausted, and with the thought of a wretched bivouac in the forefront of my mind. I tried further right but could only see shadowy outlines of cliff faces. Directly below were nasty boilerplate slabs, green with slime and polished by centuries of runoff. Beyond that, darkness. Finding another innocent-looking gully, I edged down but lost my footing and bum-slid out of control, ice-axe zinging off rock as I went. I ground to a halt. Soaked, mud-covered, almost beyond caring, I scrambled down to safe ground.

For the last hour or so, three lights had been coming off the mountain opposite and, as I fought my way down, they made their way to the base of the slope. I crashed noisily through the last clawing woodland to meet them. Although a little embarrassed that I had attracted the concern of fellow hill-goers, it was comforting to realise that in such circumstances I was not alone.

They were ice climbers who'd enjoyed a fine day on the gullies of Aonach Beag.

'We could see your light swinging about and wondered if you were alright.'

I thanked them for waiting, exchanged pleasantries, then collected my grub and headed east up the glen. No longer fuelled by adrenaline, I relaxed and immediately felt deeply tired, my legs leaden and aching for the final six miles. I even suspected I might be hallucinating when I noticed a dozen fresh bootprints heading for the bothy. They turned out to belong to a boisterous army group on a winter mountaineering course, a couple of instructors and about ten officers.

There were two days of gales and rain. The first day I lay inert in my sleeping bag nursing a screaming headache, the second I busied myself painting the interior of the bothy. It was unbearably mild, about 7 or 8°C. Outside the snow was being stripped from the slopes almost like soap suds from a car windscreen. The raging Abhainn Rath, draining the snowfields of the Grey Corries, finally gave up the struggle for containment and spilled its waters fifty metres across the flood-plain like an incoming tide. I began reading *The Worst Journey in the World* by Apsley Cherry-Garrard, but at night dreamt of a dry place in the sun.

On the third day I sought my last mountains in the west, the four peaks of the Ben Nevis range. I approached the day with something less than complete enthusiasm, affected by an ebbing motivation perhaps, or just apprehensive at the prospect of spending ten or eleven hours alone on Britain's highest peaks. I remembered a TV documentary about a camera crew who set out to film an ice climb on the north face of Ben Nevis. They failed. Having established camp by the old observatory, they were beset by weeks of storms and ran over budget. Fifteen years on, I still recall with a shudder the remarkable footage of hurricane-fuelled blizzards, reminiscent of polar regions, which daily tore across the summit plateau.

A barrage of clouds hurried in from the south, pouring over the Mamores as I made my way up sharply from the Steall ruin and into a hanging valley at 500

Treacherous walking on the Grey Corries ridge, New Year's Eve.

metres. All morning the atmosphere had greyed, and now there were mean winds and rain. Despite my brisk pace I was gradually overtaken by a figure of olive complexion, a Spanish man from the Basque country. He approached wearing trainers, jeans and a sagging pullover, and he carried a flimsy yellow knapsack. In broken English he asked the way to Ben Nevis. I mentioned the tourist path by the youth hostel. His face betrayed bitter disappoinment.

One wonders just what tourists gain from a slog up Ben Nevis. Visiting the Appalachian mountains in the US, I was shocked to discover car parks and viewing towers on the highest peaks. There may be no road up the Ben, but it was one of the least interesting mountains of the entire walk. The summit area is a slum of human detritus: a raised triangular station, crumbling walls of a century-old observatory, abseil poles and an aluminium shelter which had somehow escaped demolition after the Cairngorm tragedy of 1971. None of this belongs here, and perhaps it is time to remove the metal, concrete and stone, and let the mountain be.

I cowered behind the shelter, avoiding some excrement which the partial thaw had exposed. Conditions were vile: wet and cold with a severe wind chill. A brightly clad figure struggled towards me, and twice had to pick himself up from the snow after stumbling. An elderly gentleman, he had come up the tourist path. In a garbled voice he strongly advised me against tackling the arête, saying the forecast promised a drop in temperature that would turn the slush into verglas. He stared at his watch for a moment.

'One o clock,' he shouted, 'conditions are wild, you'd be mad to continue.'

I nodded, chatted for a while, then took a south-east bearing straight for the arête. I had absolutely no intention of returning to this group of hills. Perceptions of folly will always differ. On a normal trip I would have hurried down, but one o' clock meant three peaks had to be squeezed into the remaining three hours of daylight. The final six miles of glen bashing did not concern me, as this just meant another night march on a now familiar track.

Fortunately I knew the arête well, though conditions gave a tense and dramatic traverse. A southerly gale made up for any lack of ice, pushing each step towards the abyss of Coire Leis. Ice-axe and ski pole were replaced by free hands as I scrambled, crawled and edged along to Carn Mòr Dearg. While I was climbing the Mamores three days previously, my crampon had made a slight tear on my lightweight overtrousers. Suddenly a gust ripped the tear line from ankle to waist, and now my legging flapped and ballooned noisily, adding to the general sense of disorientation.

My first brush with this hill while a teenager proved a pivotal experience. The day was late December, windy and bitterly cold. A thin layer of old snow had thawed, then frozen again as hard as iron, leaving a skin of verglas and black ice over the rocks. I had toiled up the easy northern side with Dave Hughes. Then, to escape the gale, we trod carefully down the steep east ridge, cutting steps with our axes, for we wore no crampons.

Although highly alert to the dangers—the brittle ice that coated the rocks, the convex slope immediately below us—nothing prepared me for the sight of Dave spinning past out of control, ice-axe gone, legs and arms flailing helplessly. In a flash he accelerated into the bowl of the corrie and to an uncertain future. Sixteen years on, in my mind's eye, I can still see his struggling form and still recall my disbelief and absolute horror. I can't remember how he managed to stop, but he did, and with extreme good fortune he emerged only lightly scathed, just a little bruised and sore, though extremely shaken. In a few brutal seconds we had been taught a hundred lessons in mountain safety. First and foremost we learned respect. But more profoundly I realised that we did not belong here, would always be strangers in these mountains, that the friendly contours on the map could be lethal and capable of smashing a fragile human as easily as a foot might crush an ant.

Despite charging down the leagues of soft snow from Carn Mòr Dearg, it was three when I reached the col, much later than I had hoped. Drilling my legs up, I reached Aonach Mòr—a mountain now sacrificed to downhill skiing—in about thirty minutes, then took another thirty through raking mist to gain Aonach Beag. The cairn was buried but orange peel marked its location. Fading light and a gusty wind combined to give a descent of pure drama. I swept eastwards along the line of the glen until darkness drove me down, but managed in the process to slice a large chunk from the tedious walk back.

On 12 January, sixteen days after first arriving in Glen Nevis, I forged east. I went round the head of Loch Treig, across the northern fringe of Rannoch Moor and camped a little above Loch Ossian. Like a glow-worm, a train groaned up from Tulloch station, crossing the abyss of the moor in a narrow arc of light. I watched with a palpable sense of relief that finally I had put some miles eastwards. Already there was a change in the landscape. The mountains were smoother in profile, the summits more flattened, the narrow arêtes and ridges now mostly broad arms. And the switchbacks had gone. There were still blank cliff faces and shattered crests, but these were giant scoops taken from the high plateaux, the imprint of corrie glaciers which lingered long after the main ice-sheets had vanished.

I continued east along Loch Ossian the next day, then swung north to climb Chno Dearg (1,046m), a rather dull hill after the excitement of the West Highlands. Even at midday, heavy cloud cover lent an oppressive gloom to the day. A chain of mountains still separated me from a roof and a fire—Culra bothy—and lunching by an old ruin I considered the ways through. There were two possible routes. The northern one, though longer and partly trackless, was 200 metres lower than the well-known pass of Bealach Dubh. I felt the weight on my shoulder and noted that the steady rain was now falling as snow on the higher slopes. I went north and, as usual, regretted it.

The watershed area was a complex morass of peat ditches and clawing heather, which frustrated progress and demanded extra effort in the now-driving sleet. A path indicated by the map was an exaggeration, and did little to ease me across the worst of the bog. Now in near-darkness, a steady descent along An Lairig brought me eventually to the sheen of Loch Pattack. A strange, neon halo to the east was the lights of the new Ben Alder lodge. I turned right, away from the glow, and trudged towards a glimmer of candlelight. There were folk at Culra. I tingled with anticipation at the thought of meeting people again.

Six brassy faces were sitting on the floor around a good fire. The aroma of pine and something illicit hung in the air. They all grinned as I clumped in, hair all stuck to my brow, this shiny figure like a diver from the seabed. I lowered my rucksack with a deep sigh. One man in broad Liverpudlian shouted a wild greeting, introducing himself as 'Scouser Steve', another shoved a mug of sweet tea into my hand. Space was made by the fire and there was whisky and good humour enough for me to forget the loneliness of recent days.

8

The Worst Journey

STEVE WATCHED as I pulled on my jacket, slung an empty rucksack onto one shoulder and made for the door.

'Yer never goin' far like that?'

'Just collecting some groceries,' I said casually.

'Whaa-at?'

Twenty minutes later, I was back in the bothy, slitting open a plastic sack. An assortment of tins rolled onto the floor. Another sack was stuffed with perishables.

Steve looked at me with furious concentration, unsure whether he was sharing a room with a genius, or a complete lunatic.

'An' yer got the same buried across the Highlands?'

I nodded, opening a tin of mackerel.

'Blo-ody fooking 'ell.' he said, shaking his head.

I had arrived at the true backbone of the Central Highlands, a column of peaks and ridges comprising the greater part of 200 square miles of near-wilderness. Defended naturally on three sides by Rannoch Moor, Loch Ericht and Loch Laggan, only the railway line at its western edge gives a semblance of public accessibility. Its remoteness extends back into history; the region was never much settled due to its altitude, but provided an ideal sanctuary for lawless exiles and once, in 1746, for a wandering Jacobite prince .

It is prime mountain land. Eight of the fourteen Munros climb above a thousand metres. Two peaks, Ben Alder and Aonach Beag, have an outline recognisable from most corners of the Highlands. Some of the corries give fine winter climbing, though with most approaches requiring a day's effort, only the dedicated will venture this far. For the most part the region is left to the deerstalker, naturalist and hill-walker, or those who seek their solitude in the most austere of mountain landscapes. In 1997 the body of a young Frenchman dressed in cowboy boots and poncho was found near one of the summits, a gun by his side. An inquest recorded an open verdict. Forty-five years earlier, in what was then the worst-ever climbing tragedy, four experienced climbers were overwhelmed by a

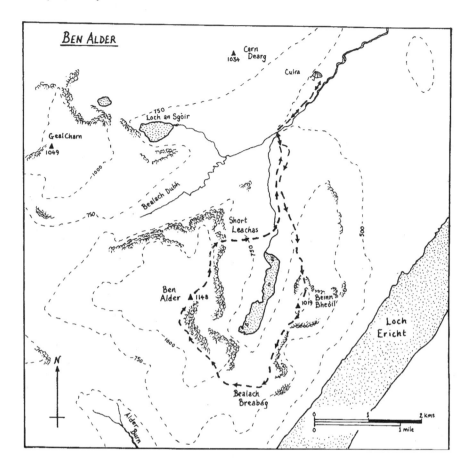

violent Hogmanay blizzard. They perished after an attempted bivouac at merely 450 metres on the floor of the glen.

During many visits here I have always been extremely fortunate: I recall either quiet mists or long sunny views, when half-a-dozen Munros yielded easily. Even during the deep freeze of a recent Christmas, when the temperatures touched –20C, I reaped a succession of clear, breathless days. With this in mind, and when pinned indoors in Glen Nevis, I had looked forward to this section with eager anticipation. On reaching Culra then, after a fortnight of snow, rain and interminable gloom, I might have been forgiven for thinking that I was due some decent weather.

Human minds, of course, are incurably irrational. My first morning was inauspicious enough: the peaks were in an iron-grip of cloud and a gusty wind brought down bruising snow showers. Jaded from last night's march, I needed immense self-discipline just to pull on wet socks, brave the chill and retrieve my cache.

The main room being busy, I had moved in with Scouser Steve. Steve was a stocky, broad-shouldered man with mischievous eyes. He breathed friendliness, talked endlessly and had a weakness for tinned steak and clean socks—eleven pairs of which were draped around the room. He spoke of painting and decorating days in London, youth work in Liverpool, a recent flirtation with Mountain Leadership. Knowing he had spent the previous week roaming the hills above Rannoch Moor I wondered what had brought him to Culra.

'Me map blew away on Chno Dearg,' he said, 'and I came 'ere to see if anyone would sell us a spare.'

The others, a collection of English, Scots and two Irish instructors, returned from Ben Alder at gloaming, their faces betraying the strain of battling against high wind and difficult snow on the plateau. Later, during pauses in our chatter, the wind was noticeable in its whining.

Steve was up before dawn next morning. He pulled on his boots and crunched around, waxing lyrical about the stars and how Ben Alder was wreathed in the most delicate mist. Then he was frying steak and potatoes and boiling water for tea. I looked at my watch: 4.30 a.m. I tried to sleep.

'Bugger,' he exclaimed, staring through the window, 'it's clouded over again.'

In a few minutes he had resumed his cocooned snoring.

He was still wrapped in goose down when later I started for Beinn a' Chlachair and Geal Charn, two peaks to the north. Having climbed both the previous winter, I set out with the confidence of familiarity, though conditions today would be quite different. My route up Chlachair (1,088m) led into a blinding vortex of wind-driven snow. Steep mountain sides offered some initial protection, but the plateau-like summit extending west for a mile was highly exposed and disorientating, and it needed an hour of meticulous navigation through drifted snow to locate the cairn. All day conditions were marginal, and many times I was on the point of turning back.

Geal Charn (1,049m) was easier, as the wind, though stronger and colder, now harried me from behind, at times almost lifting me up the slopes. I shambled towards a large cairn, desperate to compose myself for a few minutes before the final plunge down. But, as anyone who has experienced these conditions will know, a small windbreak in a blizzard is an intolerable spot in which to linger, even briefly. Spindrift pin-wheeled around the cairn, spraying my cheeks and forehead with a cold flush, finding every weakness in my protective clothing. If I opened my sack for a second, a cloud of crystals tumbled inside. A hand covering my face, I fled, once again passing Loch Pattack, which marked the final darkening mile to the bothy.

Steve had been idle again. While keen to climb Ben Alder, he would wait, he said, for a fair-weather day, readily accepting he could be in for a long wait. The others gone, we had moved into the larger room which contained the luxury of a box bunk at one end, the sole concession to furnishings at Culra. In the past I have seen benches, chairs and tables, all now having likely disappeared up the chimney. The visitor's log book testifies to the bothy's popularity, even during the short days of late autumn and winter, especially as many never mark their stay with a written entry.

Coast-to-coast walkers frequently use this shelter *en route* between the Cairn-gorms and the Nevis range, most having their first sight of it as they stride across the moors from the north-east: a one-storey wooden lodge tucked into the shadow of looming mountains. And to the traveller on a dark evening with a full pack, the distant light pricking the gloom never seems to get any nearer.

All Friday morning we lounged about listening to blasts of wind whine down the chimney. I went out to scour the bogs for fuel and Steve busied himself with preparations for his journey to a bothy by Loch Ericht. At noon the clouds lifted for the first time since I arrived, and looking west I was reminded why so many people walk the tedious lochside miles just to be here. The arc of mountains—Beinn Bheòil, Ben Alder, Geal Charn—is one of the most memorable profiles in the Highlands: Ben Alder, buttressed by the graceful lines of her two 'Leachas', was streaming a visor of snow. Further right was the wedge of Bealach Dubh, the raised loaf of Geal Charn, and in between, like a spearhead, Lancet Edge, crying out to be climbed.

It being too late for a big round I went up Carn Dearg (1,034m) instead, which rose immediately behind the bothy. This at least would shorten the list of peaks to be climbed the next day. Deep, tiresome snow combined with eddies of spindrift made for a battling ascent. But then something unusual happened. The sun, unseen for a week, came through in a scatter of blue shadows, the snow now like shiny enamel and the moorland below a hundred glittering lochans. Its faint warmth and light had a deeply restorative effect. There were views eastwards to the Drumochter moors, then beyond to the shadowy Cairngorms. South were some of the hills to come: Schiehallion and Lawers, Glen Lyon and Lochy. By contrast, ahead was a murky scene spawning the winds which gusted around the summit.

Once back at the bothy I allowed myself some optimism about the weather. The sky had cleared to a pale blue. The Lancet Edge glowed orange, then faded to an outline as the evening star climbed above the pass and seemed to hang suspended. I hurried indoors as a chill breeze sprang up. I made a small fire, placed a candle at the north window and went to bed to read—quite sure that folk would be arriving for the weekend. There was a slight moan from the wind, the fire spluttered, but these sounds barely registered. After the banter of recent evenings it felt stony quiet. No one came, and by ten I had resigned myself to a peaceful night.

I heard their voices before a torch beam was shone through the window, Scots voices, burbling and excitable. They fumbled around in the outhouse before piling into the main room, each wearing a headtorch, one clutching a carrier full of cans. Iain, Pete and Gav, a fell-running trio all in their forties, talked simultaneously with a barely controlled enthusiasm about when they were last here—in the 70s—about what had changed, and the hills they planned to climb. 'Who's nicked all the bloody furniture?', one said, casting about. There were no polite formalities. Cans of beer were passed round and the humour began. On their faces and concealed in their jocular outbursts was the sheer delight of escaping a workaday routine and gathering here with the promise of a couple of days in the hills. Three Glaswegians turned up later, billeted themselves in the smaller room and immediately generated their own merriment. Outside the frozen ground was already dusted with falling snow.

By morning the snow lay in a uniform quilt halfway to knee-height, transforming the landscape. Large flakes came down from a fog of low cloud, drifting lazily on an easterly breeze. My room-mates, a little groggy at first, were away an hour after daybreak, intent on climbing the four Munros of the Aonach Beag range. 'Might take in Alder and Bheoil if we have time,' Iain said with a grin, and then they were gone, forging up the slope behind the bothy.

With more measured enthusiasm, I set off westwards towards the pass of Bealach Dubh. It needed only five minutes to convince me that today offered nothing beyond the drudgery of effort, and I continued on upwards more in hope than in any real expectation of reaching a summit. Often progress was stalled as I sank to my waist in some drift, burning energy as I thrashed about for a sure footing. Covering two and a half miles to the bealach required the same in hours, a ridiculously slow pace, and by midday I was completely spent. My three mountains still lay miles to the west, visibility was a few metres and it was still snowing. I turned around and followed my meandering prints back to Culra.

In the middle of the afternoon with a mug of steaming tea I crawled into my sack. And there I lay, immobilised, neither asleep nor fully awake, oblivious to the world beyond the bothy, deliriously happy that all work for the remainder of the day had been cancelled. My daydreams were interrupted by Gav coming in. He shook snow from his boots and jacket, cursing the conditions as he did so. After struggling over the modest Carn Dearg he had opted to descend, while Iain and Pete ploughed on for Geal Charn and farther tops. He dismissed any doubts I might have had about the wisdom of his friends in continuing. 'No problem,' he said, 'those guys are super-fit. They do the Ben Nevis Race in under two hours.'

We set about constructing a large fire for their return, then sat around it bantering on all manner of things. Gav, from Dunblane, told of his fell-running activities. By sheer coincidence, he often partnered a friend of mine on mountain marathons. We heard the Glaswegians return. Any sign of Iain and Pete, we asked? No, they had been on a different mountain, they said.

The gloom of a short winter's day slowly filled the room. Just before dark, Gav went out to scan the slopes westwards, the direction his friends would take if returning from the pass. But there was nothing but a shroud of mist and gently falling snow.

'Do they have headtorches?' I asked.

'No, I don't think so,' Gav said, frowning, then added: 'Damn, why didn't I give them mine?'

He came in, stoked the fire, put on a brew, and prepared a meal. Time passed easily. Our fire—the best yet at Culra—crackled and spat with the aroma of pine resin and peat. Candles flickered at the windows. We joked and laughed, but unspoken, in the backs of our minds, was the image of Iain and Pete engaged in a struggle with deep drifts and darkness, likely without a torch. Six o' clock came, then seven.

'They're late. Where the hell are they?' Gavin was speaking my thoughts as much as his own. By bizarre timing a squeal of laughter came from the Glaswegians next door, warming for a long evening.

Worry is insidious. It begins harmlessly enough, a vague concern at the back of the mind, but, given time, it grows like a virulent illness until you can think of nothing else, are consumed by it. By eight we were getting a little frantic; after all, they had been out eleven full hours. We discussed how much food they had, whether they carried survival bags; and tactics: if in difficulty, would they head for the hunting lodge at Corrour? At least, we agreed, it was not particularly cold. This was no numbing blizzard, and we felt sure they could survive a night in the open. Blundering over a corniced cliff was Gav's main concern.

'Couldn't see more than a few metres when I left them,' he said, staring into the fire. 'They were walking blind.'

We decided to begin a search at nine.

'At least we can bring them a light, some grub, and stamp a fresh trail through the snow.' I said.

With a course of action agreed upon, we instantly felt better. Twenty minutes later they shambled in. Gav hugged his friends and danced a jig around the room. Their expressions were long and drawn, showing the strain of the hours since leaving their last mountain.

'Five hours from the top, *five bloody hours*, can you believe it?' Pete said wearily. 'A nightmare, but your tracks were a Godsend—kept us going, and then we saw the light. Gav, pass over some of that beer, mate.'

We relaxed. Despite their undoubted fatigue they had no plans for an early night. When Gav and myself turned in later, Iain and Pete joined the group next door and partied into the small hours. I recall being woken when they stumbled into the room for a second time—and even worse for wear—and to say the least there was all manner of shenanigans. I could only marvel at the energy of fortysomethings—and cancel tomorrow.

'What will you tell your work mates?' I asked Iain later that morning.

'There's nothing you can tell them,' he said, continuing his resuscitation of Pete who still lay in a coma.

§ § §

Culra empty again, I wandered down past a frozen Loch Pattack to gather dry branches from the small wood. Rabid squalls came down from the north. By using food the others had left, I still had enough for a couple of days at least. But tomorrow I needed to climb some mountains.

Beinn Bheoil and Ben Alder make a pleasant horseshoe circuit of some nine miles. While in summer it is a straightforward jaunt of five or six hours, I was faced with the most extreme conditions of the winter, and some of the most difficult I can remember. The hills were locked beneath half a metre of unconsolidated snow, with drifts far deeper. Much worse, though, was the northerly wind, gale force over the tops, and promising a dangerously high chill factor. Opening the door I immediately felt that wind. It swept down the shoulder of Carn Dearg carrying clouds of spindrift—and had me scurrying back inside to pull on a second layer of thermals.

The broad flank of Beinn Bheòil yielded slowly. The snow, consistently deep, demanded patience and unreasonable reserves of energy. I accepted from the outset that progress today would be hard-won and painstakingly slow, that I was terribly alone, and that if conditions worsened I would have no hesitation about turning back. But despite this, despite all the effort and uncertainty, it was exhilarating. Everything seemed on the move. Wind-blown snow and ice slammed at me from behind, hissing past and across the slope in front. Waves of sunshine flashed by like strobe lighting, dazzling and slightly disorientating. And then one of the sights of the winter: from thinning cloud Ben Alder emerged fresh and gleaming, snow streaming from her Leachas ridges and high plateau, merging with mushroom clouds above, the drama played out beneath a serene blue sky. The sudden beauty allowed me to forget the tedium of the ascent; and I thought that perhaps this was 'it', the essence of winter, a day stolen from the high Arctic and smuggled south to the Highlands. It was what I had come for.

The summit was scoured clear, but at the small col just beyond I wrestled with metre-high drifts and again considered a retreat. Occasional sunshine did nothing to blunt the severe chill, the dappled views to the south merely belying the conditions on the tops.

A horseshoe route now took me round to the south side of Alder. The steepness of the climb at first gave a pleasurable respite from the north wind, but its full fury unwound on the plateau. It now drove straight at me so that progress was only possible during the brief lulls. I pulled on my last spare garment and found the trig point in a white-out. Then I went blind on a bearing for an escape ridge, the Short Leachas, conscious always of the corniced cliff to my right. Becoming cold and uncertain, I had an overwhelming desire to get down. I needed to be out of this wind and away from this relentless noise, even though I knew a purgatory of deep snow awaited in the corrie below.

The Short Leachas, narrow and exposed, dropped away sharply. Having fixed crampons, by a clumsy step I had ripped a long tear in my overtrousers, the tattered edges now flapping incessantly. In the general confusion I then saw my compass disappear into the corrie. The ridge narrowed further, and in one place snow spiralled off the crest with such violence I could no longer see to continue; my goggles, by this time, iced and useless. For a modicum of shelter, I had no choice but to drop onto a ledge and make a painstaking detour above the corrie headwall. I regained the ridge, now at an easier angle, and ploughed down to the bowl of the corrie. I could see the short distance to Culra—about two miles, and all downhill. It was across a featureless snow slope, and this snow would be the day's last nightmare.

Deeply tired at the remorseless work rate, I ploughed on for an hour but made little real progress, less than half a mile. I appeared to be lumbering forward as if in slow motion, avoiding hasty movements, for it would be like running in sand, and leave me spent. Indeed, my movements were so laborious and my energy levels dropping so fast that I began to consider the very real possibility of a freezing bivouac, perhaps tucked into a drift by the burn. There was precious little shelter anywhere, the wind whipping up spindrift as fiercely as ever. I wondered how close I was to panic, and I tried to draw strength from previous experiences. Inevitably, I recalled reading of the 1951 tragedy when four climbers perished just a few miles away. I felt very alone and remember thinking it would be easy to die.

There was some shelter in the curve of the burn. But the snow was impossible, nowhere less than waist deep, so it was back to exposed ground and fighting the strong headwind again. I began concentrating only on reaching the next object— a rock or piece of heather poking through the surface—so I knew I was making sure progress. I found my tracks from the morning, which cheered me immensely, and followed their meandering pattern with a will. They led me to the confluence as evening darkened and at last I felt truly safe. There was a motorway of old prints from the weekend. Culra was an easy ten minutes away.

Slamming the door I peeled off my frozen outer shell. Congealed ice like plastic beads had lodged in my hair and onto the inside of my gaiters and cuffs. Blowing snow had penetrated everywhere, melted, and soaked my underclothes, giving the lie to the theory that sub-zero temperatures leave you dry. I stoked the fire to an inferno, and, cradling a mug of sweet coffee, watched the steam rise from my garments strewn along the line.

Given a conventional perspective on the element of risk that day, I might have packed my sack and headed home. But I had never felt stronger or more alive, and the 'buzz' afterwards had never been greater. The more intense the struggle, it seemed, the greater my addiction. I was intoxicated.

I fully acknowledge the very real risks associated with solo winter walking, especially when, as on this journey, it is undertaken over a long period of time. In the event of real difficulty—a broken bone, or illness—there is no one to raise the alarm, and so no chance of immediate assistance. Unless you are able to crawl to safety, the wind and cold will soon finish you off. And if you make it back to a bothy, how long before the next winter visitor? During my struggle to escape the Mamores earlier that month, I was only too aware of my sudden isolation and need for self-reliance. My brother would not be expecting a call for thirteen days, and, clawing my way down in darkness, I knew I was as alone as if I had been crossing Greenland.

It seems that our sophisticated lifestyles are in danger of spawning a dependency culture when it comes to risk. We cannot make the mountains safe. Mobile phones, VHF radios, flares and summit refuges merely encourage a false sense of security, and surely only drive another wedge between us and the mountains with which we wish to engage and which we profess to love. My own survival boiled down to a high level of fitness and basic common sense, two things that cannot be taught, only acquired. Diet, navigational skills, equipment—the commercially driven obsessions of magazines—are, by comparison, negligible. But that said, there was hardly a day when I was not reminded of how tenuous the line was between enjoyment and disaster.

Psychologically, too, solo walking is not for everyone. None of my friends were fool enough to leave their jobs and accompany me as Dave had done in '86, and at times I sorely missed a companion. But the periods of loneliness paled by comparison with the sheer intensity of the experience and the moments of ecstasy—inexpressible as they were—which had become a daily feature. There was a deepening self-awareness, a growing confidence, a selfish delight in freedom not experienced since childhood and a limitless future: '…days flashing on the heels of days like dreams'.*

An irrational side of me believed that somehow while I slept the snow would consolidate into a perfect walking surface, hard and crisp, that the wind would die and the sun show its face. I didn't deserve another day of unremitting torture among the drifts.

After a dreamless twelve-hour sleep, pre-dawn promised much. Outside was a scene of exquisite beauty. A tapestry of sunrise colours, scarlet and yellow, clustered above the hills to the south-east, while Ben Alder stood serene, wrapped in a quilt of blue snow. Above, an inky sky was broken only by a waxing moon. Was this to be one of those rare frozen days, that seemed to suspend time itself, when all that could be seen was an ocean of mountain across an unlimited horizon?

A fine thought with which to be crunching up Bealach Dubh and towards my last peaks of this section: Beinn Eibhinn, Aonach Beag and Geal Charn. To my right the yellow light on the Lancet Edge crept downwards, though I would be in shade until I breached the pass. I kept warm by working hard, but shivered from head to toe when caught full by the occasional breeze.

On most days these peaks are an easy trio: there is an interesting ridge, steep in places, and there are shapely summits, but nothing difficult or technical. I planned to climb the farthest one first, and so finish with a long descent to Culra. This morning, like the days before, I waded through deep snow, which grew deeper and more tiring beyond the pass. I was impatient to climb these hills and be gone.

*Jack London, *Call of the Wild*

Tomorrow I was due to report my safe arrival at Dalwhinnie; but floundering again and again, down to the base of my rucksack, sometimes losing balance and toppling over, made impatience a fruitless policy. My legs were heavy after yesterday's effort, and I wondered if I would be able to draw on the same reserves. The effort was unremitting. A group might have made better headway where everyone takes a turn to break trail, but it was a pointless thought. After four miles in as many hours, the day had a despairing feel to it.

Ahead, the wind-scoured shoulder of Beinn Eibhinn promised a clear, if steep, route to the main crest. The sight of it was deeply encouraging. All morning I had hoped the ridge might reward my effort with some easy walking. Looking west, there were still views of the Grey Corries and Lochaber Hills. But now a southerly breeze was bringing a dull, opaque haze, and the sun had become a white blister. A steep 500-metre pull brought me to the summit ridge, some five hours from the bothy.

After such exacting toil, I might have sought rest, but I now fought my way to the cairn in a state of disbelief. In less than an hour, the benign breeze had become a southerly gale. A scarf of snow streamed over the crest and for a moment it threatened to take me with it. I struggled eastwards along the ridge, but at a wind-blasted col my confidence disintegrated. The two remaining peaks were an impossible target, though neither could I face the hours of backtracking to Culra. I needed to get straight down. Westwards to Loch Ossian and the railway station at Corrour was my only option. I deeply resented having to take a train to Fort William. It would sour the purity of my venture but just then I could see no alternative. The thought was deeply depressing. I sank to the valley floor.

It was now past four, and very cold. Incredibly, the wind that had defeated me on the ridge had shrunk to a breeze again, and all the drama had gone from the day. I moved away from the mountains with a sense of resignation, but knowing that I would be back for more tomorrow.

I remembered there was a youth hostel at the far end of the loch. It would be closed, of course, but passing by a week ago I had seen a lighted window. The occupant might be persuaded to sell a little food, just enough to get me over the mountains and back to Culra. I might avoid the train after all.

Something was moving among the drifts just ahead. A little closer and I realised it was a woman of slight build. She was burdened with the most enormous pack I had ever seen. It must have weighed near her own body weight for she hobbled with every step. As I approached she lost balance and crumpled into a heap. I helped her up.

'Thanks.'

Her pack meant business. Attached were two climbing axes, a rope, sleeping mat, a tent, even some coal.

'Going far?' I asked. I imagined she was about to camp or bivvy.

'I'm meeting friends in a bothy by Loch Ericht.'

'What, tonight?' I was shocked.

'Sure.' She smiled. 'Why not?'

Why not?, I thought. Because the snow's a nightmare and you'll never make it. Simple. Which is what I wanted to say, my frustrations from the day, always simmering, now boiling over. Instead, I pointed out my snail's progress, and that I was probably carrying a third her weight. With some difficulty I persuaded her to head back and wait for morning

We aimed for the youth hostel, about six miles away. Her name was Kate. As an outdoor leader she had frequently trekked in such exotic places as Nepal, Karakoram and Patagonia. We swapped stories of travel on the subcontinent, but the lochside miles and cold eventually stifled any desire for conversation, and we only wished the light at the end of the loch would get a little nearer.

Approaching the hostel I saw that the door was ajar. Light flooded out, and just beyond, a bearded figure was standing .

'Open?'

'Not officially. Come in.'

A wall of heat cushioned our entry. In the middle of the room was a coal-burning stove, and on one of the hot plates a large iron kettle was hissing. Laid out on a table were three mugs, some milk, a jar of coffee. We had been expected.

The place was indeed closed (unless specially booked by groups at weekends), but Alan, the resident warden, made us extremely welcome. A shy, quiet man in his fifties, he loved the place like a home, and obviously enjoyed the company of winter visitors. I was able to phone my brother, and helped myself to food left by previous visitors.

At breakfast I noticed Alan slicing up old vegetables. Surely he wasn't going to eat that lot? He cleared a space on the tiled floor, poured out the scraps, and opened the door. After a minute I jumped out of the way and Kate gasped as a fully-grown stag ambled in to munch his breakfast.

'Feeding time for Windswept,' Alan said, 'but careful, she doesn't like to be stroked.'

It was turning mild and already the snow by the loch was wet and thawing. With no compass and the hills enveloped in thick cloud, I would need to be extremely cautious, being dependent only on an altimeter and previous knowledge of these peaks. I climbed Beinn Eibhinn again just to be sure I hit the ridge, then followed it by going over Aonach Beag and blindly onto the whale-back of Geal Charn. With visibility down to a few metres, I aimed in what I perceived to be a south-easterly direction, leading to Bealach Dubh and yesterday's tracks. But, some-how in the confusion of the white-out, I strayed round to the south-west, got completely lost, and dropped to near the morning start point. I found my tracks eventually, but by that time had added a couple of unnecessary hours to the day's weary tally.

I made Culra at dark and slept until two the following morning. I cooked a large meal, then slept on until eight. After drying some clothes over a fire, and with the thaw continuing, I walked the ten easy miles to Dalwhinnie. Construction vehicles prowled the private lochside road to and from the site of a multi-million-pound rebuilding of Ben Alder Lodge. Despite the lavishness of this venture, the development seemed to underline that sense of mediocrity I always experience when approching 'civilisation' after a spell in the mountains.

§ § §

If An Teallach and Ladhar Bheinn rank among the most spectacular of Scottish peaks, the hills climbing wearily from the Pass of Drumochter are probably the most dreary. They are without doubt the best argument against the indiscriminate collecting of Munros. Of the seven summits, fortunately for me only a single one, Beinn Udlamain, poked above the 1,000-metre contour. I would need to visit this ocean of moorland, but was thankfully spared a longer stay.

There were two other reasons why I sensed the walking was going to be an ordeal. First, I was without a compass on a day of thick, low cloud. Secondly, my new boots, collected that morning from the post office, were less than comfortable. Despite my breaking them in with a 150-mile walk during autumn, already, after a mile, both heels rubbed painfully. Another mile and I stopped to soak the leather in a burn, bandage the areas of soreness, and thought soberly about the Cairngorms soon to come.

To avoid the busy A9 I followed the railway to the deserted Balsporran cottages. A crudely bulldozed track led me to a broad, featureless col, the heather here mown to its roots by the wind. Much of the snow had been stripped away, but the temperature was falling again, and now a damp wind began to coat me in sticky rime.

The way to Udlamain (1,010m) was confusing: I meandered along a flat-topped ridge which altered direction three times, and three times I strayed off course. My altimeter was vital in locating a snow-swept summit, and there I lingered awhile, the tiny cairn scant shelter from a bitter wind. The irony was that my lack of a compass had made the day an intriguing route-finding challenge. But that aside, my feet ached with a vengeance and I tried hard not to think about retracing every inch of those nine miles back to Dalwhinnie.

9

Cairngorm Odyssey

'The Good Lord didn't create this beautiful country for some rich landowner to fence it off.'

The lady at the post office was adamant when referring to the owners of the Ben Alder Estate and the thirty million pounds being 'squandered' on the new lodge.

'Think of the schools and hospitals that money could have built…'

Her words ringing in my ears, and on a morning as fine as any that year, I moved steadily uphill towards a row of bow-shaped hills. The growl of traffic on the A9 was now a distant murmur, the air breathless, and a low sun was making little impression on the hoar and water-ice that glazed the track. Tawny-coloured heather gave way to sugary corries and an opaline sky. The landscape had the polish and gleam of newness.

There being no obvious route between Dalwhinnie and upper Glen Feshie, I aimed to stitch together a network of diverging paths, estate tracks and one section of unmarked moorland.

Reaching the col beneath the Munro of Meall Chuaich meant the last of the easy walking. I traced the line of a burn, passing the gruesome remains of a stag, and entered the confines of a shady gully. But I drifted too low. In a lung-bursting effort I hauled myself up a precipitous bank using my ice-axe on the hard snow rim. A bulky white upland, unseen before, filled the skyline to the northeast: the Cairngorms.

After a long acquaintance with the spiky, jumbled ranks of the west, the emergence of this landscape had all the strangeness of a mirage, though a beautiful one. From this perspective you realise the Cairngorms exist as a single entity: Cairn Toul, Macdui and Braeriach were merely features of the same upland, like the many living parts of a single organism. Despite years of familiarity with these mountains, their sudden appearance was still a revelation.

I crossed countless burns and the view shrank as the slope tipped me down by the River Tromie, low and easy to ford. As yesterday, my movements were still hampered by ill-fitting boots. Towards late afternoon and in some discomfort I

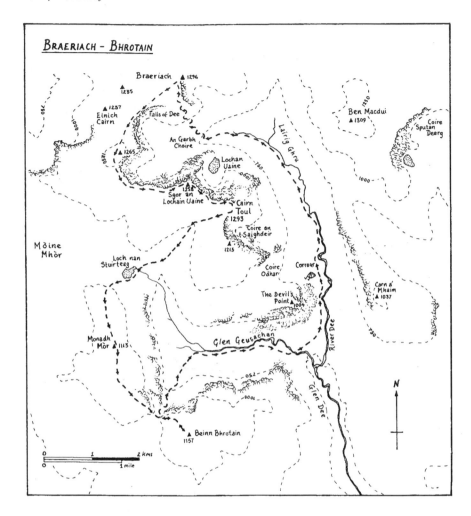

BRAERIACH – BHROTAIN

crunched up frozen snow at the edge of a plantation, latched onto a track for the final bealach and dropped low as the sunset shimmered across the vast Atholl moorlands to the southwest.

Darkness came with the promise of a severe frost. Passing the lodge in Glen Feshie, though I trod soundlessly, the peace was shattered by a commotion from kennelled dogs. There was a bothy nearby but instead I opted to pitch beneath one of the finest night skies I could remember. My tent up and my gear inside, I turned my attention to the one remaining task of the evening.

Just by the path I climbed into a small pine enclosure and slipped into the murk among the groves. I counted the trees to my right: one, two, three…, stopping at the tenth. Apprehensively, on my hands and knees, I scooped away handfuls of frozen needles and soon found what I was looking for: two plastic sacks;

one full of tins, the other wrapped tightly around a picnic box, itself bound securely with waterproof tape. Everything was intact. There was gas, candles, a new torch battery and enough grub to see me well into the Cairngorms.

After the coldest night of the winter, I wandered four sunny miles down the private road to meet friends Antony and Ursula Ranger. Finding no sign of them, I went back, packed the tent and made for the bothy. Woodsmoke rose from the chimney. My friends, having come all the way from Glasgow, had got there before me. Antony, a close friend and mountain companion since college days, was now convalescing after a serious back operation. Not being able to share mountain days in the north-west with him—as previously planned—was a huge disappointment, but his offer of some moral support was gratefully accepted. Antony asked about peaks climbed, routes, gales, encounters—that sort of thing—while Ursula, a doctor, commented with some disgust on how 'bloody healthy' I looked. Their presence was uplifting, and they brought with them that item of equipment without which I could not have gone a step further, a compass.

Mullach Clach a' Bhlair (1,019m) was climbed on a morning of near-perfection. Accustomed as I was to fighting for my mountains, the peace and ease of the ascent was fully relished. Ski tracks led away across the Mòine Mhòr and towards the barrier of the High Cairngorm tops, sunlit and beckoning. The dark fabric of my garments soaked up the warm sunshine, and, had the temperature not been well below freezing, I might have dozed by the cairn. The gale on Alder seemed months ago, not six days. On their winter round of Munros in 1985, Martin and Joy Moran had been plagued on this same hill by 80mph winds and –30°C wind chill.

Three tiny, black shapes were moving very slowly up the snowfields to the north. In no hurry I followed, idling over frozen snow to Carn Ban Mòr. I might have overtaken them because, at the summit, unseen voices, crisp and clear, drifted up from the corrie. Surely it was too soon to be heading down?

There was a novelty in loitering without fear of freezing, and at a tiny stone howff, half-filled with drifts, I wasted a happy hour excavating a way in, trying it for size. I lay back on the snow pleased with my work, pleased that everything, for now, was going well. There was such an intense contentment that I could not imagine the wars, famines, droughts, storms which surely just then afflicted corners of the globe; could not imagine the hordes of office workers or the silent tedium of a commuter train, or a single person with a long face, having a bad day. Chinks of sunlight came through gaps in the wall to cast pools of phosphorescence on the snow. Hardly the place to pass a wild night, but on such a day, perched above a high table-land, it was a palace in the sky.

Sgor Gaoith, the second Munro of Feshie, is a nose of pink granite nudging above the general plateau. Her elegant profile is seen to best effect when approaching, as I was, from the south. The slight breeze now carried with it a bitter chill. I pulled on my fleece. My hills climbed, I might have hurried down to Feshie but, instead, retraced my steps the miles over the plateau back to Mullach and marvelled at the myriad shades of sunset. The last rays gone, I jogged down with some haste to the sombre embrace of the valley.

For a couple of days I had been mulling over possible routes into the Cairngorms. One obvious option was a twenty-mile slog tracing the watershed around the bulk of the massif: safe, but unadventurous. More interesting was a direct line across the Mòine Mhòr, a near-featureless plateau hovering around the 900-metre level. Although not a route for poor conditions, as your escape hatch to the Lairig Ghru is a narrow col at the eastern rim, the idea of crossing the Mòine Mhòr in winter had intrigued me for years, and so, in fact, the choice was easy.

Hoisting an unaccountably heavy rucksack I began a gruelling climb. While I detest the mark of man in wild places, I will admit the crudely cut track which ascends Glen Feshie did ease the burden a little. I pulled to the snowline and onto the plateau. A bearing led me north-easterly for four miles and into an impenetrable mist. The slightest features were useful as navigational aids: the line of a meander, tiny ice-covered lochans, a change in the angle of a slope. In the middle of the Mhòr, about as far away from anywhere as I could be, a breeze sifted ice particles along the ground. And if the wind died, silence reigned. The naturalist Jim Crumley claimed that the silence here once stopped him dead: 'Incomprehension held us for a few seconds, then we heard nothing. No sound. No shred of wind, no whisper of it round a rock or through a tuft. Nothing. No fall of water, neither trickle on rock nor slap on shore. No cataract, no single syllable of water.' In nearly a thousand miles of walking it was more barren and desolate than anything I had encountered.

My boots were growing more comfortable by the day, but, as I dropped sharply to Glen Geusachan, it was the burden on my shoulders that became the problem. Each footfall came down hard on frozen peat, jarringly, my tendons straining to make every step precise and steady, for among the heather were lethal sheets of water-ice. It was a miracle I avoided a serious tumble.

Beneath a darkening sky, I swung left into the Lairig Ghru for the last mile, a difficult one tracking the meanders upstream of an infant Dee. In the gloom, Devil's Point had an intimidating presence. A little further was the familiar outline of Corrour bothy. There being no light I thought the place empty so was taken aback at the sound of a voice from the shadows—an Outward Bound instructor from the Lake District. He was in the Cairngorms to prepare for a Winter Assessment in Mountain Leadership. A congenial soul, he had recently swapped a career in engineering to train as an instructor, and while he had no regrets, he was finding that the commensurate drop in salary called for some lifestyle adjustment.

Dawn revealed a shabby-looking Corrour. Notices threatening its closure and demolition, due to the 'well-known fecal and litter problem', had been placed by the window. The grate was piled with half-burnt rubbish and there was the usual row of empty whisky bottles—useful as candle holders it is true, but who carries that many candles? A couple of hours with a broom and a spade, and I had made it feel more like home.

On a gentle, cold morning I went up the Tailor's Burn in firm snow, and practised some step-cutting on the way to Ben Macdui. Half-seen from across the Lairig Ghru were the fine high corries of Cairn Toul and Braeriach, separated by the colossal bite of the Garbh Choire. But the high plateau was always wrapped in drifting cloud, denying my ascent any real logic beyond an exercise in navigation. Macdui's summit did prove difficult to locate in the thick, freezing mist. For the second-highest peak in Britain, there is a strange lack of elevation. Perhaps because thousands who make this ascent are helped by the Corrie Cas chairlift, the Ordnance Survey confidently mark the summit as a 'viewpoint', but Cairn Toul, just opposite, is by far the finer.

To climb Carn a' Mhaim (1,037m) from the north is to tackle the only significant ridge in the Cairngorms, this one sporting a number of false tops. Now below the cloud level, I had a fine view southwards to the great waves of the Grampians, snow-splattered and messy, as if two giants had fought to the death with white paint. An innocuous-looking gully gave a fine glissade, tipping me out a mile from Corrour, which was a speck in the distance.

If you pulled down an entire house leaving just a small room intact, fixed it with a simple roof, then you would have an idea of the dimensions of Corrour. But, tucked proudly beneath the weeping cliffs of the Devil's Point, and surrounded by a wilderness of snow and scree, it is the sheer audacity of its situation that leaves the most enduring impression. The bothy is rightly part of mountaineering folklore.

Built in 1877, originally as a deer-watcher's cottage, it is now probably the oldest bothy still in use. As early as the 1920s in an average year three hundred people would record overnight stays—today in summer the same number may pass by in a week. Even for a bothy, it is a simple, spartan affair. An aluminium roof and granite walls keep it weather-tight; the concrete floor, stone table and fireplace give it a degree of comfort. Its present austerity stems from the renovation project just after the war, which saved the bothy from certain extinction after years of neglect and vandalism. But the aura of this place, like that of any historic building, can be conjured up by a little imagination and knowledge of its past. There is a dwindling band who still recall with affection the 'old Corrour'.

Mountaineer and poet Sydney Scroggie first entered its confines in 1938 and found it in a 'beautifully dilapidated condition... We surveyed the torn-up floor with joists and bent nails exposed, moist walls of quarried granite with the protective panelling gone, the underside of a tarry felt roof, the waterproof qualities of which were merely retrospective...'. He tells us of the paraphernalia left by the last deer-watcher: rickety string chairs, an old press, sacks of oatmeal; how the interior had an eerie presence, so that on opening the door you might find a fugitive Jacobite or hairy cattle-drover.

Scroggie returned with a friend seventeen years later, now one-legged and blinded from the war. He was saddened to discover a clinical, soulless place, as if the planners had moved in. Open the door now and you might encounter a 'sanitary inspector, truant officer or occupational psychologist'.

I arrived back as three red-faced walkers trailed in from the north, having come straight off Macdui. Inside were two others, Mike and Guy, young students from Aberdeen University. I wondered how many more might show, and whether it would be a repetition of a Hogmanay years before. On that occasion three of us, being first in, had secured floor space by the hearth. I lost count of how many others joined the celebrations, but by midnight Corrour resembled a busy nightclub. There was neither room to cook nor space to lie on for sleep—when eventually it was time for sleep.

Mike and Guy were back after an abortive attempt to climb a gully in Coire Bhrochain. 'Couldn't find the bugger so did Braeriach instead,' Guy said. Then, with Mike chipping in, he gave an entertaining account of their day. When relating a story, Guy would gesticulate madly with flaying arms and bulging eyes, his enthusiasm sometimes distorting the telling. Later, around the fire, their student tales of epic climbing escapes, missed lectures, parties and freezing digs, were a reminder of my own misspent college days. They watched hungrily as I tucked into a jar of marinated peppers, then managed to relieve me of a bag of muesli. 'Sure, if you want it, but it's been festering underground for three months,' I said.

An overnight snowfall transformed the appearance of the Cairngorms, and as I left the bothy, powdery flakes still floated down from a mantle of cloud. I stole up the Lairig Ghru bound for the Braeriach–Cairn Toul plateau, then hopefully further on for two lesser-known peaks. Before the pass I veered into the jaws of Garbh Choire, into the cloud base and up the southern flank of Braeriach, which steepened to a lip. The summit was a frosted world of rime and quiet mists. The ground here is level, but always, just a few metres from your feet, is the invisible abyss of Coire Bhrochain with its promise of cornices and sheer faces. Setting a careful bearing I began to traverse the table-land I had first seen as a nine-year-old from the old A9, the highest few miles in the country, the roof of the Highlands.

Enveloped all day in a ghostly shroud, I had no view, could barely see a thing. It was a world without a single reference point. I would scrutinise my surroundings for some irregularity: the mark of a concealed boulder, a stipple of snow, a slight decline, anything that might ease route-finding and guide me safely round to Angel's Peak. But, beyond my own extremities, I could not distinguish air from earth, the two elements blending perfectly as one. For much of the time I was walking blind. Had I been able to relax, I might have remarked on the strangeness of the experience. Gone was any sense of time and place. The gentle breeze, the ring and crunch of my footfalls, the freezing fog, it all lent the plateau a universality and dredged up far-flung landscapes from my memory: equatorial ice, a French glacier, a snow-covered Manchester moor.

Many times I had to remind myself that every step led irresistibly towards the yawning mouth of Garbh Choire, that this plateau, contrary to appearances, was guarded by headwalls and cliffs. And the mist was so thick I would not be given much warning. On a mountain in Glencoe, twice in ten minutes I had drifted too near an edge and sunk to my waist in a cornice fracture. Now as I began to descend the ground vanished. I pulled up a couple of metres from the rim of the corrie. I put away my compass, and giving the cornices a wide berth, followed the rim to the finest of Cairngorm tops, Cairn Toul.

Someone was there ahead of me, and for a few minutes my strange lonely vigil was broken. Richard, who was staying at Corrour, had come up the ridge straight from the corrie.

On a memorable winter ascent seven years before only the curve of the earth seemed to limit a panorama which unfolded at every point of the compass. Ben Nevis at fifty miles was a sharp outline, whilst a tiny white pimple, like a mast of a ship far out to sea, I later identified as Bla Bheinn on Skye, ninety miles as the crow flies.

A bearing now should have taken me to the small col above Loch nan Stuirteag but I strayed too far south and ended up on the unsafe ice of the loch itself. Monadh Mor and Beinn Bhrotain are two far-flung peaks reminiscent of Cairngorm scenery but without the sweep of corries. Little known and suffering from the popularity of their famous neighbours, they are rarely climbed. I was surprised then to cross a fresh pair of ski tracks. Crampons came on for the initial steepness and I nearly lost myself on a flattened and featureless two-mile crest where only a spirit level would have indicated if you were rising or falling. Beinn Bhrotain was more straightforward, and the gully tucked into its north face provided the perfect escape route.

A short, sunny interlude next day gave a pleasant climb to Devil's Point, a simple matter of about 50 minutes. Here you stand at the southern edge of this great dissected plateau. Although it is dwarfed by its mighty neighbours there is a familiar view of the Dee escaping south in a series of looping meanders, like so many ribbons of white silk. Cloud and cold rolled in with a rising wind, and I left as two small groups were toiling up. I packed and walked the few miles to camp by old Derry Lodge.

Seven peaks in the eastern Cairngorms were still to be climbed, and my anticipated base, the tiny Fords of Avon refuge, lay seven miles to the north. I woke early with nausea and a migraine, so put off any walking for the day. As if to rubber-stamp my decision, an overnight deterioration in the weather now brought loud gusts whistling through the pine groves, kicking up snow like dust. Little snow actually fell but the squalls blotted out all views of the mountains. The pines bore the brunt, and I was spared my tent being shaken to a deafening crescendo as it would have done in the open.

In the afternoon, feeling much improved, I went to investigate the 'new' Bob

Scott bothy. A whole literature, fact and fiction, has grown up around the late Bob Scott—gamekeeper at Derry until 1973—and the famous bothy he ran for visitors. His house remains but the original bothy was burnt to the ground in 1986. The new place was empty and I found it a dispiriting hovel: walls festooned with all manner of graffiti, much of it carefully cauterised with hot pokers. I wondered what Scott himself would have thought of it.

In sharp contrast, the encircling stands of Caledonian pine—like those in Glen Luibeg and Lui—are some of the most beautiful woodlands in Scotland. Beyond their ecological significance as a 'window' to the past, is the purely aesthetic pleasure of just being among them. Perhaps it is their range of bizarre growths, Rodinesque almost, which even in death take on a melancholic beauty; or how in certain light the greens and rust-browns seem the purest pigments of nature. Like a visual metaphor, in one relic we telescope time and see the cycle of life, from precocious seedlings, to maturity, to graceful old age and the grey bones of death.

The complete absence of pine woodlands today in most Highland glens reflects the plundering of centuries and the continuing mis-management of sporting estates. Overgrazing by deer on Deeside is reducing the capacity of these remnants to regenerate, and in recent years the vast increase in deer numbers has merely accelerated this decline. Some woods, it is true, have protective fencing, and a part of Upper Glen Derry, barren for centuries, has now been planted with seedlings. But to the casual eye these are piecemeal measures and do not address the Highland-wide problem of overgrazing. One hopes the new owners of Mar Lodge Estate, the National Trust for Scotland, have taken some inspiration from the success of Creag Meagaidh.

Continuing strong winds in the morning delayed my start, and it was noon before I shrugged off the last pines and went north over the pass. Lairig an Laoigh, 'the Pass of the Calves', is the longer but lesser-known route through the Cairngorms, and probably carries a tenth of the traffic of its more famous sister.

Crossing the Avon, itself choked with ice and drifts, I found the refuge empty. With my only previous stay being a July heatwave in 1986—when we sought the confines more for shade than shelter—I had forgotten the utter bareness of this place, and was suddenly apprehensive at the prospect of spending a few nights alone here. In terms of size, if Corrour could be likened to a single small room of a house, the Avon refuge would have been the toolshed. It is a tiny, windowless space enclosed by a wall of loose boulders, and resembles nothing so much as a prehistoric burial chamber.

For the seven peaks I allowed myself three days, including the walk out to Derry. The first morning, though, made a nonsense of any schedule. The wind moaned in from Loch Avon, and I needed to gather up all my confidence to brave it. Cairn Gorm (1,245m) was only three miles distant and little more than 500 metres of ascent, but I had to face into the teeth of this gale. With the high

Above Devil's Point with Carn a' Mhaim in the background. (Clive Dennier)

On Devil's Point with the Feshie Hills behind. (Clive Dennier)

verleaf: *Limits of the naked eye. Sandwiched between a blizzard and the aurora was this exceptional day in 00 where I made out the Skye Cullin from Cairn Toul—a distance of nearly 100 miles. This view shows the opposite direction, looking south-west down the Lairig to the snowy Grampians.*

Lairig Ghru, February

Opposite page, top: *Approaching the summit of Stob Binnein in early March.* (Mark Tagholm)

Opposite page, left *Built in 1877 to house a summer deer-watcher, Corrour bothy in the Cairngorms is now the oldest bothy still in use.*

Overleaf: *From Ben Challum at sunset, a last look west to unclimbed peaks Ben Cruachan and Ben Lui (left).*

A glance back from Ben Oss to Lui's south-east ridge and the sliver of Loch Awe beyond.' If I felt a twinge of melancholy once back it was because the scenes of mountain and light that had so moved me had irretrievably gone, now consigned to bright memories.'

Ben Oss and the hills of Perthshire seen through snow clouds near the summit of Lui.

plateau lost in a ceiling of fast-moving cloud, there were ominous ribbons of spindrift spawning from its edge. The deep, powdery slopes leading to it were a temporary haven, wonderfully sheltered, and from their safety I caught a remarkable display of shifting light as if a spectator at some fantastical stage drama: cloud curtains rising and falling, great wedges of light gleaming in relay from Macdui to Mheadhoin. But I seemed the only beholder, and it emphasised my solitude. Loch Avon below had an opaque, crusty surface, like a dried-up salt lake.

The plateau rim was a blizzard of ice pellets that flayed my eyes. Cupping a mittened hand over my face, I continued onwards in a clumsy and haphazard manner. Many times I crouched low, back to the wind, waiting for some particularly vicious gusts to pass. In the freezing air I was chilling rapidly, but to pull on my last remaining fleece I first needed to remove my over-jacket. During ten chaotic minutes, my jacket flapping in a frenzy, it was all I could do to hold on, all the while exposed to 70mph of abominable cold. My protective shell back on, I struggled for another twenty minutes before admitting the folly of it, and fled.

Fighting against this wind was pointless and dangerous, but at least I might go with it. I sailed back over old ground and carried on for Bynack More (1,090m). Conditions were little better. The wind threatened to dislodge me even on gentle slopes, and the last half-mile to the summit was marginal. I sought immediately the shelter of the glen 400 metres below. After a week of bleak monochrome, my eyes adjusted to splashes of colour, the view northwards unrolling to toffee-coloured moors, and, in the distance, a green lacework of fields.

Though I felt weary after the fight, the refuge was not much of a place to return home to. Situated at a touch below 700 metres, at the crossroads of two glens, it was particularly exposed, and in the time I was there I found the immediate vicinity to be a fierce wind-tunnel. Gale-force westerlies roll off the Cairn Gorm plateau, sweep unchallenged across a frozen Loch Avon, and are then squeezed to a bottle-neck by the confines of upper Glen Avon. They finally shriek past the refuge standing at the cork end—as they did all that evening, night, and into the next day.

I lingered over breakfast before making another attempt for Cairn Gorm. It was hard to tell, but I sensed the wind had eased slightly, and once outside, it felt less cold. I still wrapped myself to a state of suffocation. Here and there small pockets of life cheered me immensely: the green of a dwarf juniper pushing through a drift; a family of ptarmigans croaking angrily at my approach. On reaching the exposed edge of the plateau, this time I knew I could traverse the upper slopes and reach the summit.

On one of the busiest tops in Scotland I was alone. Barely able to stand, it was inconceivable that fifteen minutes away—had it been open—I might have sat down to a cooked meal in a heated restaurant, scribbled a few postcards and stocked up on chocolate. And doubtless in a few years, after the construction of

Cairngorm Automatic Weather Station at 1,245 metres. The Cairngorm tops have a sub-arctic climate similar to Greenland's coastal regions, and reaching this spot on 4 February required a two-day assault against winds in excess of 80mph.

the state-funded funicular, I could be whisked down to the fleshpots of Aviemore twelve miles away. A bizarre thought as I lunched in the shelter of the automatic weather station and watched an anemometer emerge cleanly from accumulations of rime and spin crazily in the wind. Clouds hovered at summit level. There was a sprinkle of sunshine and half a view down to Corrie Cas and the deserted pistes.

Backtracking, I dropped to Loch Avon, and climbed Beinn Mheadhoin (1,182m) opposite, but it was a weary ascent for which I had little enthusiasm. The wind had strengthened again, and the contest was draining. Only by keeping leeward and fighting hard was I able to reach the granite tors that adorn the summit. Attempting to scale the ice-plating and reach the true summit was out of the question. Nor would I return later. Munro-bagging, peak-bagging, mountain climbing solely to reach the summit—at times like this it all seemed pretty absurd. I flew down the east flank, sinking to my knees in heavy drifts, but just relieved to be out of the gale.

Beinn a' Chaorainn, a mere 300 metres above the pass, would be the shortest climb of the entire winter, but there was nothing more to be squeezed from the day. I had taken enough punishment, was sick of being the wind's punchbag. I trudged back to the refuge. I would crawl inside for sixteen hours of recuperation, and, hopefully, rekindle some interest for another assault tomorrow.

Approaching the small hollow where the River Avon flowed, I heard voices and saw two walkers below having some difficulty with the crossing. One was teetering midstream on an ice-plated boulder, while the other, already across, shouted instructions. He cackled with laughter as his mate, mistiming his leap, plunged in up to his knees. They ploughed up the slope towards me.

'D'you know what the Hutchison Hut is like?', asked the leading one, a tall fellow with a West Country accent. His mate was considerably shorter, and they both wore a lot of expensive, shiny gear.

The Hutchison Hut is a bare concrete cell about three miles away, and on my last visit I recall it stinking badly of stale urine.

'Hot showers, full breakfast and TV in every room I should think.'

They laughed and we bantered for some minutes, but with only an hour of daylight they pushed on for the pass.

There was an ever-changing sky and a raw, elemental beauty. Mheadhoin appeared to be bellowing steam like a volcano. Hoary clouds massing in the west were edged, at times, in silver and those floating across the north, a mustard yellow. Beyond them all a sky scratched with a thousand cirrus trails. Beneath this drama was the white presence of Cairn Gorm, serene, and from this side, quite unrecognisable to the thousands who play in her northern corries. For half an hour I stood there until the moon appeared as a thin sickle and my feet were so numb that I needed to thaw them over the gas burner.

The cirrus clouds, of course, were bad portents. All night I had been entertained by a booming wind, and now I stared glumly at chutes of rain and sleet sweeping the hillside opposite. Spreading pools of meltwater made a moat round the refuge. With no climbing possible, I weighed what limited options remained. The Beinn a' Bhuird-Ben Avon massif could logically be tackled from Braemar. And with just enough grub for an extra day, I could take in the two remaining Munros on my way out tomorrow. While it was the obvious course of action, I had begun increasingly to loathe this place which now felt like a prison, its dimensions reminding me of the solitary confinement cells from films about POWs. There was a sense of suffocation, as if the weight of the wilderness pressed in from outside, and it took everything to overcome the desire to escape to Derry.

Of course there were other ways of escape. I had my book. Meticulous planning for the winter included a careful selection of reading material, and for some weeks I had been rereading one of the great works of exploration: *The Worst Journey in the World*, by Apsley Cherry-Garrard. The author, a member of Scott's last Antarctic expedition of 1910–1913, chronicles the events of three pioneering years on the continent, culminating in the tragic deaths of the Polar Party on their return from the South Pole. While the narrative and Scott's diary extracts are unbearably poignant, it is not—most will agree—the highlight. An earlier chapter entitled 'Winter Journey' is the most implausible tale I have ever read, a masterpiece of understatement.

Garrard, with friends Wilson and Bowers, set out on a midwinter expedition to collect Emperor Penguin eggs, something that had never been attempted before. While ostensibly done in the cause of science, the element of adventure was undoubtedly a huge incentive. After only a few pages it is obvious that Garrard cannot quite find the words to convey the experience: hurricane-force blizzards, −60°C temperatures, the claustrophobic living conditions, what perpetual darkness and the proximity of death does to the mind; and how in the end it was only the bond of friendship that pulled them through. The story lent my own experience a sobering perspective.

And there were daydreams. My mind drifted to that leaden December day when I visited the Hertfordshire village of Wheathampstead, a prosperous place where old half-timbered cottages and smiling gardens rub shoulders with modern, red-brick semis. In the centre stands the church of St Helen's. My interest in the building lay within its north transept, for beneath the large stained-glass windows and set on a small plinth is a statuette of Apsley Cherry-Garrard. He is a noble figure, wrapped in thick polar clothing, so thick it distorts his natural proportions. But what is arresting is his facial expression: his youthful features exhibit a remarkable serenity; an untroubled mind, eyes penetrating far beyond the gloomy interior and resting on some distant ice-scape. It was easy to imagine the bronze breaking into life, this figure leaving his plinth, and in a slow, determined gait marching off into the polar night.

By morning it had turned colder, the moat frozen solid and covered in a few inches of dry snow. And after a week's absence the sun returned. On the climb up Beinn a' Chaorainn, much of the new snow scoured clear leaving verglas and old *névé*. Crampons were needed even on gentle slopes. Everywhere wild and raw vistas opened up: the Northern Cairngorms etched hard against clear skies; Ben Macdui and her satellites lost in a haze of cloud and spindrift. It was the sixth continuous day of gales.

An incised stream course gave a sheltered descent to the first skeletal pines of Glen Derry. Hardly stopping, I wrestled up the steep east flank of Derry Cairngorm (1,155m), the lower reaches guarded by bristly, knee-length heather. Utilising the shelter I maintained a leeward approach, only exposing myself on the final hundred metres. I wasn't alone. Just below, three fumbling shapes emerged from the melee, resembling a trio of bow-legged martians. From the summit I had wanted to stay high and continue along the ridge, dropping to my tent via the top of Cairn Gorm, but instead the wind marshalled me straight down.

I broke camp, made a phone-call from the lodge to confirm some accommodation and set off into the dark for Braemar. There were still ten miles of track and tarmac to town and it needed all my willpower to refuse lifts from generous Braemar folk, especially as by the end I was limping painfully with newly-formed blisters. Though I didn't fully appreciate it at the time, I remember it as a magical night to be out: the gleam of stars and the faint orange brush of the aurora.

10

Grampian Spring

MIDWINTER IN Glen Callater in the heart of the Grampians was a fact, the date on my watch confirmed the truth of it, but none of my senses could quite believe it. Winter had vanished like a retreating army, with only small pockets of resistance in high corries. During the early hours I'd woken drenched in sweat and was forced to make the first adjustments to my sleeping bag since the balmy nights of early November. After overcoming the psychological barrier of the Cairngorms there was now a sense of anti-climax and disillusion. I was like a sailor, who, on reaching the Cape Horn finds, not all the winds of the world, but a gentle swell and idle breeze. While I was not necessarily wishing to court blizzards and storms, nevertheless these were expected and prepared for. Their sudden absence was a profound disappointment.

I was camped at 500 metres, at the head of the glen, and as I gazed from the vestibule the snowless hills were brushed with a drizzly cloud. The tired, spring-like weather had an apathy and indifference about it, neither quite winding itself up to the interest of a full-blooded gale, nor breaking to give rekindling sunshine. Despite these feelings I had looked forward eagerly to this day, for somewhere in the mist and away to the east was the finest peak of the Grampians: Lochnagar.

Like all illustrious mountains Lochnagar has an allure that far transcends the simple experience of climbing to its summit. Viewed from the south, she is merely a belly of granite rising slightly higher than the folds of rolling plateau that typify this region. By contrast, from the north, she is an imposing sight: a crescent ridge climbing high above the outstretched palm of a great corrie; and you suddenly comprehend how a mountain profile can inspire such a blend of artistic, literary and royal endeavour.

With all this in mind, I climbed eastwards from Loch Callater with a sense of expectancy. Not since a scorching June day a decade before had I set foot on this mountain, and never from this approach. While Lochnagar is hugely memorable, the same cannot be said for her Munro acolytes to the west and south. If Sir Hugh had applied a rigorous logic when tabulating his 3,000-foot peaks, then surely these knolls that poke their noses above the granite table-land would have

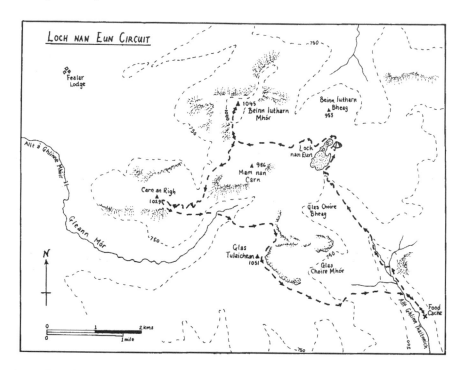

been listed as 'tops' and not 'separate mountains'. But they were on the sacred list and so, like a myopic trainspotter, I went my weary way to tick them off.

The first, Carn an t-Sagairt Mòr, was remarkable for its aircraft wreckage, some items of which had been unceremoniously placed in the cairn itself. Scattered widely about the Highlands, these alloy remnants from the War have become such a hackneyed part of so many peaks they no longer evoke any morbidity over the fate of those aboard. This plane had sadly missed clearing the top by only a few metres.

A fierce wind hurried me over the White Mounth and prodded me roughly onto the last slopes of Lochnagar (1,155m). The actual summit is a tumble of boulders jutting above the main crest. The mildness gone, it was an unpleasant place, a west wind shrieking around the wet slabs, whistling through gaps and stealing my body heat at an alarming rate. Cowering behind the largest of the boulders, I shivered and stared vacantly into the mist, part relieved, part wondering what on earth I was doing there. Incredibly, a middle-aged couple appeared from nowhere, both wrapped in identical green cagoules. They staggered towards me, animated and grinning like a couple of guilty school children, doubtless also wondering what they were doing there.

I can't imagine Byron would have been moved to write the words: 'crags wild and majestic' on such a day. Nothing could be seen beyond a fuzzy outline of cliff. Instead, I felt a strange affinity with Queen Victoria who climbed to this exact spot 150 years ago, observing prosaically: 'On the summit was a thick fog… the wind was blowing a hurricane.'

A horseshoe route of a few miles led to the rocky crest of Cairn Bannoch. These hills, being gentle and broad-sided, afford little shelter, and I now rather struggled against a lashing headwind. Through cloud tatters were glimpses to the Dubh Loch and its ring of cliffs, some marked with impressive waterfalls. Oddly, conditions of near-calm prevailed back at Loch Callater. With lengthening days, arriving home before dark was becoming more usual. The last mile I carried that familiar feeling of being short-changed from my day on the hill, that the effort expended had given but scant reward. I was hungry, foot-weary and sought my tiny green shelter with its promise of rest with a childlike craving.

Leaving the Cairngorms had also marked a change of accommodation. Since early December I had pitched my tent perhaps a half-dozen times, but from now on, due to the scarcity of bothies and howffs, I would have to become more accustomed to its cosy dimensions. After hours of continuous movement the smallness was no hardship. With the cessation of all effort it was easy just to lie completely inert and be nothing but utterly contented. Though still early, all sounds conspired to pull me to sleep: the breeze sifting through the heather, the rustle of dry grass on nylon, the clamour of moorland birds—grouse, curlews, golden plovers—some launching an evening lament, others an irrepressible babbling. Above all came the never-ending sound of a nearby burn. At first it was just a murmur and tinkle of running water, but, straining my ears, I began to decipher the odd syllable and word—strange, idiot words, like those of a foreign language vaguely remembered, but real words all the same. Sometimes I would doze, and on waking hear, not water, but voices so real that I sat upright with a start, waiting for the approach of heavy boots, an angry landowner perhaps, someone wanting assistance, an intruder—but only for a few seconds. If indeed these were spirits whispering, then there was nothing malign or unsettling about them, for they always sent me straight back to sleep.

South of Callater the hills comprise a large, grassy table-land, and are one half of a great amphitheatre sweeping round eventually to the A93 and Carn Aosda ski runs. Primarily managed as deer forest and grouse moorland, the heather on them is carefully burnt into long strips, like stubble clean-shaven from a cheek, and on a misty, dour day I was numbed by their lack of character. But they would also be the easiest and most gentle hills I would have to cross.

After traversing the moorland anonymity of the Munros Carn an Tuirc and Cairn of Claise, I struck out for Glas Maol (1,068m) and bumped into a stalwart Scottish gentleman up from Dundee. We took refuge from the tedium by chatting for thirty minutes in the shelter of a drystone wall. On a survival course here a fortnight ago he'd taken part in a snow-holing exercise, excavating a small cave on the east side of Glas Maol. It had taken hours of labour, and he laughed at the prospect of anyone in real peril having the energy for such house-building.

'Is it still there?' I asked.

'Just about,' he laughed, 'but going fast.'

§   §   §

While at Glen Callater I had become engrossed in a remarkable book: *The Big Grey Man of Ben Macdhui* by Affleck Gray. The Big Grey Man or 'Am Fear Liath Mòr', has come to mean the range of mysterious phenomena claimed by some to have been experienced on Macdhui and its environs: echoing footfalls, malevolent voices, unearthly music, sensations of unease and terror, even an apparition of a humanoid creature with 'pointed ears, long legs, and feet with talons'. The author, agnostic on the matter, nevertheless questions why so many such phenomena should be reported on this particular mountain. In recent years the sightings seem to have dried up.

'What's happened to the Big Grey Man?,' I asked in the pub when next in Braemar.

'Haven't you heard?', the barmaid said, 'Macdhui's way too crowded these days, he's gone to live on Beinn a' Bhuird.'

In terms of sheer muscle Beinn a' Bhuird and its neighbouring Ben Avon comprise the most colossal upland in Scotland. Their form is seen from a great distance: a collection of bulging shoulders, some scooped into corries, others sweeping down in convex slopes to pine fringes and river courses. Natural defences of remoteness and inaccessibility have made this the last bastion of true mountain wilderness in the Cairngorm area, and, in winter, these peaks are a serious undertaking. I left Braemar with provisions for three days.

By wading the Dee down by Braemar Castle I could save four miles and head straight up Gleann an t-Slugain, gateway to these hills. I crossed the grassy flood plain to where the river split round a small island, a likely spot for fording, I reckoned. But the waters were deep and murky, so instead, I followed the meanders downstream to Invercauld Bridge, now conceding that I would have insufficient time for the high tops that day.

It didn't matter. Gleann an t-Slugain is a dramatic place, the path squeezed until you find yourself at the bottom of a gorge-like cleft. Among the acres of heather and peat I found what I thought to be the perfect camp spot, a sheltered, grassy bowl which cupped a baby lochan. I pitched on some level sward at the near end. While streams flowed into the lochan, none emerged, and I concluded it must have a hidden outflow. Later, just before nightfall, though I heard nothing, I glanced out to see that a red dome tent had mushroomed nearby.

After a stormy wet night, I had cause to regret my choice of pitch. Unzipping the vestibule I was shocked to see that yesterdays' miniature lochan had doubled in size, the water now lapping barely a metre away, and rising. My neighbour had vanished; where his tent had stood there was now only a sheen of water. With the hills strafed with gales and periodic downpours I stayed indoors but I got no peace. The tent shook and flapped, the water edged closer until wavelets brushed the sides of my groundsheet. Cursing, I pulled on my boots and searched the sodden vicinity, but nowhere was there any room for a tent. I was contemplating packing up and retreating back down the glen when the rain ceased and the water mysteriously ebbed away.

The following day the clouds lifted clear of the peaks, and the winds relented somewhat. Emerging from the confines of the glen you are suddenly confronted with a vast sweep of hill, Beinn a' Bhuird's South Top and the cliffs that fall from A' Chioch, 'the Nose'. A splendid seven-mile traverse can be made of all the tops beginning at the southern rim of this peak, but perhaps the finest approach is to traverse beneath the immense bowl of Coire nan Clach, gradually rising above the snowfields straight to the North Top.

Winter had almost entirely vanished from the plateau, the hills giving a general appearance of May or early June, but the west wind was now strong and bitter. Clouds heaved a little above the tops, affording gentle, panoramic views. The plateau is broad and spacious, and you walk with long energetic strides, as if moving over a vast table-top with invisible edges.

Ben Avon is peppered with strange granite warts like barnacles on a humpback whale. The actual summit, reminiscent of a Dartmoor tor, was today an easy scramble, but I wondered if I could have coped with the savage winds and ice of a week before. There is a lunar feel to this bare landscape. To avoid facing the wind, I swept southwards, then steeply down a snow gully. Collecting the tent, I went over the moors in the evening sunshine and made another attempt at fording the Dee, this time at Allanaquoich where I hoped the river would be weaker and shallower. I succeeded, though at some cost. By midstream the icy cold had drained all sensation from my ankles and feet. The thigh-deep flow tugged at my balance, my feet finding every sharp stone, and I reached the far bank yelling with agony.

I might have camped hereabouts as tomorrow I would head up Glen Ey to the Central Grampians, but the attractions of Braemar—bath, cooked meal and pint—were too great. And I was also due to meet Gavin, last seen in the wilds of Glen Nevis. Around the final bend was the glow from streetlights. Gavin was already in the pub. His greeting was short and to the point:

'You smell like something they pulled up from the bog. Get a bath.'

§ § §

'Skiing for six months, drifts as high as houses…'

In the small village supermarket the winters of yesteryear were being discussed with the nostalgia and affection one might feel for an old friend who had recently passed away. The talk became increasingly more technical and intense: global warming, climate change, the need to diversify, the future of the skiing industry, and so on. There was no skiing at Glenshee. Patchy at best before this week, the season had now come to an abrupt halt.

'Half-term and this place should be buzzing with skiers,' someone said emphatically.

'Mildest February week on record, worse even than last year,' another said, looking at me. I nodded absently, and mumbled something about the poor fare for ice climbers.

' If you ask me it's global warming. Skiing in Scotland is dead.'

'…which is why Aviemore want their funicular,' the first man chipped in.

As he was leaving the shop I happened to ask whether he agreed with the funicular scheme.

'Of course, it's year-round tourism, regardless of whether it snows. They can't lose.'

'Shouldn't people walk?', I suggested. 'They might appreciate the mountain a little more.'

He shook his head with a dismissive swagger, and we became embroiled in a frank exchange of views. Right from the beginning we were poles apart.

'That's an elitist viewpoint,' he said, 'the hills are for everyone.'

'Everyone willing to make the effort.'

'Including those in wheelchairs, the old, the blind?'

'Wait a minute. How can you really appreciate a mountain without spending a little time getting to know it?'

He shook his head again.

'That's like saying you can only appreciate the view from a tall building by flogging up forty flights of stairs.'

I tried another tack.

'What about the fragility of the Arctic plateaux? The habitats for wildlife? It's all going to be damaged, and probably for good.'

The man shrugged his shoulders.

'Look, let's be honest. Who really cares about a few birds when jobs and prosperity are at stake?'

'But shouldn't we be saving the Cairngorms for *everybody*, for the future, not ruining them for the few. Mountain railways are just not compatible with conservation or wilderness, they don't belong.'

'Tell that to the unemployed lift operators or hoteliers with empty rooms.'

'But aren't we making economics into a god? What of the landscape itself?'

He gave me a look of incomprehension, as if I'd slipped into a strange dialect. 'Meaning…?'

'Well, hasn't it got a right to be itself? Everything we humans have done has been a violation, from bulldozed roads to blanket forestry, to the overgrazing of deer estates.'

'A landscape with rights, eh?', he said without trying to conceal his sarcasm. 'Your kind are on a different planet.'

We parted amicably enough but the difference of opinion left a sour taste in my mouth. The attitude of 'using the Cairngorms solely as a resource to be exploited', I found deeply depressing. But this is one viewpoint. Another is that the

Cairngorms are a unique and priceless treasure, that any man-made structures on the mountains are anathema to the landscape, aesthetically and ecologically, and should be removed. Man-made structures would include ski developments, bulldozed tracks, bridges, purpose-built bothies, waymarkers. Easy access should be denied, allowing the mountains to defend themselves naturally with wearying miles. But this can only be achieved if the Cairngorms are afforded real 'protected status' which countenances no development and seeks to restore the land to its natural state.

Perhaps we are already too late. In terms of the forthcoming funicular development, the words of Jim Crumley, written in 1991, already have a prophetic ring: 'Existing legislation is no match for the commercial pressures which well up around the fringes of the Cairngorms, and without stronger legislation it is a question of time before the heartland of the mountains is breached again as massively as it has been on Cairngorm itself.'

§   §   §

Midway through a turbulent first year teaching adolescents the mysteries of physics, Gavin perhaps needed a gentle introduction. As he rode in the post bus to Inverey, I walked the miles of tarmac some distance behind. It was a calm, chilly morning, with a lazy sun filtering through milky cloud and casting indistinct shadows. Few people were about. An estate track up Glen Ey led us deep into the hills. After a few gently ascending miles our route followed a foaming burn, crossed a broad strath overshadowed by scree and rubble-strewn slopes, and aimed for a profile of shapely peaks. A solitary walker was coming down, all smiles, pleased at having 'knocked off a handful of Corbetts' about the glen head.

This region of wilderness lying south of the Cairngorms, while less dramatic, is vaster in expanse and far less frequented. The land is distinctly softer and more fertile, the skin of vegetation thicker, and, for the most part, covered in a glut of crisp heather moorland. The hills rise like a lumpy ocean swell, no towering breakers, but with some slopes climbing to scree and rubble and broken ground above nascent corries. It boasted seven peaks, scattered widely.

Up ahead was the ruin of Altanour wrapped in a grove of singing larches. They swayed in the wind, and seemed particularly forlorn against this relic of a once grand lodge. We munched sandwiches in the lee of the west wall by the old fireplace, sheltering from the sharp breeze. A Land Rover and trailer were parked nearby. The wind carried with it the scent of burning heather, and we noticed a pall of smoke about a mile to the west. Moving on, we stopped to chat with a tweed-clad gentleman manoeuvring an Argocat back onto the trailer. He'd had, he said, an excellent day's burning. 'Dry with a fair breeze. Let's hope it continues. Have a good walk.'

Leaving the track we continued southwards, threading a steepening burn, the terrain ever rougher and more tiring, as, at the end of the day, a little fatigue was creeping into our limbs. Taking advantages of the fine conditions we camped high. It is no secret that Loch nan Eun is an idyllic spot for wild camping. No path goes there, it is many miles from any road, in the wild heart of this region, and it nestles beneath three fine Munros.

Gavin, being more of a caver and rock-climber, did not possess a tent, so we had to share mine, and only then did I fully realise how exaggerated the claims of the manufacturers were that their nylon shelter could accommodate two full-sized adults. There was space to lie completely still, but none left to manoeuvre, certainly insufficient for two people to co-exist comfortably. Nor was the discomfort equally distributed. The vestibule side was by far the more spacious, and thus became eagerly sought after, despite the condition of having to do all the cooking.

Apart from the squeeze it simply felt novel and strange to be sharing my tent with another person. Though a good friend, Gavin was someone I didn't know particularly well outside my immediate social circle, and certainly not in the context of hill walking. Our forays together had been limited, amounting to a few caving excursions, a short ski tour, and those few days in Glen Nevis.

A short while ago a close friendship almost disintegrated during a trek across the mountains of Corsica. The first couple of days we lugged full packs over high passes and in blistering heat. Hardly a gentle apprenticeship, it was true, for someone whose previous backpacking experience was a few strolls in the Peak District— but he had been desperately keen for me to take him on a 'real trek'. With the realisation of a gruelling week ahead, my friend that night went to sleep in an irritable and disillusioned state of mind, silently cursing me for bringing him there. The nadir was reached the following morning.

During the night wild pigs had raided our vestibule making off with my friend's new rucksack and his entire food supply. Searching nearby bushes at first light, I found the remnants of a riotous feast: the food gone, his rucksack chewed and smeared in excrement, his spare clothes bitten to rags. With my own gear and grub safe inside the tent, I returned to face a stream of Mancunian invective and a bad temper that rumbled on for days.

Gavin and I awoke to find our piece of heaven embraced in greyness and drizzle. If the three Munros and loch make up four points on a circular route, then Beinn Iutharn Mhòr stands in the northern quadrant, a bulge of scree-strewn moorland whose most notable feature is an immature north-facing corrie. We found the top in a shivering mist. Carn an Righ, 'the Hill of the King', is slightly lower, but well defended on all sides by steep flanks. There is no gentle way up. By now a sleety rain and freshening breeze had combined to squeeze much of the pleasure from the day. Gavin, who had toiled behind me on Carn an Righ, now turned back not halfway up Glas Tulaichean, fed up with the miserable conditions.

Aptly translated as 'the Green Hill', Glas Tulaichean is the highest and by far the most beautiful of this trio. Given a clear day you will see a fine angular peak supported by curling ridges. Two grassy corries are tucked away on the eastern side. But this layer of vegetation also makes it a fragile peak, and I was depressed to find Land Rover tracks cut into the soil close to the summit. In Victorian times a private railway took shooting guests to the now-ruined Glenlochsie Lodge in the valley below, and here the walking started. Today, it seems, the idle are driven to wherever the deer are, disfiguring the mountain for decades to come in the process.

I now had a slight dilemma. There was a useful cache in Gleann Taitneach, but retrieving it would involve a six- or seven-mile detour, then a 400-metre re-ascent with a considerably larger pack. Alternatively, I could be back at the tent with hands wrapped round a hot drink in forty-five minutes. Recalling the grim weather forecasts in Braemar, and mindful of being delayed in this wilderness, I opted to scamper down for the grub.

I rummaged about the scree a little apprehensively. Back in October an old shepherd had seen me from a distance rolling over boulders here, so I hoped there had been no disturbance. Some mice had punctured holes in the plastic but it was all intact. To lessen the weight I immediately ate three tins of fruit, peanuts and some chocolate; then I hauled the rest back to share a gourmet meal by the loch.

One liability of a high camp is exposure to the elements should they turn nasty. On our second morning we woke to filthy conditions: rain of a flogging, relentless nature being driven by a rude west wind. It clattered the tent with venom, the wind punishing us for daring to camp in such a perilous spot. Not surprisingly, with the promise only of a great deal of discomfort, we packed and dressed for battle with an air of resignation, saying little to each other. Once outside we collapsed the tent, which shook and flapped like a wet rag. When folded and stuffed into my sack it felt twice the weight. Setting off, our minds dealt only with the simple necessity of getting down as fast as possible.

At least navigation would be straightforward. Reaching the path for Glen Tilt and Fealar Lodge would be just a case of rounding the loch and then contouring south-west for a quick mile—forty minutes at the most. An hour later we were completely lost. South-west led us not down a gentle slope but up a steep flank. Where there should have been bogland we found a scree slope; and a large flooding burn that was not marked on the map. In a calm mist it might have been an intriguing navigational problem, but in driving rain, with Gavin having a coach to catch, it was becoming something of a nightmare. We contoured on blindly, Gavin by now losing faith both in his compass and in my route-finding ability.

'Perhaps the rocks round here are magnetic?'

A physics teacher, he obviously knew about these things.

'No, we've just been walking about half-asleep, like a couple of zombies.'

That was the truth of it.

'You mean *you* have,' Gavin said. 'Navigation is your department.'

We scrutinised the map endlessly, checked and double-checked our bearings, cast about for any feature or landmark that might reveal our location. Patience was running low.

'Look,' Gavin suggested, 'I'm getting cold with all this mucking about. Let's go back to the loch and start again.'

'What, and waste another hour? You must be joking.'

'So, what do you suggest?'

His spectacles had misted up and rain dripped from his nose.

'Bugger it, we'll just head south-west. It's bound to lead us into the Tilt.'

But we were soon climbing steeply up scree again, still utterly lost. Then I realised our mistake. As the map indicated Loch nan Eun as being squarish, we had aimed to leave it at the second corner. But, in reality, on the ground, the loch is circular and we had drifted away too early, peeling off into Gleann Taitneach, naively heading south when we needed to be going west. In the numbing downpour, when all thought is focussed on getting down fast, it was an easy error.

The rain gave way to blustery showers of hailstones which ushered us to Fealar Lodge and beyond. The path, now high and airy, traced the edge of a deeply incised river, stupendous were it not for the foul conditions. At a confluence we were delayed again. All the burns were foaming in spate, and this one, though narrow, seemed barely fordable. After a while of plucking up courage, I managed a frantic lunge across the boulders, while Gavin removed his footwear, and with a painful grimace, waded through the thigh-deep, brown liquid.

We crossed the much larger River Tarf by Bedford Bridge, just below the falls which churned and boiled with menace, then turned to head down Glen Tilt. A further mile and I camped, while Gavin, wishing me well for the month ahead, continued on for the miles to Blair Atholl. There was no real envy in watching him go.

§   §   §

With its near-precipitous sides, and capped with a summit crest like a baroque dome, Beinn a' Ghlo, 'the Hill of the Veil', is one of the most singular and beautiful hills in Scotland. Perhaps this can be best appreciated from the Cairngorms where she pulls free of her anonymous neighbours to rise in splendid isolation. Any traverse is enlivened by a covering of snow and ice, and yesterday's rain had left a wintry coat on the higher flanks.

After crossing the River Tilt I launched myself at the uncompromising slopes. They eased for a while and I made my way up a broad, little-walked shoulder, then into a mask of cloud and falling snow. It was an unorthodox way to reach Bràigh Coire Chruinn-bhalgain, my first top. I immediately dropped to the col, which was a severe wind-tunnel, and began the stiff pull to Beinn a' Ghlo. It being a Sunday I expected people. Sure enough, up ahead, their backs to me, three humanoid shapes loomed from the spindrift—arms attached to thin sticks that moved rhythmically like metronomes. I crept up behind but they were unaware of my presence until I fell in step, shouted a greeting and, for thirty minutes, enjoyed the conviviality of complete strangers. Two adults and a teenager, friendly folk from Dingwall, and ostensibly preparing for the rigours of a guided climb in the Himalayas later in the year.

Perhaps it was the sheer scale and loneliness of the Highlands in winter, but contact with a fellow human in a wild and barren place always had great significance for me, even if only for the chance of a minute's idle chat. Silent for hours, locked into your thoughts, initially the tone of your voice strikes you as peculiar, the first words spluttering out like an old car exhaust. Every day all manner of dialogue and discussion would rattle about inside my head, but there was a primal need to communicate and hear the resonant sounds of my own voice, which, for much of the time, had become like a record that never gets played. The friendliness of the people I met during this journey, their generosity and unfailing good nature, never ceased to be a source of inspiration.

The final slopes were a tussle in the wind, now raking tatters of cloud across the summit ridge. It was colder than it had been for a week. The Dingwall group picnicked in the partial shelter of the large cairn, while I continued along the ridge northwards and slipped down a long, heathery arm back to the Tilt. Midway, a melancholy view opened up to the endless grey moors of the north and east, the hilltops white and contrasting with the dull conveyor belts of cloud.

Next day, 23 February, the cloud became rain and its persistence delayed a walk until afternoon to the Tarf Basin, a little to the north of the Tilt and perhaps the last word in unfashionable country. As far as you can be from a public road, the interest here lies in the scale of remoteness, an uninhabited, treeless world, but with the added spice of a couple of high peaks, An Sgarsoch and Beinn Dearg. Under a good covering of snow the landscape becomes a white, polar desert.

Yesterday's snow, however, was but a memory. After a brief wintry spell, spring had reasserted herself in a vibrancy of colour. I was crossing a shallow basin from where I could see nothing beyond a rim of undulating moorland. I moved with an energetic stride, leaping peat ditches, dodging the wetness, and, whenever possible keeping to the crisp, dry heather which allowed for fast, easy progress. There are moments when, buoyed by the conditions and my own feelings, I seemed to be walking not on the ground at all, but cushioned on a bed of air, every decision instinctive, every action automatic and effortless.

An Sgarsoch (1,006 metres) sprouted like a giant mole from a carpet of heather, intersected by grassy streamlets and topped with a nose of scree. Bloated clouds were carried east by the breeze that rippled the vegetation in one continuous breath, and I could add yet another glorious day to the repertoire of fine days among these hills. I remember well one March weekend skiing up from Blair Atholl, bivouacking at the high bealach east of An Sgarsoch, then pushing on over deep powder through the Cairngorms for Aviemore. This high wall of moorland defeated General Wade's roadbuilders back in the eighteenth century. In their plan to link Inverness to the Lowland cities, the direct route would have had to breach the Minigaig Pass at over 800 metres, so they opted for a long detour over Drumochter instead, the line of the present A9 trunk road.

Retracing my steps back to the Tarf, I went due west, over some low watershed hills and towards the hunkering profile of Beinn Dearg, 'the Red Mountain'. I was now toiling somewhat, this being one of the few occasions that my route led me over an actual summit with a full pack. No peak east of the A9 now remained unclimbed. Beinn Dearg was the last of the Grampians.

Tomorrow I would continue southwest, weaving through glens Lyon and Lochy, south towards Loch Lomond. From there I would loop north in a great sweep of the peaks fringing Rannoch Moor, finally to end at Glencoe. But I could not conceive of ending. And though I was familiar with much of the route, and knew the immensity of it, I was still not given to thinking too much about it. I rarely gazed more than a day or two ahead. The future was irrelevant; only the 'now' mattered: how to tackle the next incline, this ridge, that river, to keep warm and fit and motivated. I accepted the days as they appeared to me, smiling or sad or mean, and while I planned ahead, I lived now, existentially, stoically accepting my lot with the weather, the discomfort when it came, relishing with unspoken gratitude the satisfaction that inevitably followed.

In deepening gloom, I peered into deepest Perthshire and to the peaks for the coming week. I greeted their familiar shapes as old friends: Schiehallion, Ben Lawers, the Glen Lyon Hills, all in darkening silhouette as the declining sun was lost behind ashen cloud banks. Hauling a full pack up here had knocked the stuffing out of me, but it was impossible to linger even for a minute on the freezing summit. With little food left there was no prospect of a celebratory meal, only a cheerless night in a nearby bothy. In a cutting wind I made my weary way down to Glen Bruar.

11

Second Winter

THE WAY to Blair Atholl was a straight track across miles of swelling moorland. After weeks of bleak mountainscape, below was a soft, green strath fragmented into regular-sized fields and cut by a meandering River Garry. On the last mile through woods came the sounds and odours of nearby habitation: of woodsmoke and coal-fire, the stench of silage and livestock excreta. Through the trees was the disturbing whine of a chainsaw, and from a distance came the steady grumble of traffic on the A9. The first person I met was a smart, elderly gentleman with a stave and glengarry, attired, it seemed, for a wedding or church service.

'Been over the hills, have ye?'

I told him of my walk from Braemar, the high camps and the hills I'd climbed. He listened with curious eyes, acknowledging my words with a faint nod of the head. He'd worked as a stalker in the Cairngorm area in the 1950s and '60s, and reeled off a litany of corries and glens I'd never heard of. There was a genteel wisdom about him, and he reminded me, in a peculiar way, of an elder from one of those wild mountain communities on the subcontinent, where the old are revered and their opinions sought.

I asked him about the way to Tummel Bridge.

'Aye, there's a Right of Way to Tummel, up this road, left over the Garry, then cross the main road—careful mind, there's lunatic drivers on that road...'

This was one of the very few sections of lowland walking I was unable to avoid when planning my route. Schiehallion, my next peak, would be a day's journey to the south-west, past farmsteads, rough pasture, and blankets of conifers. Crossing the busy A9, I went up a muddy farm track, passing the rusting hulk of a combine harvester. I weaved through skeletal birch and climbed steadily, then emerged onto open moorland to meet a louring sky, the din of engines and farm odours all now behind me. The way led through a gloomy plantation, over the crest of a gentle hill and finally down to Strath Tummel where I camped among some roadside pines.

It had been the easiest of days for quite some time but, as always, after much pounding on tracks, my feet and calves were complaining. My stiff-soled boots,

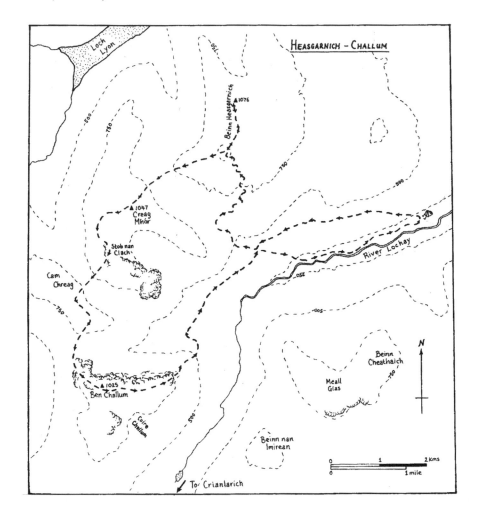

designed for winter mountaineering, were hardly appropriate for stony paths and hard roads. I had seen no one since leaving Blair Atholl.

At first light I awoke to a chorus of chaffinches and the tinkling of a burn. Above, the canopy of conifers swayed in the stiff breeze, and immediately I realised the air felt different, thin and chilly, and for the first time in a fortnight it had an arctic bite.

On the road, the wind was full in my face, and reaching Tummel it became a common vandal, knocking over road signs and dustbins, scattering litter in a flurry of anger.

'That all you need? There's no shops where you're heading,' the lady had said. Admittedly, the shelves of goodies were tempting but I had an excellent cache a few miles further on.

Passing the power station I crossed an aqueduct, fought my way tooth and nail through thick birch, then up knee-length heather to be greeted by vicious hailstorms. Finally, as I topped the crest of some moorland there was a view of a snow-covered Schiehallion.

Schiehallion at last! I'd first seen her from the Mamores two months ago, a perfect snow-capped cone rising like a distant Fujiyama; I'd seen her from Ben Alder on that wild day, a fleeting window in the spindrift; from the Feshie Hills in the pink of sunset, and from Beinn Dearg at gloaming. Now she was before me. Is this the most satisfying way to climb a mountain? To approach her slowly and cautiously, circling almost as if you are stalking her, then to climb her alone and without haste. Perhaps only then can you really know her. In equatorial Uganda the five-day climb to Mount Stanley (5,102 metres) took us through fantastic vegetational zones, from lush rainforest and past mountain scrub and scree to hanging glaciers, so that reaching the summit was merely the culmination of an unforgettable experience that lasted ten days. Having no really high mountains in Scotland we have to make them so.

Schiehallion is also, I am told, the first mountain I ever set foot on. My parents cajoled my brother and me about a third of the way up before a mist rolled in and hastened an early return. And though I remember nothing directly about the day, I like to think that even at a tender age, something of the beauty triggered a fascination for mountains and wild places. Like most who climb often, I would find life without mountains unimaginable. I do not know why mountains became an obsession for me while my older brother, after his Ben Nevis experience, never set foot on another hill. Or why some of us are drawn to the high places, whether this desire is lodged in our genes, or nurtured by an early experience. I like to think that even before Schiehallion, when gazing from my bedroom window I saw, beyond a dreary suburban backdrop, a horizon of unclimbed peaks, the same way a sailor born in the middle of a continent hears the roar of the ocean. Today, a mantle of bellowing clouds shoved along by the wind had already lopped off the summit and the prospects for an ascent looked exceedingly grim.

Another mile and I was at the Braes of Foss eagerly rooting among the stones of a collapsed wall. But I found only piles of chewed paper and plastic and a few rusting tins. It was the first cache where the perishables had been completely destroyed by mice, and its demise made me fear for other larger and more crucial ones ahead. Some children were returning in dribs and drabs to a yellow mini-bus, the only vehicle in the Forestry Enterprise car park.

A further blast of hailstones terminated any vestigial desire I might have had to climb the mountain that afternoon. Instead, I contoured a few miles round the base of the hill, following tiny beast trails to the headwaters of Gleann Mòr at 500 metres. Here I cast about for a place to camp. The entire glen was a wind-tunnel. Eventually I pitched in the lee of a disused sheep fank which afforded some

marginal shelter from the north-west, carefully securing each peg with a gener-
ous-sized boulder. Food had become a major concern. With no cache my larder
was near empty, and that evening I dined on soup, custard and a few biscuits,
leaving only some porridge and a snack for tomorrow. I could either climb
Schiehallion the next day or retreat ignobly for provisions at Tummel.

All night a gale came down Gleann Mòr, robbing me entirely of sleep and
making for a disturbing and hellish experience. There were moments when gusts
half-collapsed the tent, pushing the fabric onto my face; when, for minutes at a
time, I grasped the single supporting pole lest it snap and plunge me into disaster;
when the din of thudding hailstones was so great I could neither read nor articulate
a coherent thought. And I thought nothing beyond wishing the hours away and
hoping my tiny home would somehow survive the night. Many times the demise
of my tent seemed imminent and, as a precaution, I lay fully clothed with my bivvy
unfolded, ready to dive inside should the unthinkable happen.

By first light the gusts had eased slightly, allowing me to snatch a couple of
hours' sleep. Having forced myself awake, and after a few mouthfuls of watery
porridge—all that remained—it required a serious effort of will to pack a day
sack, pull on frozen boots and set out wearily through the snow for Schiehallion.
Lack of sleep had left me deeply jaded, and I hoped it would not affect too much
my agility over steep ground. The southern side of this mountain is notably steep,
but scree gullies do break the line of crags in a few places and allow for a scrambling ascent to the ridge. While the sensible route is the well-beaten path from
the road at Braes of Foss, at least my line afforded temporary shelter from the
bitter northerly airstream.

By gaining the ridge, perhaps half a mile from the top, I became immediately
exposed to the full fury of the gale. At first I merely stumbled forward, boots
skidding on iced rocks, quite unable to peer ahead. I stopped, and with my back
to the wind I crouched low to pull on an extra layer. Blown snow was ferreting
inside my sack the second I opened it, finding its way onto exposed flesh and
instantly melting with a numbing cold. Again I went forward and again I pulled
up behind some shelter, this time ready to concede defeat. I felt I could struggle
against the wind, but not the driving snow which was peppering my face like fine
gravel. It was just not possible, so I dug in and waited. Perhaps after twenty minutes
the snow let up, leaving only a turbulent wind, and I was able to fumble through
fresh drifts to the summit.

Once back, and having forced down some unpalatable soup, I packed and
moved off with thoughts only of reaching my cache in Glen Lyon. My original
route had involved heading west over the Lyon Munros with full equipment
before dropping into the glen itself to camp. But now, tired and weak from lack
of sleep and nourishment, I would struggle just to make the 800-metre watershed over to Lyon. Snow was falling thickly and already lay inches deep, but at
least the wind was less harsh, and the sheer effort made it seem less cold as well.

The passes were drifted knee-deep which slowed my pace where I had expected to speed across. I contoured steep ground below the Munro of Carn Mairg, to another col, then sharply down the east ridge of Creag Mhòr. After the barren hills the civility of Glen Lyon was a pleasant contrast. Here is a rural softness, clumps of woodland fringing the fields that stretch level towards the river-bank. The road is lined with busy farms and prosperous-looking hamlets.

Evening had settled into darkness when I passed Camusvrachan, crossed the river and sought my cache at the bottom of an embankment. Up on my left were the gaunt shapes of the Ben Lawers range. Stars emerged one by one. I trod warily, as when stashing these provisions last autumn I'd managed to cut my foot on a rusty nail. Thankfully the cache was as I had left it, and four days' food meant three days over to Lochy and a day's grub spare.

The wind had died, and the ground was already freezing hard as I searched for a spot to camp. Occasionally snowflakes swirled in the breeze, like thistle-down, dazzling white as they passed my beam. Camping might be a problem, for this glen was heavily cultivated and there was an occupied house directly ahead. Not wishing to arouse attention, I turned off my torch and clambered uphill, crossing rough pasture and disturbing some cows, and pitched behind a small knoll. I was entirely hidden, but a metre away was a commanding view east and west along the length of the glen. It was 8 p.m.

The thud of boots and chatter of early morning walkers reminded that I was camped beneath some of the busiest hills in Scotland. On a fine summer's day the number of people encountered on the main Lawers ridge can resemble a human chain. Of course, Ben Lawers has always been a popular hill, climbed in the past primarily by botanists, but now more commonly because, at a shade below the magical 4,000 feet, Ben Lawers has the status of a 'high' mountain. It has also been made one of the most accessible mountains in the Highlands, and the inevitable cost has been erosion.

It is perhaps unfortunate that Ben Lawers should be composed of mica-shists—a parent rock which supports a rich diversity of alpine plants—for its ecological uniqueness has been the cause of its partial deterioration. The National Trust for Scotland (NTS), bought the estate ostensibly to conserve this rare ecology. In their haste to bring these riches to the public, however, they have merely aggravated the erosion problem by the thoughtless location of a car park and visitor centre high on the mountain's southern flanks. Increased access and the endless promotion of fragile regions can only result in their degradation. It is true the NTS's present aims are more inclined towards the needs of landscape protection and repair, but relocating the visitor centre would go some way to restoring some wildness to Ben Lawers.

Some, particularly in the tourist industry, have long campaigned for the establishment of National Parks in the Highlands.* For many, the very word 'park'

*Loch Lomond and the Trossachs was formally inaugurated in 2000 as Scotland's first National Park.

smacks of recreation and visitor services as its highest endeavour and not protection and restoration of wildlife and habitats. The establishment of a park, say in Glencoe or the Cairngorms along English lines, would merely cause a massive acceleration in visitor numbers and worsening of problems already experienced. By their very status, and sometimes regardless of their scenic worth, they inevitably create honeypots—note the vast difference in the numbers of walkers visiting the rather dull 'High Street fells', just inside the Lake District, to those walking the spectacular Howgills, just outside. National Parks give status to a piece of landscape in the manner an attractive label or piece of packaging makes an ordinary product more saleable.

Frozen boots and gaiters, which I had to thaw slowly over the gas, rather delayed my start. Following a large burn, and after passing a dozen ruins, I slowly edged up the ridge which connects to Meall Corranaich, my first Munro of the day. Beneath a ceiling of milky cloud stretched an army of white mountains, growing increasingly rugged towards the west, with buttresses, spiky ridges and crests like a medieval skyline. It was strangely comforting to identify hills I'd climbed six weeks previously, their clean shapes as I remembered them—a mirror on my past. In these, the most delightful winter conditions for some while, I was determined to enjoy myself. From the summit I bounded down with some abandon on heaps of drifted snow, each footfall accompanied by a hissing noise; then, suddenly, I was in some difficulty.

The snow on the east side, my descent route, had developed a hard, icy crust. Expecting only drifted powder, I had left my crampons in the tent. Below, the ground steepened or broke away altogether into small tumbling crags, some sheathed in verglas. I tried one flank, first turning to face the slope, and kicked steps in a cautious, steady fashion. But the snow was hard, my feet felt numbed, and the angle steepened unnervingly. I could see people casually ascending Beinn Ghlas a mile away, while others stood motionless on the summit, probably watching my crazy antics. I gazed through my gaping legs at the rocks below. A slip here would be extremely nasty, and I had begun to feel unsteady and vulnerable. Traversing left gave no safe descent either, so I climbed back up and detoured round, finding a much safer route down. On Beinn Ghlas, a couple just coming down admitted they'd sat shivering on top watching, wondering what the hell I was up to. Other small groups were returning from Lawers, more people than I had seen on any hill that winter.

Few of those who climb Lawers bother to continue along the ridge; a shame, for arguably An Stuc, a mile and a half to the north, is a much finer peak. After the ice on Meall Corranaich I approached the ridge with some trepidation, as I knew from experience that her north-east spur is fearsomely steep and rocky. Hamish Brown, during his Munro walk, tackled this section on a wintry day in early May, and claimed it gave the most dangerous minutes of his entire journey. Fortunately there was more rock than ice and, with my axe to hand, I made a safe, if awkward descent.

A continuation of the ridge took me over the unsung Meall Garbh and Meall Greigh, lower and more rounded than their more distinguished neighbours, but quieter. I now followed only a single pair of footprints. Sunlight on the fields by Loch Tay turned them a luminous green, and whitewashed farmsteads became specks of brightness. Orange peel clouds drifted behind the crest of Lawers before the sky darkened and I made my way down as the ridge was immersed in a snow shower. Gloom crept upwards and overtook to first greet, then swallow me as I found the upper edge of a plantation; I completed the last miles under starlight and the first sliver of a waxing moon.

For half an hour the next morning I sat shivering on a small rocky perch from where I had a commanding view along the glen. The ground was cold to touch and stony hard. A clear, frosty night had given way to a crimson dawn, but already the sun had vanished and clouds were gathering on the Carn Mairg Hills opposite. But for the occasional car plying up the glen, vanishing then reappearing as it passed through clumps of woodland, the quiet was absolute. At last, a tall figure clad in black came into view, striding purposefully along the track below, completely oblivious to my presence. 'Looks like him,' I thought, and bellowed a greeting. It was . I'd last seen Antony in Glen Feshie more than a month ago, and the prospect of friendly company cheered me immensely. Two days before in Tummel Bridge, and purely on the off-chance, I'd left a message with a time, date, and six-figure grid-reference, but it was anyone's guess whether he would turn up.

He brought with him a pile of deep-fried, carbohydrate-rich snacks from the deli, and a grim forecast: 'Heavy snowfall, blizzards on the tops, and a warning for hill-walkers.'

I shrugged my shoulders. 'They err on the side of caution, don't they? If things turn nasty we'll get down.'

In the context of my journey, weather forecasts had long ceased to have any meaning. No decision was ever based on one. If, according to the weathermen, a band of rain or snow was 'expected', then it came, giving me a soaking or a hiding or forcing me down, but its arrival was completely out of my control. I carried on until it became too dangerous or unpleasant to continue; I knew my limitations. Predicting accurately the weather conditions in any mountain area is also notoriously difficult, as local topography can deflate or exaggerate any general forecast beyond recognition. My scepticism of forecasts, particularly 'mountain activities' ones, is admittedly irrational and subjective, but more times than I can remember I've been disappointed when the expected improvements failed to show, or when the early promise of challenging conditions would die to a whimper.

Weather forecasts can also be completely wrong. In the Cairngorms one February, conditions on the high tops were looking particularly uninviting so we phoned a well-known information line before setting out. I distinctly remember the cheery tones of the voice on the recorded message concluding with the phrase: 'breezy and cold, but a fine day to be out'. So, with skis attached, we aimed for the Lairig Ghru with the simple ambition of crossing over to Deeside. After being blown to a standstill and losing the fight to gain the pass, we retreated to excavate an emergency snow-hole, the wind-chill being probably the worst I'd ever experienced.

Striking up Carn Gorm, the first of the Lyon Munros, was refreshingly direct: no niggling false summits or long drawn-out ridges, just a mile-and-a-half grind up to the snowline and a damp wind that coated our jackets with rime. We'd already secured the best spot behind the cairn when a party appeared from nearby Rannoch School, two staff and about six adolescents. There being too many of us to crowd against the cairn we watched them form a well-drilled protective huddle, like a herd of musk ox, but the mournful sight of volleys of snow whistling past the youngsters was enough to propel us on. Between here and Càrn Mairg the ridge dances over a confusion of bumps and tops, twisting willy-nilly and trying to shake you off at every turn. Navigation is aided in places by the remnants of an old boundary fence. Some of the iron stakes had been shoved into a cairn, like needles in a pin-cushion, to resemble a bizarre piece of sculpture. A young couple crouching behind had 'had quite enough for one day' and were heading straight down.

Conditions had gradually worsened so that now as we bowed into the wind approaching Càrn Mairg there blew up a gale and full blizzard. The summit was no place to linger. A final bearing and we bailed out like a couple of robbers leaving the scene of a crime, leaping over compacted snow to the basin and relative shelter of the corrie. Unable to stop at any point on the ridge we indulged in a late lunch in a dilapidated bothy. Two members of a party we'd met earlier came in behind, brushing snow from their cagoules, huffing and puffing and rather cursing the conditions. I chatted to an animated, bearded fellow in his fifties.

'You're camping tonight in *this*?' he exclaimed, showing his teeth while emphasising the last word. When strangers meet in the hills, there will inevitably come the idle question: 'Been out for long then?' And from my appearance it was obvious that I'd not left my car down in the glen after a morning drive from Edinburgh. Nearly two weeks of growth sprouted from weather-beaten cheeks, my hair was an unkempt mop with sun-yellow streaks, my nose red and peeling from continued exposure to the elements. I possessed no mirror but Antony assured me that I would 'scare to death a bingo hall full of old ladies'.

To avoid overreaction, as a rule I tended not to give the whole truth. On the few occasions that I did, I received a mixed bag of responses. Most were warmed and cheered at my eccentricity; others peppered me with questions on equipment and details of my route; some changed the subject. But on this occasion, before I could open my mouth, Antony chipped in:

'He's been out since November.'

And the response? A long pause, the snow outside falling as thickly as ever, and our bearded friend repeated gravely, shaking his head: 'And you're camping out in *this*?'

With evening falling we emerged from woodland that reminded me of an Alpine valley, the snow now so heavy we couldn't see to the other side and already thick on the road. Concerned at being stranded, Antony left me to half-jog the three miles to his car, and wheel-spun his way to safety for the long, difficult drive to Glasgow.

While during the night the snow eased, it was replaced by a malignant wind that forced me awake and for long hours pummelled away causing an unending commotion. Icy currents ferreted about the interior so I withdrew any exposed flesh, my head and hands, to the protection of my sleeping bag. The wind died as suddenly as it had arrived, and on opening my eyes I did actually wonder if it had not all been some nightmare. The air was warm, the sun radiating heat as it came through the nylon skin of the tent.

How rare an experience had this been? To be gently woken in a sun-warmed interior, to gaze outside, screwing up your eyes in the brightness, and to see the lovely Glen Lyon, its broad strath, its woods and hills, under a quilt of snow and an empty sky. It was in a buoyant mood that I ploughed down to the road, then west up the glen.

If any length of road is worth walking then it is Glen Lyon, for the scenery simply makes you forget the tarmac. I walked the entire length of it one day in late May, and remember the sheer explosion of new growth and blossom along the verges. The friendly lady who ran the tearoom and tiny store at the Bridge of Balgie agreed, saying proudly: 'The loveliest glen in Scotland.' Moving here with her family thirty years before, she talked of jobs becoming scarcer and winters milder. But I kept quiet when she strongly berated walkers for being on the hill in yesterday's snow. Her husband, a shepherd, would 'never have gone out,' she said.

On a slightly gloomier note Glen Lyon was home to Captain Robert Campbell and his men, who in 1692 massacred forty unsuspecting MacDonalds while garrisoned in Glencoe. Clan Campbell and Clan Donald had feuded for generations and there was no love lost between them, but historians have rightly pointed out that the Campbell garrison was acting under direct orders from the Scottish Secretary, John Dalrymple, the real murderer of Glencoe. As if to exorcise the guilt of so heinous a crime, Robert Campbell's son and grandsons joined the Jacobite cause in the '15 and '45 rebellions, fighting and dying side by side with the MacDonalds on Culloden moor. Clan Campbell has gone, and today, despite its low-lying fertility, the glen is probably quieter than at any time in the last thousand years. The school hangs on with five pupils, and except as summer homes most of the cottages now stand empty.

The Bridge of Balgie to Loch Tay road was blocked with drifts and the absence of traffic only emphasised the peace. I plodded my way up to camp in the dramatic amphitheatre of Corrie Riadhailt, overlooked by the Tarmachan ridge and my next target, looking all bumpy and saw-toothed. A grey ceiling had sullied the sky, first filtering, then blotting out the sun. It was the leading edge of a weather front, and before it arrived I went up the ridge for Meall nan Tarmachan. Monochromatic views embraced a sweep of Munro shapes from Ben Nevis to Ben More, and before my eyes the air became thick like a fog, hiding the shapes one by one. I hastened down but the snow had stolen a march on me and I arrived back sodden.

Only a little snow actually fell and in the morning I pushed on for Meall Ghaordaidh (1,043m), a bulky brute of a hill sandwiched between glens Lyon and Lochy. With a 300-metre start most people do the climb up from Lyon. To save a little time, it was my intention to undertake an east–west traverse of Ghaordaidh under the burden of a full pack, and the south-eastern arm, being exposed and windswept, appeared a good option for this ascent. Silhouetted against an emerging sun, a tiny figure was bounding down, then vanished from sight; at least I would have some prints to follow. The sunshine came as a mixed blessing as it now softened the snow, making the going particularly slow and tedious. I traversed exhaustingly at about a mile an hour and then began the upward grind.

At some point, about midway up, perhaps, I entered the freezing level, but, in deep snow with every sinew straining under a heavy pack, it failed to register. The grinding effort kept me warm, so warm in fact I wore only a single thermal layer, perspiration running down my back, face and arms, and dripping from my nose. Then it was as if I'd been ambushed. You are never quite prepared for this. Approaching the top I was suddenly exposed to sub-zero winds and shivered uncontrollably, the wind like a steel blade, sharp-edged and ruthless. It was cold in the peculiarly savage way of a Scottish peak, the bitter wind infiltrating uncovered flesh as if a living thing, my clothes, a second ago moist and warm, now feeling like icy blankets. Eagerly I made for the meagre shelter afforded by the cairn, oblivious to the glorious views westwards and quite unable to believe how a marginal rise in altitude can bring about such a transformation of conditions, how these summits manage to breed such a vile concoction of wind, cold and damp.

My face twisted with the discomfort of it, I pulled on three extra layers, a balaclava and overmitts and gulped down some tinned tuna and chocolate before feeling better. Traversing westwards, I hurried down, finishing up below the snowline and a good way along Glen Lochy. After retrieving some food—all untouched—I continued west, camping on rough pasture at the head of the glen. By now, three hours from Ghaordaidh, I was hungry again. Delving into the cache I piled a huge meal onto my tiny cooker: fish, peas, tomato, pasta, almost all of it emptied from tins and ready in ten minutes. When packing these caches I threw in an extra day's food for every third day, so that in theory every cache was overstocked. I remember wondering how I would ever eat so much, but in practice an ever-growing appetite dealt with any surplus, and delays meant I could stretch the grub a day or two longer.

By morning I was eternally grateful for this generous policy. I was also intensely happy. Outside heavy snow was being driven by a strong wind, obliterating the hills and forcing on me the unexpected luxury of a rest—a complete, clear-conscience, uninterrupted rest. I could easily have slept, but to avoid a sleepless night I dozed instead, neither asleep nor fully conscious, but awake enough to relish the tranquillity of the hours as they slid slowly by. Occasionally I rooted about for something tasty to eat, sometimes I read, but mostly I just lay wrapped in my sleeping bag, unmoving. Did Blaise Pascal say 'complete calm is death'? But to lie utterly still and not be compelled to pack and walk and climb, not be compelled to move for one entire day, was an intense experience of living. The stillness was an ecstasy. Nothing mattered beyond rest, not the blizzard outside, not the hills tomorrow, nor even the fact that I was ill-shaven and evil-smelling, that my clothes had deteriorated into grimy wrappings giving off offensive odours, that I'd become a slave to unsavoury habits.

By morning the weather had improved enough for me to set out for my last peaks before Crianlarich. It was cold and raw and snow clouds threatened, but I couldn't string the food out for another day. On the face of it Beinn Heasgarnich, Creag Mhòr and Ben Challum was not a difficult round. There had been accumulations of fresh snow, but the peaks were steep and rocky, and once high I hoped for windswept crests and ice, making for fast, easy walking. With only sixteen or seventeen miles to cover I expected to be back before dark.

However, miles worked out with a piece of string became meaningless when, an hour from camp, I found myself ensnared in drifts, sometimes to my hips, and was forced to move face down into a snowstorm. In thirty minutes I'd managed maybe a hundred metres, most likely less. Whenever the wind and spindrift intensified to make progress impossible, I would huddle in the lee of some drift, wait for a lull, then lurch from foot to foot, cutting a bizarre, zig-zag line. The surface never advertised its depth or softness, or what manner of danger it concealed, whether snares of running water or hollow ditches. Ordinarily I would have turned back, the investment in effort not justifying the meagre gain in distance, but I pushed on because I was stubborn, and probably a little reckless. At the end of my second hour I was still not halfway to climbing Heasgarnich. At one point in this madness I thought I saw three figures struggling some way behind me. But later when it cleared they were gone. Perhaps they had overtaken me, or given up. Had I really seen them? In these abysmal conditions I couldn't be sure of anything.

Finding a steeper, more direct line, I attached crampons and went up easy snow ramps, threading some outcrops. While for the time being I was perfectly sheltered from the vicious north-westerlies, I knew the last mile would be a fearsome tussle. And so it was. The summit is out on a northerly limb, and for an age I was thumped, harried and exhausted in my quest, but otherwise not defeated. As the crow flies, Heasgarnich lay less than three miles from my tent but the mountain had consumed more than four hours of labour.

At least the wind was now coming at me from behind. The snow squalls had petered out and the clouds were clamouring to get free of the ridge. And then, something unexpected. Immersed in dense clouds for hours, the sudden dramatic appearance of the sun was magical and revelational. One moment your whole world is the claustrophobia of a white out, the next there is an explosion of vision limited only by the horizon, and you see sixty or seventy miles in the clear maritime air. The ground below vanishes, distant valleys and troughs remind you how high up you are, and everywhere there are mountains gleaming in sunshine, pale blue cloud shapes rushing across laundered white slopes. In an arc from south to north, a hundred peaks make a multitude of sharp ridges, fine lines, blue shadows: Ben More, Ben Lui, the Black Mount and Bridge of Orchy Hills, north to the Mamores, the Grey Corries, Ben Alder—most mountains, I fancy, this side of the Great Glen. The landscape was entirely white, like a polar wilderness, and with such an array of peaks, it seemed more like part of Arctic Greenland.

Three human forms were now approaching, surely the same three I'd seen earlier. They were being thrown sideways by the wind and moved with an erratic gait as if dodging bullets fired by an invisible enemy. In a garbled conversation in which we strained to hear one another above the wind, they said that they'd also sought shelter and crept up the southern flanks and were now going to 'bag the bugger and get the hell down'.

In thirty minutes I found the relative shelter of the col, but Creag Mhòr (1,047m) gave another struggle. The wind had dumped huge quantities of snow on the east side and again I toiled to gain the long summit ridge. Cascades of blue-grey ice hung like an old man's beard from some of the crags, and on the high wind-shaved crests verglas coated the rocks in lethal fashion. My crampons were on and off all day. Miraculously, on approaching Creag Mhòr the wind had died to a breeze, and the sun, brilliant as ever, cut long, slanting shadows on every piece of relief. The snow, untrodden at my feet, rippled like sand at low tide, the mountains everywhere were sharp and edged, fiercely bright or deeply shadowed.

It is not possible to describe the experience of crossing unmarked snow to a high summit in the Western Highlands. For hill-walkers this is simply the greatest joy. It was mid-week in early March; all morning and early afternoon had been wild, but now I reaped the reward of persistence, and had the mountains to myself. No car or road, or house, nor any mark of man blemished the view—I was quite alone.

It was now 4 p.m., seven hours since I'd left my pitch, and Ben Challum still lay some three miles to the south. I studied the distance on the map. There would be much descent and re-ascent, the peak of Cam Chreag (884m) would have to be traversed, and every step south led me further from my tent. But I knew the moon would rise tonight, and I wanted to see the sun go down whilst high in the mountains.

By racing up the last slopes in a lung-bursting effort I reached Challum just as the sun was lost behind flesh-coloured clouds. The peak of Ben Cruachan glowed orange for a minute, then a gloom settled around the summit. With no wind at all now, it was still and utterly soundless. The snows became the colour of the sky, still strangely resplendent as if keeping alive the memory of daylight, and very quickly, like something tangible, night began advancing up from the valley below.

With all haste I jogged for a mile down the east ridge on perfect snow, dodged steeply through some crags and ploughed through drifts to the snow-covered track maintained by the hydro-board. The track was endless but the moon had now risen to show the way. At last I picked up my faint boot marks from morning and knew these would lead to my tent. And it was only 8 p.m.—home in thirty minutes, I reckoned. I'd made good time from Challum, though was now tired to the bone. Then the moon went behind a cloud and I lost the trail. With my headtorch I searched wearily for that tiny wedge of nylon. It was, I recalled, up from the main track, hidden behind a small knoll, and by a trickling burn. But the darkness had rearranged things so that in a maddening search lasting nearly two hours I found twenty such places, but no tent. My wanderings created a confusion of prints which now probably obliterated earlier tracks. The night was horribly cold. Close to tears and about to give up and sleep in a shed full of cow-dung, I did one last sweep and literally stumbled over the guyline. I had saved some tins for a huge meal but was so tired that I could barely think to co-ordinate the cooking. I thought of little beyond sleep.

Next day, the way to Crianlarich was a small matter of ten miles, but things are never quite so straightforward and conditions precluded any normal pace. There was a long, flat bealach choked with soft snow, and the weather had turned mean again. A raw east wind scurried down the glen from behind, whipping up mini-tornadoes of loose snow, while from above a sunless grey sky came down like a lid, turning midday into evening. Ben Challum was lost in cloud and I was deeply thankful not to be climbing its endless slopes today. After I'd extricated myself from a drift for the umpteenth time it began to snow, the flakes blowing horizontally and making pattering noises on the back of my upturned hood. I ploughed clumsily on as a line of pale-rumped deer skipped away with arrogant ease.

At the farm beneath the railway arch four hysterical dogs barked their greeting to this unkempt stranger from the hills. A young man emerged behind them, a convivial fellow, his face half-muffled in a green and white scarf, and his hands dug deep in pockets. He grinned broadly and told me of the floods they'd had in February.

On arrival at Crianlarich the snow was inches deep and still falling. As the youth hostel, one of the busiest in Highlands, had room only for one night, I fixed up a B & B for the other. There is no doubt this hostel feeds off the popularity of the West Highland Way, and nestling in the shadow of high mountains it is an ideal base for hill-walkers too. It was our starting point for the Munros in 1986, and judging to the number of walking and climbing guides strewn across tables, the clientele seemed almost exclusively hillgoers, some having had epics that day, now licking their wounds in the warmth of the lounge while planning for more of the same. Among them were Ian and Mark, and later we joined the throng in the tiny pub. Both, still with the clutter of a week's work in their heads, had been turned back by foul conditions on nearby Munros. I was buoyant and in high spirits. Crianlarich! It had seemed a fantasy place when setting out from Sandwood last autumn, and even now it took a while to sink in that I'd actually arrived.

12

West Highland Journey

CLIMBING BEN More had been a brutal thousand metres of unrelenting steepness.

'My wife thinks I'm crackers,' Mark shouted up between gulps of air, '…you know, coming up here in the middle of winter. You must be off your *head*, she says. Did you get a view? No? Then why the hell bother? What's the point of it? If you want to get fit, go to the bloody gym, it's a damn sight cheaper… Are we at the top yet, leader?'

'Five minutes, I reckon, it's beginning to level out, so we must be close,' I said, screwing up my eyes to see through the mist.

'But she does have a point, doesn't she?'

'Who does?'

'My wife!'

'Umm… yeah, she does, of course she does.' I could now see a vague outline of a monolithic shape. The cairn, surely!

'I've just slogged my guts out, and for what?' Mark went on. 'A load of snow and mist.'

'It might clear, the bloke on the forecast seemed to think so,' I said, though I didn't believe it for a second.

'Pigs might fly. So how you feeling, then? Bet you've not even broken sweat. You've been moving like you're on a mission, and I'm knackered 'cos I've been trying to keep up,' Mark said with a mischievous grin, still puffing hard.

I'd bumped into Mark Tagholm at the hostel and, after a night at the pub, persuaded him to accompany me over a couple of Munros. For him it would also be a chance to exact some revenge. In yesterday's blizzard he'd been turned back on this hill not halfway up the northeast ridge.

'Thought the ridge would give shelter from the prevailing westerlies; trouble was, the blizzard came in from the east, ambushing me from behind. Bloody desperate.'

'Coming over the pass from Lochy was no picnic either,' I added, shaking my head in sympathy.

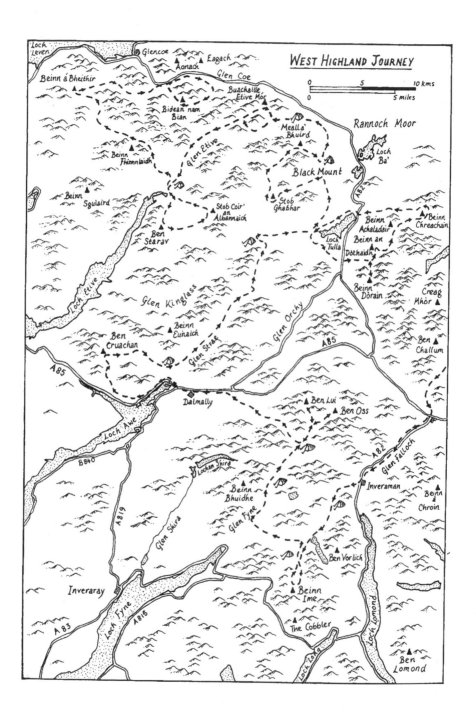

WEST HIGHLAND JOURNEY

0   5   10 kms
0   5 miles

Loch Leven

Glencoe
Aonach   Eagach
Beinn à Bheithir
Glen Coe
Buachaille Etive Mór
Bidean nam Bian
Meall à Bhuird
Rannoch Moor
Loch Ba'
Glen Etive
Beinn Fhionnlaidh
Black Mount
Beinn Sgulaird
Stob Coir' an Albannaich
Stob Ghabhar
Beinn Achaladair
Beinn Chreachain
Loch Tulla
Beinn an Dòthaidh
Ben Starav
Loch Etive
Glen Kinglass
Glen Orchy
Beinn Dòrain
Creag Mhòr
Beinn Eunaich
Glen Strae
A85
Ben Challum
Ben Cruachan
Dalmally
Ben Lui
Ben Oss
Glen Falloch
Loch Awe
A85
B840
Lochan Shira
Beinn Bhuidhe
Glen Fyne
Inveraman
Beinn à Chroin
A819
Glen Shira
Ben Vorlich
Inveraray
Beinn Ime
Loch Lomond
A83   A815
Loch Fyne
The Cobbler
Loch Long
Ben Lomond

On the summit—at 1,174 metres, the highest in Perthshire—there might have been no view, but this strange world of blue ice and rime-plated boulders had an ethereal beauty. Only a soft breeze swirled around the cairn carrying tiny snowflakes. We ate our sandwiches unmolested.

'Who needs a view anyway?' Mark said with his mouth full. 'Just being here is enough.'

We went on for Ben More's twin, Stob Binnein, slightly lower, though by far the more interesting. Like Schiehallion, both peaks are easily recognisable from a great distance, but whereas Ben More has muscular bulk, Stob Binnein is shapely and elegant, a compatible couple if ever there was one. Reaching the final crest we had good reason to hope there might be some reward for our toil. For some moments a pale shining disc tried to pierce the mist; there was a filtering of light and the faintest of shadows, but we waited in vain. Mark peeled off, heading back via Benmore Glen quite happy with his day's haul. He'd lost fitness, he said, since his marathon trek across the length of Scotland a year before.

In the time since I last traversed these hills, I'd obviously forgotten just how much of a 'pull' it was to Cruach Ardrain, climbing without a break for 500 metres. Initially I clambered over the top of Stob Garbh, whose northern crags held long snakes of ice, then crossed a tricky ridge to a tiny col with Ardrain looming directly above. I'd also forgotten how steep this mountain was, clear of cloud and in Alpine regalia, and it was here that I ran into some difficulty.

I didn't much like the look of the north-east ridge. An easy scramble in summer, I could see grey sheaths of verglas poking through the snow cover. A smooth snow flank to the left seemed better, and, with crampons attached, I began kicking my way up. The snow texture was perfect for crampons, crisp and hard, my boots making a reassuring sound as they were thrust into the snow, and I sank into a comfortable upward rhythm. From below the slope had appeared relatively short and I had assumed the summit was just over the lip, but after a hundred metres I realised that I was barely at the halfway mark. As it steepened, the snow grew thinner, my crampons scraping the rock beneath. A number of times I skidded and wobbled and had to throw my axe in quickly. Seeking better snow I veered further left, but this was a mistake for it steepened still and directly below were the beginnings of crags. A slip now didn't bear thinking about.

The first flicker of worry pulsed through me and I suddenly felt exposed and vulnerable. Though I love mountains and read climbing books endlessly, I have an almost pathological fear of steep faces. Photos of climbers clinging like bats to overhangs always leave me nauseous. In winter I have never been on anything more challenging than a simple 'grade three', and on that I was pretty much winched up like a sack of potatoes. An irrational fear continues to undermine my attempts at ice climbing, and I persevere only in order to notch up winter skills.

Real fear arrived the moment I realised that I would probably be unable to check myself if I slipped more than few metres, and it manifested itself by turning my limbs to jelly. They shook uncontrollably. My legs and arms suddenly weakened so that my stance seemed even more precarious, and into my head came a vivid image of a helpless body hurtling out of control. I could reverse my line and go back but it appeared a very long way down. Looking up I could see that the slope, now about forty degrees, steepened menacingly to ice and bare rock. To my right was the ridge that had initially so repelled me and this I now aimed for. My heart pounding, I traversed the slope with the utmost care until a near-vertical snow lip of a few metres barred the way. I made tentative marks with my axe but it was just too precarious. Retreating a little, gasping with nervous exhaustion, I aimed instead for a snowy ledge. I climbed to this, reached the point of no return and scrambled belly first onto the ridge, my boots treading air. I rolled onto my back and laughed with quiet relief.

The top was clear but not a single ray of sunlight softened the harsh landscape. It was cold and bleak-looking; it was also late. A curling route took me into the bowl of the corrie then north towards Crianlarich, darkness catching me as I reached the edge of the forest. Not having come this way I was unsure of how to thread a route through the ranks of fir trees and did not relish the prospect of another tooth and nail struggle, not now, so weary after a long day in the snow.

For some while now I'd been following fresh bootprints, and just ahead was a dark figure, slightly squat, and moving very slowly. He vanished into a dense grove. Not wanting to startle him I called out in a friendly manner:

'Hope you know the way to town.'

He replied without turning round or stopping: 'Should do. I came this way earlier. That was you on Ardrain, wasn't it?'

I admitted it was and made a joke about hill-walkers needing to get their kicks somehow.

The conversation was strange because, it being dark, I couldn't see his face so it was like talking to a shadow. Nor was he particularly talkative. First I followed him down a steep fire-break, our thoughts drowned by the roar of a nearby burn, then we wove through interlocking branches that scratched our faces until we finally emerged onto a track beaten by many feet. We walked side by side in an awkward silence. Just before the lights of Crianlarich he pointed to a thicket saying: 'My tent's in there somewhere,' and disappeared.

Often, in idle moments before sleep, I'd consciously name each peak that I'd been over, climbing them again in my memory, recalling with delight their shape and character. They had long become old friends, and in my mind's voice I uttered their Gaelic names almost like an incantation, for the likes of a Seana Bhraigh or Sgurr nan Clach Geala seemed to resonate with a kind of mystique. But as the journey unfurled and the list grew, it became increasingly difficult to reach the end before sleep took hold, and on reaching Crianlarich it was easier to concentrate on those I still had to climb.

And now I realised there were just sixteen to do. It didn't sound like many. A keen, car-based walker could polish them off in under a week. But I knew there was much walking to connect these peaks, a great deal of it trackless; and, with only a single shop en route, I would be dependent on food which had now lain buried for five months. While I gave myself a fortnight to finish, I was not in any kind of rush. With mountains such as Lui, Cruachan, Stob Ghabhar and Starav still to come I just wanted a little fine weather, some views. If I harboured any complacency about the task remaining then it was fully extinguished by Mark who reminded me of just how uncompromising March weather can be. During a ten-day spell based around Fort William a few years ago they'd not managed to climb a single hill. 'Conditions were bedlam,' he said, 'totally vile, day after day, and that was at sea level.' The one afternoon they did venture above 300 metres they were literally blown off their feet. It was a salutary warning.

§ § §

I left Crianlarich on the second week of March, late on a Sunday morning, the hills resplendent and bristling with the mantle of winter. Beneath lazy white clouds and bright sunshine was an almost endless stream of traffic heading north. A local lady pointed me in the direction of the West Highland Way going south. I went up porridgy snow through conifers then began an easy descent of Glen Falloch, the smooth man-made surface giving some of the gentlest off-road walking of the journey.

In its early years this and other parts of the West Highland Way became an eroded quagmire, a victim of the Way's own popularity; and these manufactured sections, while artificial in appearance, have at least prevented a total collapse of the footpath. The concept of long-distance paths in Scotland has come in for much criticism, not least because of unsightly erosion caused by hemming thousands of feet into narrow corridors. Many see little merit in the Way itself, and have rightly pointed out that anyone could have walked from Glasgow to Fort William *before* 1980. Crossing private land in Scotland—unlike in England—is not, in itself, an act of trespass so no 'right of way' need be established.

We certainly don't need any more of these paths. In Scotland there will always be more miles of footpath than there are people to walk them and these days when walking guides proliferate to the same extent as books on cookery and gardening, there is a vast spectrum of 'recommended' walks to choose from. Even better, anyone with imagination and a few OS maps can conjure up their own walks—far more interesting than anything the local bureaucracy could create. Notwithstanding this, the West Highland Way is a very fine route indeed. It threads along glens and lochsides, taking advantage of old military roads and cattle-droving routes. And while it has given thousands immense pleasure, it has also, no doubt, bolstered the viability of a number of remote hostelries such as the hotels at Inveroran and Kingshouse. There is certainly no lack of refreshment *en route*.

Scotland's other official path, the Southern Upland Way is quite another matter. In September, a full two months before starting this journey, I set out along the Way, ostensibly to break in some stiff-soled winter boots, but also to explore a part of Scotland I hitherto knew little about. It was a massive disappointment, utter tedium in the end forcing me to abort at Melrose fifty miles from the finish. The Way takes one past a grotesque wind farm sited on a hill top, and through a region devastated by lead mining. Of the 160-odd miles I did cover, nearly half were through dreary plantations and, incredibly, thirty were on hard tarmac, about the same amount I covered later during four and a half months in the Highlands.

Today, despite the chill, I moved briskly in the calm of the valley, wearing only a single thermal top, something I'd not done since that balmy day in early November. Few people were about. I passed some French lads with packframes and cricket hats, then a couple of attractive ladies, but no one else. The car park by the Inverarnan Inn was jammed with vehicles and only when I stopped for a short break did I realise that the temperature was barely above freezing.

A group of well-dressed customers hovered by the entrance and seemed not to notice a walker cross the road, disappear into the scrub on the far side, crawl beneath a railway arch and sweat his way up to the snowline. The reality of walking every inch of this journey meant that once again I was able to leave the road and vanish into a mountain hinterland, this one as empty as any wilderness in Sutherland—and it would likely be four days before I emerged again, at Dalmally, in the shadow of Ben Cruachan.

This land immediately north of the Arrochar Alps is probably as little visited as any in Scotland. With not a single Munro or Corbett, and steep forestry tracks hardly suitable for mountain biking, there is perhaps little reason why anyone would want to come this way. Sadly for those who do, the scenery is marred to an extent by huge pylons and plantations.

With my legs still sore from yesterday's ten-hour exertion, I was being cautious with my walking; as I was already tired, Beinn Ime in the Arrochar Alps now became tomorrow's objective. Sunlit green fields by the River Falloch as it managed one last loop before Lomond gave a nostalgic yearning for lazy summer days. My memory is crammed with such days. Before the responsibilities of adulthood during the early and mid-'80s, I'd spent a lifetime of summers, mostly in July and August, walking and camping in the Highlands. Today it didn't feel right to be rushing up mountain sides in a sweat, and like the folk gathered at the Inn, I longed for once just to be doing nothing.

The going along the snow-covered tracks, always tiresome, now became a grind. The snow surface had begun to freeze hard, forming a crust, and with every step my boots plunged through, finding the soft underbelly and reducing my progress to the pitiful speed of a crawl. Taking twenty minutes to struggle less than a quarter of a mile was the final straw. I dumped my sack, cleared a space in the snow and pitched right there high on a shoulder at nearly 500 metres. Though I was extremely exposed to any change in the weather, the full moon over Ben Vorlich promised only a calm, clear night.

After a hard frost I continued south next day, making equally slow progress and, for a while, becoming equally frustrated. I traversed steeply through a young conifer planting and dropped to the watershed of Strath Dubh, a lonely and strangely inaccessible spot. No track or path comes here, the eastern approach from Lomond is barred by outcrops and the nearest road is a dozen miles to the west. A track does begin after a mile or so, winding through a plantation, climbing, then falling to the head of Loch Sloy. I recognised the paw marks of a wild cat and saw a herd of about twenty hungry deer. Beinn Ime (1,011m), highest of the Arrochar Alps, now loomed directly into view. A watery sun, which all morning had struggled to find its way through, now gave up the ghost as dirty cloud rolled in over the tops. A murky, sullen atmosphere prevailed. I pitched above the roofless shieling known as Abyssinia, had a meal and set off for Ime.

With barely a shred of wind and the feeling of being imprisoned by an oppressive mist it was an eerie ascent. There were no sounds save my own footfalls, and no other feet marked the wind-packed snow on this northern arm of the hill. From my position this had seemed the obvious route to the top. Doubtless a finer climb would have been to tackle the narrow north-east spur, but just to reach it would have involved two miles of bashing through soft snow—and by now I was quite sick of soft snow. Unavoidably, I went over Beinn Chorranach first, then tracked the final icy slopes to Ime.

For a Munro group not thirty miles from a million people these hills are surprisingly quiet, and in half a dozen previous visits I can recall only rarely meeting other folk on the main tops. Probably the vast majority who come here test their nerve on the Cobbler instead, a touch below 3,000 feet but bizarre in its summit architecture, the crest looking like a lower gum of broken and missing teeth. I knew it well. Working in Dumbarton one summer I would often drive up for an evening scramble and be back home in Glasgow before dark. Beinn Ime was the most southerly peak of my journey.

The dense pall had been an approaching weather front, and during the early hours I was woken by the din of torrential rain on nylon. Come morning, a grey light revealed a desolate world, the nearby burn having swollen to bursting, its roar so overwhelming I stuffed my ears with cotton wool and tried to read. There was a temptation to stay put and hold out for something better, but I'd run out of food and the next cache lay just eight miles over the watershed in Glen Fyne. In the great scheme of things, running out of chocolate and teabags cannot rank very highly, but just then on a wild day with few comforts, it was demoralising. All the same I put off going until I absolutely had to move lest there be no daylight.

Though it rained it did not feel in the least mild. It was a cold rain, which very soon ran down my neck in icy trickles. Whatever the claims of manufacturers, no jacket in the world could have kept me dry that afternoon; with the downpour, the saturated air, and me having to toil up a slope of thick slush, my cagoule had simply stopped 'breathing'. Condensation so soaked my undergarments that when pausing for a minute's respite I immediately began to shiver. Only by moving continuously could I keep warm, but at least not stopping for idle breaks would shorten the overall purgatory.

The watershed to Glen Fyne was a few misty miles of melting snow and peat bog. Navigation was easy as a line of electricity pylons more or less went in my direction. A west wind blew rain into my face, and growing increasingly hungry, I thought of nothing beyond reaching my cache and savouring its contents. It was the first one I'd placed, and I recalled well its preparation, grinning to myself at the trouble I'd taken to make it rodent-proof, and to conceal it cleverly. Plans for tomorrow and Ben Lui were irrelevant; it was only the cache that spurred me on.

A very steep 500-metre descent landed me in a snowless Glen Fyne. From here a private tarmac road leads to the lodge, then rather deteriorates into a muddy lane as it climbs northwards into wilder country. A mile past the last estate cottage I put up the tent, then eagerly went to retrieve my food. Shifting some mossy stones from a tomb-like space beneath an overhang, I rolled up my sleeves and reached deep into the gap, feeling about for a plastic sack. I pulled, but it disintegrated immediately. My heart sank. It had been chewed to confetti. The plastic picnic box I had so carefully packed with perishables also felt horribly light and a hole underneath indicated where the mice had gnawed their way in. And they had been indiscriminate, for everything was eaten and shredded; only the few tins remained, and after months in the ground they were grimy with rust. I washed them in the stream and tried to be philosophical about the loss—after all, at a pinch, there was still enough grub to see me to Dalmally.

Of course now I had nothing to drink other than cold water. I lay there, my wet gear a sopping pile in the vestibule, and wondered how much hard cash I would have parted with for a single mug of sweet tea. Then I remembered that Scott's party would drink plain hot water mixed with a little sugar. My sugar was gone so I boiled water and mixed it instead with sweetened condensed milk. It sounds disgusting but just then it was a revelation—I downed three mugs of the stuff. Outside the rain had nearly stopped.

I woke first at a little past midnight; the moon filtering through some high clouds had given an impression of the coming dawn. Seeing the moon was a promising sign and I went back to sleep in a happier frame of mind. At least the portents were good. When I opened my eyes again and saw the arrow head of Ben Lui freshly snow-covered against the palest of blue skies, I was transfixed, the beauty of it extinguishing in an instant all the dreary wet days there had ever been. After a meagre breakfast it was suddenly no hardship to pull on two pairs of half-frozen socks and wrap myself in a cold, wet thermal top. I broke camp and went north.

Perhaps because of the intense variability of weather conditions and scenery, any walk through the Scottish Highlands seems always to be remembered as a collection of remarkably distinct days, each day burning a place in your memory when much of the repetition of life blurs to nothing. And often, much later, you recall vividly these events as if they'd occurred just yesterday. The late W. H. Murray, when imprisoned by the Nazis, took refuge in his recollections of climbs with friends in the Highlands during the 1930s. Years later in his classic *Mountaineering in Scotland* he described those days with such clarity and freshness that it was easy to believe his tales were pure invention. Some days in particular stand above others. For me Ben Lui would be one of those days.

Without doubt the finest approach to Ben Lui is from the north-east where, if fortunate, you are presented with one of the most beautiful sights in Britain: a canopy summit with five steep spurs slung like guy-ropes. The folds inbetween hold a number of dramatic high corries, particularly Corrie Gaothach, which gleams with snow well into summer.

Today, unusually, I was approaching from the south. As Glen Fyne twisted westwards I continued straight on, losing sight of the mountain while toiling up a steep flank by an incised burn. It burst into view again when I moved onto gentler ground, its great southern slopes rising inexorably for three miles to a shiny, white crest. Ben More and her satellites, peaks I'd climbed some days before, poked all in a row above the near horizon, dazzling, then grey with shadow. I was crossing a hummocky wasteland, almost a plateau, where large drifts choked stream courses. Somehow in this great space I found the perfect pitch: a green cushion of sage and rye grass by a bend in a burn, sheltered from the west by an old river terrace.

After a tinned meal of pasta and fish there was sunshine for the climb to the wide bealach dividing Lui from her less illustrious partner, Ben Oss. As I started up her long south-east ridge, clouds ominously rolled in, blotting out the sun. It began to snow, this time earnestly, and there was a dreadful feeling of permanency about it. In near white-out I moved cautiously, alert to cornices that had been growing to my right and now overhung the eastern face. Whirls of snow came at me like dervishes, showering me, so I paused and stared at the ground to avoid a face full of stinging ice. I found the summit as the clouds tore clear. Snow plumes danced around and ice particles glittered in the sunshine but there were strikingly clear views of yesterday's peaks to the south and east. The land from where I had just come seemed a level plain littered with a million snowdrifts like fallen cherry blossom. To the north, the higher hills of Glencoe and Rannoch remained consumed but occasionally a radiant ridge or flank would emerge highlighted by a declining sun.

I lingered until the bitter cold drove me on for Ben Oss. Still wearing crampons, I raced up with the sun emerging from a cloud bank in great orange shafts before vanishing again. The climb to the summit is something I will never forget. So much seemed to be happening: the entire panorama was a fast-moving scene, the atmosphere like a spot-lit stage, the lights flashing and fading, intensifying again, staining the clouds and hills the most exquisite colours I'd seen since November days in the Monar Forest. The sun slipped from view. A full moon rose above the frozen lochan of the corrie, and for a while it seemed to hang suspended by an invisible cord. There was something mysterious and magical about its sudden appearance, and later the light it gave allowed me to descend to the tent without a torch. If I felt a twinge of melancholy once back it was because the scenes of mountain and light that had so moved me had irretrievably gone, were now consigned to bright memories. For nearly an hour I watched the moonlight on the symmetrical form of Lui until the frost had me scurrying back to the warmth of my sleeping bag.

The splatter of rain and a curtain of mist at dawn almost convinced me that the light and colour that still buzzed in the forefront of my memory had just been a vivid dream. Large droplets of condensation, which last night had frozen on the inside of the nylon like marbles, now ran down in tiny rivulets. My food gone, I was keen to get down. In driving rain and an unpleasant headwind I shuffled to the broad watershed and over to Strath Orchy. Burgeoning streams were everywhere, coursing down soggy hillslopes, undermining drifts and becoming traps for the unwary. There is normally no way down to Orchy as blanket forestry has effectively denied all western access to the Lui group, but now a line of electricity pylons snaking up from Loch Lomond has scythed a broad route through. After a desultory mile in the shadow of these monstrously ugly towers, a good track peels off to the lodge and slips beneath the railway line, past a cottage whose walls are covered in large murals, and finally to the small community of Glenview.

An inebriated gentleman clutching a carrier bag was the first person to welcome me from the hills. Crossing the road he wobbled towards me so I was unable to avoid him in the way you might a drunk in a busy street. His tatty blue parka, many sizes too big, covered him loosely like a gown or cloak. Beneath a bush of dark hair protruded a ruddy face whose eyes bulged with delight when I asked him to point me towards the shop. With the hand grasping the bag he gesticulated flamboyantly at a row of houses, delivering a monologue of barely audible directions. He managed to ask where I was heading.

'Cruachan!', he exclaimed, wide-eyed again, then crooned wistfully. Another monologue. 'Aye, a great wee hill, great wee hill, aye. Doin' Cruachan are yeh? Been up myself dozens of times, aye, great wee hill that...'

I found the shop tucked away in a backstreet and, inspired by the hours of hunger, reprovisioned beyond all economy, buying two kilos of fresh fruit, more tins, a bottle of olive oil, vegetables, biscuits and snacks. The storekeeper recommended various routes up Cruachan.

'Go by the dam, its easy and direct. There'll be plenty of folk about, always are on a Saturday; mind you, more people take the special bus up to see the power station.'

13

Last Storm

IN THE days when the arguments of utility prevailed over those more airy ones of conservation, Ben Cruachan, as a mountain, was damaged irreparably. They have dammed its lonely corrie to create a high-level reservoir, laid tarmac roads up its flanks, erected great steel pylons, built concrete platforms and sluice gates. The eastern sides are scarred by crudely excavated tracks. Disused quarries are now used to shelter cattle, and there is still much rusting industrial garbage strewn about. One hopes that such exploitation and schemes like the Cruachan project, inaugurated by the Queen in 1965, could never again happen, that never in the name of 'development' could we leave such indelible wounds on a natural and beautiful landscape.

Notwithstanding, Ben Cruachan is still one of the jewels in the West Highland crown, an untamed giant of a mountain whose main ridge and six tops make for a classic winter traverse. Like Liathach in the north, Cruachan has one of the most familiar settings in Scotland, particularly the view of her rising from the waters of Loch Awe and as a backdrop to the fifteenth-century Kilchurn Castle. One envies the early tourists who came up the loch in their pleasure steamers and made the ascent before the plantations and hydro developments. There are historical connections with both William Wallace and Robert the Bruce, the latter having his famous victory over Macdougall of Lorn at the Pass of Brander.

From my pitch in the early morning I had a fine view of the plain of Strath Orchy, towards the flickering lights of the farmsteads, the road and railway. Cattle bellowed and someone started up a tractor. My tent, though exposed on a small knoll, blended invisibly into the rough pasture—a case of 'see and not be seen'.

By the shores of Loch Awe the breeze rolling off the water was balmy and mild, an auspicious start, and I hoped the cloud might lift from the ridge and allow me some of the seaward views for which Cruachan is justly famed. A local man polishing his large bay windows waved a greeting, the last person I was to see all day. The attractive village of Lochawe is strung out along the road, having been built, literally, on the side of the mountain. At St Conan's Kirk I left the village and took the hydro road which eases you the three miles to the dam and reservoir.

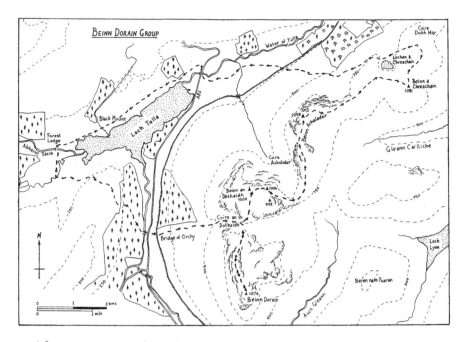

After so many months in the hills, the sudden impact of the disfigurement of the landscape is always much greater, and rounding the last bend you are suddenly faced with the full extent of the hydro-electric scheme. Man-made concrete and metal structures—whatever their function—can be beautiful, but in Cruachan's case it is their utter incongruity when set in a natural mountainscape that depresses, their harsh lines at odds with the folds and curves of the land, their uniform colourings set against the myriad shadings of rock and moor. And when high on a mountain it is a bizarre experience to walk the arrow-straight wall of the dam.

From the dam the path led steeply into Coire Dearg and to the snowline, the sea-level warmth now having vanished. Soft snow filled the corrie and fearsome cascades of ice clung to east-facing cliffs. Some of the ice, dismantled by yesterday's thaw, had lanced into the drifts at the base of the cliffs. At the rim of the corrie, and exposed to the west, I found a gusty wind that would plague me all day; but I had been wise to choose a west–east traverse. I reached the summit exactly four hours after leaving my pitch and for the second time on Cruachan was left to imagine the view below of an island-studded loch, then across the ancient lands of Lorn to the Hebrides, the islands of Mull, Jura and Islay and, on an exceptionally clear day, the hills of Antrim in Northern Ireland. Allowing myself only a minute's contemplation, I picked my way cautiously along a narrow ridge heaped with snow and rime.

A little way ahead the ridge threw up an impasse, and at its narrowest point I had to choose between climbing a vertical block or edging down and rooting

'Despite it being "home" for almost five months, I never really grew fond of my tent.'
Another cold night, this time in Glen Strathfarrar.

about for something easier. No doubt a climber would have taken this section in his stride, but the consequences of a slip would be pretty awful. Dropping a little I scrutinised a collection of giant slabs for an acceptable line. It seemed marginal but after a few fumbling moves I committed my shaky limbs to some icy shelving and groped my way back to safety.

Under snow, and in fierce, gusty conditions, the ridge gave me an intriguing tussle, my reward for the hours of toil from the lochside. Alone and with no distracting views I became completely absorbed with the immediate terrain, my thoughts concerned solely with the next step or move, the choice of line across a slab, round a block, continually wary of cornices, alert always to hidden verglas—absorbed, because in conditions like these you are compelled to make a hundred snap decisions every minute. Cruachan that day gave a classic winter traverse, but the Jekyll-and-Hyde wind did its best to torment and unsettle, clubbing me on the back, knocking me sideways, then, in seconds, calming to a whisper. It chased me along the ridge, snapping at me from all sides like a pack of terriers.

At one of the knuckles of the main ridge I naturally followed the crest round. In a minute I was dipping into the wilderness of Glen Noe, going north when I needed to be moving east. In fact many go wrong here. A spur invites you north but the main crest swings to the right, and a south-easterly bearing is what is needed—a row of way-marking cairns is definitely what is *not* needed. It was a steep and awkward descent to the col, folowed by a precipitous pull to Stob Diamh. From here, of the three spurs that would lead eventually to the tent, I slid down the most northerly one, a great winkle-picker with a toe of gnarled ash that I rolled off, and onto the floor of the glen.

From Dalmally the long trench of Glen Strae marching north-eastwards provides a logical—if little-used—way to the Bridge of Orchy and the Black Mount Hills. That morning a rather intimidating sign greeted my entry: 'Danger: High Velocity Rifles in Use'. Whether this was really a euphemism for 'Walkers: Enter at your Peril', I could not tell. There was no information as to when, or what, they were shooting, and, it being March, I assumed the season for hind culling was over. In any case, after the main stalking season in October the public have a perfect right to roam anywhere in the Highlands. Some signs are obviously intended to cause uncertainty among visitors and so dissuade people from entering. Of course, many estates have cultivated very cordial relations with walkers, providing information on stalking dates, contact numbers and occasionally even assisting in the maintenance of bothies. While I detest what many of them have done—and are doing—to their land, my own encounters have always been extremely friendly.

The overwhelming majority of hill-users abide by the unwritten agreement to avoid private land during the early autumn stalking season. Having no natural predator the deer must be culled, and no one begrudges the right of any land-owner to charge clients hefty sums to undertake the task. There is local employment, and if the land was not deer estate it would more than likely be blanket forestry. In fact, most estates are not culling nearly enough. According to the Red Deer Commission the present deer population of 350,000 is roughly two-thirds above what the Highlands can comfortably sustain. The consequence has been overgrazing and further ecological degradation.

For a while after I'd entered a field of shaggy Highland cattle I believed the sign should have warned instead against these fearsome-looking beasts. I tried to slink by anonymously but a large group, having reluctantly let me pass, now trundled after me. In a disturbing way they mirrored my movements: I quickened my pace, they did likewise; I stopped and turned to confront them and they stared back. Had I fled then I am sure I would have started a stampede. Working as a conservation volunteer on the Isle of Rum I once tended these intelligent creatures so I knew they were only expressing a natural curiosity, but those vicious horns always seem like a lethal weapon in the hands of a playful child.

Escaping their attention I passed the last plantation to enter a wide-open strath dotted with ancient birch. The many moss-covered ruins suggested that a considerable community must once have existed here. In the upper reaches I was saddened to see the ditches and lines of yet another new plantation, which, in less than a decade, will change the unique character of this lonely glen, transforming it to become like so many others.

The path lost itself among more old shielings, leaving me to cut across some bogland then clamber steeply to a 400-metre bealach. Having packed much fresh food bought from the shop at Loch Awe, I was hauling quite a burden, but once up moved with ease over the trackless ground. Some miles ahead a hazy light had found its way onto the snow-splattered flanks of Stob Ghabhar.

A few more miles, and I looked down onto a magical setting: the plum-shaped Loch Dochard, fringed with a pocket of Scots pine and set in a natural amphitheatre of wild mountains. That this residual woodland is now fenced and protected from grazing beasts is a fine thing, and a landowner with vision would see it is a nucleus for a future forest, spreading like wings around the loch, then miles beyond to clothe the hills themselves. In a rising wind I went down to seek a sheltered camp. A favourite pitch was occupied by one of the only other tents I'd seen all winter, so I made do with an uneven spot in the lee of a great boulder.

It rained all night and by morning the day was one of forlorn wetness. Across the loch, fingers of snow-melt poured down the mountainsides, and even from a distance the burns brimmed with a raw power. The rate at which cloud scudded across the hills gave a clear indication of wind speeds at the summits. I didn't pull on my waterproofs, but lay back, had a late breakfast and waited. While the rain did ease after midday, the wind actually strengthened, so that it now came round the boulder and tried to root me out like a reluctant weed. It rattled the tent so viciously that there came a point when I could take no more. Packing the sopping nylon, I sloshed the few miles to the Inveroran Hotel and for the first time since starting the walk slipped into a daydream of finishing.

Tucked into the cosy bar with a pint and a plate of steaming food, the mountains and all their nastiness, at least for a while, were quietly forgotten. The Inveroran, though not having the facilities of some larger establishments, is a home in the wilderness, and Anne Marshall the proprietor had given a generous welcome. Between mouthfuls I chatted with the only other customer. When I arrived, this chap with his pony-tail and greying beard had his eyes fixed on the tiny television that buzzed away in the corner, and for the first time in a long while the words 'mountain' and 'climb' were entirely absent from a conversation. We trawled over a medley of topics: local land ownership, politics and sport, especially fishing, for which he had a passion. He lived alone in a nearby estate-cottage.

'To deter the bastards I've got the place like Fort Knox,' he said, referring to the thieves who streamed up from the city and invaded the Highlands every weekend. 'The other day a bloke from Preston was caught nicking sheep for his restaurant. Found his transit van stuffed full of the smelly buggers.'

Gusts were still shaking the conifers next day as I dropped to Bridge of Orchy, having come the short distance from Inveroran via a section of the West Highland

Way. Quite obviously it was an insane day to be out, and during the course of winter only the Fannichs or Cairn Gorm probably gave me a worse battering. But it was a measure of how hardened—or reckless—I'd become that I matched the foul conditions, at times even revelled in them.

An air of weekday normality presided over the small community. Oblivious to the rain a group of small children was engaged in a noisy game in the school-yard. A resident in a yellow mac, his back to me, worked slowly on a wire fence, while some delivery men at the hotel were shifting crates of foodstuffs. One of them flashed a grin as I crossed the main road and went beneath the railway line to the open hillside. The path that led up towards the cloud-wreathed Beinn Dòrain had, I noticed, widened considerably from when I last climbed here more than a decade before.

My route today included the four main peaks, and along with most walkers who tackle this round I intended to take advantage of the wind and pursue a west to east line. Of course, this inevitably meant finishing on a mountain far from any road, and as darkness fell I would have to find the resources for the eight-mile trek back to Inveroran. This probably explains why the complete traverse is an unpopular venture in winter. These are very fine mountains indeed: Beinn Dòrain thrusts nearly a thousand continuous metres from the flood-plain of Auch and is a compelling sight for any northbound traveller on the A82. By contrast, Beinn an Dòthaidh, Beinn Achaladair, and Beinn a' Chreachain stretch a muscular arm across the southern fringe of Rannoch Moor, forming an unmistakable trio when viewed from Glencoe and the Mamores.

It was not so much that I'd become battle-weary that I expected so little from this group, but that I could not recall ever having a fine day here. My first teenage round was a stormy affair, the conditions more than a match for our jeans and leaky waterproofs. Then in May 1986 I got halfway up Dòrain before retreating in agony with a ligament strain. I went back some days later but a fierce blizzard chased me off the same mountain. A week after, and now into June, I struggled to the last Munro in another freak storm which by morning had left half a foot of snow on the tops. Nothing about the weather convinced me that today would be much different.

Hemmed in by steep ridges, the tiny col above the corrie channels any west wind into something much more violent, and this morning it was no place to hang around, even for a minute. Cold drizzle mingled with mist swept noisily up gullies and crags. It spilled over the ridge, hindering my movements to such an extent that I seriously doubted whether I could sustain the effort for very long.

At some point I bumped into Mike and Ben, first year students from Edinburgh University. They appeared suddenly through the mist on my right—having been blown off course, they said. Strange how perfect strangers can meet in such circumstances and subsequently be locked in trivial conversation for the next hour or two. In the circumstances collaboration seemed a good thing, but there was also an inherent danger that, for the sake of maintaining good humour and polite interest, the vile conditions would be ignored. Close to the summit a cloud window revealed the dinky proportions of a sunlit Bridge of Orchy Hotel. A tiny truck slid by noiselessly, heading towards Glasgow. Mike leaned into the wind with whoops and cries, as if in the park on a breezy day. Twice he was knocked to the ground, but he merely rolled over, picked himself up, laughing, and did the same again. The window closed and we got no more views.

Away from the ridge the soft snow still lay thickly, and through this we rather struggled to the cairn. Ben played with his fiddly compass as we shivered behind the poor windbreak, our good humour draining from our faces. Then we followed him back down like a couple of sheep. Back at the col I reflected that if any of us had been alone then the pressure to descend would have been overwhelming, but being a newly-formed group, if any of us had privately considered a retreat, then no one would have wanted to be the first to suggest it. I led the way up the ridge. Beinn an Dòthaidh yielded and here the students decided to bail out. They had a dinner party to prepare for, they said, and the chap left in the flat couldn't be trusted with anything more than a tin-opener.

Another of Ben's meticulous bearings and they scurried off downhill, leaving me to ponder the sense of continuing. The weather, if anything, had deteriorated; but the company had enlivened me, perked me up. I felt fit, had kept relatively warm, and after two summits had gathered a certain momentum. To go back now meant an almost equally long day tomorrow. Up until that moment escape was a simple matter of slipping down to the road, but now in the middle of a vile afternoon I pushed on east, and with every step moved further away from home.

Finding a safe way to the bealach from where I might continue the traverse was a tricky business. Initially, to avoid the northern cliffs, I over-compensated and steered too far south, finding myself teetering on steep snow and lost among dripping outcrops. Some dainty traversing got me out of danger and to the bealach, from where I could see the ridge sweeping away towards Beinn Achaladair.

Whether it was a change in topography or an increase in the pressure gradient of the storm I could not tell, but the wind, which continually harried me, now suddenly started jostling me from behind. Then a gust almost lifted me so that for brief seconds I became weightless, my legs thrashing out of control until I tumbled to the ground. I lay there for a minute, breathless, the wind tearing past, shaken and troubled. It had also became cold, and now mixed in with the drizzle were volleys of sleet. There is a thin line between a merely miserable day and one fraught with danger, and the danger lay in being exposed to these conditions for very long.

While it is true that part of me relished the struggle, being pushed about and flung to the ground by a volatile bully also incensed me. I kicked back and decided I wouldn't retreat until forcibly expelled. In a strange way the battle became personal; I felt under siege, at war, and by giving the elements a malevolent face I found I could fight them more effectively.

Somehow I made Achaladair, but passed the cairn without stopping as the dip in the ridge beyond promised some respite. To drown out discomforts when walking a track in the rain, my mind would usually drift into daydreams. But not here. The noise of the storm assailed my eardrums and I thought of nothing beyond keeping a good pace, maintaining my balance in the gusts and achieving my next target.

Beinn a' Chreachain was my final objective, now only a simple climb from the last bealach. Here I couldn't have escaped even if I'd wanted to. North, the way home, was barred by a ring of cliffs that extended all the way to the summit of Chreachain, while south led only to the wilds of Upper Glen Lyon. The cold was such that part of my face had grown numb. Wet snow was whipping sideways at me across the ridge, and, soaked in perspiration from the continual effort, I had taken to shivering involuntarily at every halt.

Still an hour from dark, I made the summit by half-crawling the final metres, then crouched behind the pile of stones to compose one last bearing. All about was a chaos of blowing snow and never had I wished so keenly to be down. On a north-east bearing I peeled away but immediately the wind swept me sideways, the eastern cliffs coming towards me like gaping jaws. The risk of being hurled over this face was terrifying and real. I crumpled to a heap, crawled back from the edge, then tore down the ridge into the teeth of the storm. In what seemed only a few minutes, I dropped 400 metres to the relative safety of the lochan. Here was another world: less cold, less windy, the snow now coming down harmlessly as drizzle. I traversed westwards, endlessly, dropping at last to below the cloud base, and slipped through a dying birch wood. I ran and jogged more from relief and euphoria than any need. Darkness would greet me at the railway line where even then there were still many miles to cover, but I was safely down; the miles to come were not difficult miles, and how much easier they would be now with the day salvaged from near-disaster.

From Achaladair Farm in dim twilight I cut over boggy pasture, crossed the main road, then followed the track by Loch Tulla. As I passed the tiny estate community of Black Mount, security lights flashed on to dazzle me. I tensed, expecting the usual eruption of barking dogs, but no sound was added to the rush of swaying trees. Inveroran shone warmly from across the dark waters, still a mile or two away, but close enough for me to entertain the luxurious thought of a respite.

Anne welcomed me back with another large meal. Too tired to make much conversation with the other guests, my eyes settled aimlessly on the small TV. During twenty minutes of mindless trivia was an 'in-your-face' promotion for a new set of channels. 'Digital TV,' blared the voice. 'Now you can interact with the environment without leaving your chair.'

§ § §

If you are walking the eighty-five miles from Glasgow to Fort William, your first day on Rannoch Moor will likely be the one you remember. Pulling up the old track from Loch Tulla you at last exchange the long, dark glens for a moorland expanse and a horizon of encircling peaks. While officialdom has turned this old military road into the West Highland Way, for centuries it was the main arterial route to Glencoe and northern Gaeldom, carrying greater numbers of Redcoats, Jacobites and drovers than it does walkers today. The dry, stony surface, immune to erosion, at first takes you effortlessly into the embrace of Corrie Bà a wide, watery basin ringed by a proud sweep of mountains. Beneath towering skies the views are gloriously open. Looking ahead, an ocean of moor tapers to distant hills, while a few miles west the Black Mount grows in the classic Highland form of corrie, ridge and buttress. There is a quintessential Scottish grandeur about the place, and to those for whom travelling up the A82 has become something of a habit, it is one of the most intensely familiar of all mountain landscapes.

Sometime during the night the wind died, and now in morning sunshine I passed by Forest Lodge, left the rhododendron shrubbery and strode across the miles of stark moorland. In the distance a pyramidal peak crowned in white showed above the crest of near moorland like some Himalayan giant. But in less than a minute the track dipped slightly and the Tolkeinian peak vanished. Mysteriously, I never saw it again. Later, I examined my maps but couldn't fathom what I had seen. Was it a trick of my imagination? Had I seen not a real peak but just a gable of white cloud? I was unsure and the thought of it gnawed at me all day.

I strayed off the track and camped at an idyllic spot in Coire Bà, the hills now resplendent in sunshine, while overnight snow had left white smudges on the some of the cliffs. There was time enough to tackle the Black Mount, but the memory of yesterday's mammoth effort lingered on in stiff muscles and a weary gait. With the gurgling of a nearby burn for company I lounged in my tent and read the afternoon hours away. At around six o' clock I lit my candle and began what was to be my last book, a novel by François Mauriac.

Of one thing I was convinced: that when I did finally finish and the reality of the walk faded to fragments of memory, I would remember the books I'd read with almost as much relish as the journey itself. Apart from Cherry-Garrard's odyssey I had got through novels by Endo, Chatwin and Herling. I also reread some classic epics: *Annapurna* by Maurice Herzog and *The Long Walk* by Slavomir Rawicz, books which informed my attitude and unfolded in tandem with my own wanderings. Their words were always my silent travelling companions. During the long hours between my evening meal and sleep, night after night, I entered other worlds: a Tokyo suburb, the Canadian tundra, a Welsh hill farm, and in the complete absence of any distraction these stories became my reality. They clothed my days with rich imagery and bright themes and were looked forward to as much as any meal or mug of sweet tea. And on so many mornings I remembered not the dreams that coloured my sleep but last night's reading, which quite transcended them.

That night a frost was prevented by incoming cloud cover, though thankfully conditions remained settled. By morning the only disturbance was a light breeze drifting down Coire Bà; it was thin and chilly but carried no threat. Stob Ghabhar, (1,090m), was climbed by scrambling up her cornice-lined east ridge, and I revelled in my first clear summit for over a week. There is a dramatic sense of elevation on this peak, especially when casting an eye across the swelling moor, or south beyond Glen Orchy to Ben Lui, Ben More and the Cruachan range, and at last there was a clear view of Bidean nam Bian.

The Black Mount Hills form a high-level traverse with a panorama that is always changing. The summits today were cold but there was no wind, and if I wrapped up I could linger over the views with impunity. Not since that day on the Tarf watershed had my mountain walking been so relaxed. With absolutely no urgency I idled northwards along the broad ridge of Aonach Mòr. From the last bealach I gazed into the chasm created by the torrents that ran down these precipitous slopes, then further into the gulf of Glen Etive, itself squeezed by spurs truncated during the great ice movements. The signature of the ice was everywhere: wide-bottomed glens, hanging valleys, ice-scoured bowls, a landscape first sculpted by crude bulldozing, then chiselled to some form of perfection by subsequent millennia of frost and rain. An infinite patience had been at work here, and on this quiet, windless day it was easy to believe the mountains were immutable and changeless.

A member of the Ladies' Scottish Climbing Club was already at the red cairn of Clach Leathad, and with her scientist friend we discussed an out-of-print gem of a book.* It was indeed an afternoon when to sit quietly and contemplate the vista with a notebook or sketchpad would have been more appropriate than marking off yet another group of hills.

The ski mountain of Meall a' Bhùiridh with its cables, cafes and concrete is best forgotten. Recent rain had broken up the runs and the lifts were silent. I ploughed down untrodden snow on one of the steeper pistes, finishing up at the ruin of Bà Cottage, and walked the last mile to the tent in a mood of deep contentment.

Next day I realised why the hills were so empty this winter, why I had met so few other people: they all seemed to be on the Buachaille in Glencoe. The popularity of this mountain is not surprising. Buachaille Etive Mòr, 'the Big Shepherd of Etive' (1,022m), appears to have been transplanted from an altogether more monumental landscape, a Death Valley or Sinai Desert perhaps. A starkly beautiful peak, its great cliffs are riven with long columns or grooves which, in the morning light, appear like giant fluting. To my mind, the east face has the single most intimidating aspect in Britain.

Walkers with climbing aspirations sweat their way up Curved Ridge, an exposed scramble that splits the great east face. I settled for a modest ascent of the southern flank. Below, weekend drivers were idling along the single-track road. On the River Etive a large group of canoeists became bottle-necked at the rapids, their yellow and orange buoyancy giving splashes of colour on an otherwise grey and overcast day.

*Poems of the Scottish Hills (see Further Reading, p.163)

Immediately above were six figures silhouetted against the mist. On the two-mile section of ridge to Stob Dearg, the highest point of the Buachaille, I passed perhaps two dozen people and a dozen more were milling about the misty summit. Heads continually popped up from the eastern cliffs, red-faced, perspiring and relieved, almost all having come up Curved Ridge. Some grasped ice-axes, though there was little snow about. The mountain was so saturated with folk that few bothered to greet or acknowledge those they passed, as if when a place becomes crowded we humans gather up the inhibitions we usually reserve for the city.

Some loose scree led me rudely down to the floor of the glen. I collected my tent and trudged westward, beginning a seven-mile glen bash. The canoeists were, by now, in a state of some disarray, many strung out like brightly-coloured flotsam along a mile-long stretch of the river, their excited screams and yelps echoing round the glen. Others dragged their craft the short distance to the road where two minibuses patrolled back and forth collecting the stragglers.

As if something ominous were about to happen the atmosphere thickened so that a gloomy pall hung over the valley. On both flanks great, steep-sided peaks slowly lost all detail and became shadowy outlines. It was quiet in an uncanny and oppressive way. I had drifted past hamlets, some with cars parked outside, but this seemed a ghost glen. Glen Etive is part of a vast estate comprising some 88,000 acres, roughly the size of Greater London, though the comparison ends there. Despite being a remarkably mild and sheltered valley, a place where you might expect a thriving community, Etive is sad, lonely and almost devoid of occupants. Historically the glen was decimated by successive cholera epidemics, and those who survived were promptly exiled by their lairds to make way for sheep pasture. Much of the best land today lies smothered in conifer plantation; in fact the first people I passed since the canoeists more than an hour before were itinerant forestry workers mooching in front of some caravans. Their week of clear-felling had turned great swathes of valley into barren, brown patches resembling a test ground for biological weapons.

It was hideously ugly. One-time forestry contractor Steve Tompkins described commercial afforestation in the Highlands as 'theft of the hills', others talk of aesthetic and ecological vandalism. It is hard to disagree. Aesthetically, the harsh lines and evergreen appearance are an affront to our sensibilities, diminishing our sense of wildness, replacing an ever-changing moorland cycle with an alien monoculture of sitka spruce or lodgepole pine. The modern practice of planting a few deciduous species to soften the fringes does not hide the truth that this is still blanket forestry. The land is emphatically lost, and no walker can penetrate it, no animal can live in it. Ecologically, afforestation has been disastrous, its impact on wildlife communities, particularly moorland birds, being well-documented. In the words of the Royal Society for the Protection of Birds, 'broadly speaking afforestation replaces the threatened and vulnerable with the commonplace and adaptable'. New forests have also been shown to exacerbate the effects of acid rain, acidifying streams and lochs and generally depleting the land even further of essential nutrients. By the late 1990s over 15% of the Highlands was already forested, the massive expansion fuelled for a time by a ridiculous tax loophole whereby the government handed landowners and speculators 70% of the planting costs. Public outcry plugged the loophole, despite vociferous opposition from vested interests, though there still remains a generous system of grants favouring forestry over more diverse and people-friendly forms of land husbandry.

Of course, most environmental issues boil down to questions of landownership, and given that Scotland's landownership laws are some of the most feudal, elitist and archaic in Europe, it is not surprising the land has suffered a terminal decline, our native woodlands are almost extinct and our moorlands near-deserts due to over-grazing. That there has been a need for land-buying conservation bodies such as the John Muir Trust and the National Trust for Scotland to reverse such a decline, is a reflection of the failure of generations of landowners and the system which produced them. Glen Etive is a case in point. It is surely absurd in a modern democracy that such a vast tract of land can be bought and sold at will by any individual or organisation, that there are no environmental safeguards nor conditions of any kind attached to the purchase. Etive should not be empty. Given reasonable investment and a wholesale reform of landownership laws, there is no doubt that even remote Highland glens can prosper on a par with similar locations in Scandinavia, but land must be made affordable and available to smallholders, crofters and the rural community in general.

Ben Starav and tomorrow's peaks towered their full thousand metres at the head of the glen, growing ever larger, and now appearing quite forbidding in this dull light. Crossing the river to seek a place to camp I went downstream to where the mild winter had hurried spring along, and here by the warm Atlantic there was already a dusting of green on skeletal alders.

It is a fine thing to sleep so soundly and wake with no stiffness in your joints, to pull on your boots and be immediately into your stride; a fine thing also to be moving so well and making light of the ridge that coiled down two miles from the summit of Starav. And I moved at a pace well within my abilities so, like a shepherd, I could climb for two hours with barely a minute's rest. Clambering up a ridge first thing in the morning had long become the natural way of things, my body expecting nothing less. To speak of physical communion with the mountain may be fanciful, but over the months my body had become so attuned that my feet seemed to have developed their own tiny minds, knowing exactly where to tread, where to avoid. It had not always been like this.

Except for a few excursions with my father, my first real forays into the mountains were always with a peer group from school or college. Our hill-walking apprenticeship entirely escaped the culture of the 'Outward-Bound school', and perhaps because of this I have never been much interested in detailed plans with their lists and guides. We could take a bearing and knew all about gravity—there didn't seem much else worth knowing. We learnt through trial and error, through blisters and soakings, and going hungry. Sometimes we carried too much—or too little—and while we had our share of luck we were never unduly reckless. More importantly, we went to our hills at every opportunity, and sometimes to the detriment of work and career ladders. Our walking was a constant source of challenge, the mountain environment, its features and wildlife, an inexhaustible store of wonderment, and I had felt it these last months as strongly as ever.

Shortly before the summit I was enveloped in a freezing mist which left frost feathers on the grass and turned the snow to concrete. I placed my boots in a line of old prints and these led easily to the trig point. Starav's summit crest is a classic tent shape, a slender ridge slung between two tops. It remains narrow and broken while dropping eastwards, changing direction as it climbs again, now seemingly endlessly, for Glas Bheinn Mhòr. Snow had vanished from much of the crest and it was easy to follow as it turned abruptly, swinging northwards and dumping me onto a tiny hemmed-in col. A convex slope of 300 metres led up and over the rather featureless rump of Stob Coir' an Albannaich (1,044m).

By now some loose snowflakes were being driven by an increasingly bitter wind. The tops had suddenly become wintry. In a moment of chaos I removed my cagoule to pull on another layer, then fled into the teeth of the weather, making a bee-line for Glen Etive. There are few easy ways off Albannaich. The map contours here are so bunched they appear as shading, but as no outcrops were marked, I simply plunged down.

There were indeed no outcrops, but the slope soon became frighteningly steep, so steep I pulled out my ice-axe, ready to ram it into the turf should I stumble. Confidence returned as the slope eased, and for once I threw caution to the wind and came down like a runaway train, barely in control. While my speed was slightly reckless, I returned knowing I still had another pass to cross and miles to cover before nightfall. By now the day had its own urgency and momentum. Away from the forestry I could make out two men igniting the heather. In thirty minutes there was a line of flames and a thickening scarf of blue smoke streaming away along the valley.

The way north from Etive to Ballachulish, never a logical route, has been further complicated by plantations, which now cover much of the ground hereabouts to 400 metres. And while operational tracks penetrate deeply into these forests they rarely reach open ground beyond, leaving you with a desperate fight along a stream course or a crawl up a drainage ditch.

But from the hamlet of Invercharnan I beat up a westbound track that seemed to offer a way through. The track, obviously little-used, climbed rather tediously, now over gravel, now on a carpet of moss, and to keep my interest I moved at a pace that would soon tire me. But I didn't tire. Again—and how often has this happened?—I was swept along as if by a heaving wave, endlessly rolling and breaking. The track became a path that toiled through a dark fire-break, vanishing altogether as it merged with open moorland. Free of forestry, I continued at a blistering pace, mindful that daylight was running out and that my headtorch battery had long since died. There was no need to consult the map, for the bealach sandwiched between two obscure Munros was obvious; it was straight ahead. Even then I didn't pause. I hurtled on downhill towards Glen Creran, faster and faster, a drizzly breeze on my face, the heather and hill moving past in a blur, my ears filled with the roar of the tumbling burn which, for the final hour, became my noisy companion. So many days had been like this; my feet in tune with the bogs and the earth's undulations, leaping ditches as if the burden on my back had at last become weightless, moving unharnessed, swiftly and easily, treading a carpet of air. To stop now was inconceivable, and I felt I could just carry on going into spring and summer, then another winter, never arriving.

In two days I was in Glencoe.

14

Glencoe

DESPITE IT being 'home' for almost five months, I never grew fond of my tent in the way one may grow to love a much-used car or boat. However sturdy in appearance, it never quite guaranteed womb-like security, never convinced me it would survive a really wild night. Waking to a tangle of torn nylon and bent aluminium was surely only a matter of time. Only exhaustion made me truly content within its meagre dimensions, and to delay otherwise quickly made life intolerable. Now as I waited by the River Laroch, longing for dawn, the joys of camping had worn very thin indeed.

Just the day before I had come over from Glen Crenan on a wave of optimism. Beyond Loch Leven, new snow was splashed across the Mamores and spring sunshine played on the hills to the west. In no great rush to reach Glencoe, I decided my penultimate Munros, the two peaks of the Ballachulish horseshoe, could wait. But the night had been a wash-out. Unwisely I had chosen to camp on a small alluvial bank by the River Laroch, the only pocket of flattish ground in the valley. Woken in the early hours by the roar of the river in spate, I prodded the groundsheet and realised half of it seemed to be floating. Through the downpour I saw that a small overflow had broken free of the main channel and was sloshing around the tent. If the river, now almost brim-full, burst its banks, then I was directly in the line of fire. I stuffed everything into my bivvy bag, pulled on boots and made ready to evacuate but, by some miracle, the worst never happened, though I passed a sleepless night convinced it would.

The gale continued through morning and into afternoon when, irritable from lack of sleep, I went a few weary miles to Ballachulish for supplies, promising myself that tonight would be my absolute last under nylon. At the tiny grocery my sour mood turned to one of embarrassment. Queuing for the checkout, the silent locals stood at a respectable distance as rank odours escaped from clothes not washed since Crianlarich a fortnight before. Clambering back I found myself craving the simple comforts of civilisation—bath, clean garments, an uninterrupted night's sleep—with a longing not felt throughout the winter.

I did manage sleep, and then, as always, the promise of a new day wiped clean the slate of yesterday's frustrations. Shifting back to the north-west, the wind peeled off old layers of grey to reveal a gleaming underskin, and the sun, not felt for days, came through the trees to cast a lacework of shadows on the sodden ground. The light had a rejuvenating effect; for now it was easy to pull on wet socks and boots, probably for the last time, and take my first steps uphill, the sudden brightness dazzling and forcing my gaze downwards.

The two peaks making up the Ballachulish horseshoe—Sgorr Dhearg and Sgorr Dhonuill—stand prominent above the neck of Loch Leven, a crest of bleeding scree which holds an elegant arc of snow well into the spring. Although access to the ridge in recent years has been made difficult by encircling conifers, the climb direct from Ballachulish gives a fine traverse with some awkward scrambling. Certainly the mountain deserved better than today's top-bagging mission, for which I climbed a line of least resistance, direct and with little to commend it.

A rag-tag army of adolescents on an Outward Bound course brewed up where the path entered a plantation. They grinned as I lumbered past and struck directly up the hill. As on so many climbs that winter the going was pathless and unforgiving, a case of keeping my head down until I was able to measure my progress on the Munro of Sgor na h-Ulaidh opposite. Mostly the tops remained hidden, but below were dollops of sunshine and roving shadows. I found the ridge in a fierce shower of snow and hail, and, judging from the moisture-clogged west, more seemed imminent. Exposed and quite cold, I moved swiftly along the crest, first to Sgorr Dhonuill at barely 1,000 metres, then backtracking to Sgor Dhearg. My descent route was a mistake, for somehow I had been enticed into a loose gully of sharp rock; a twisted ankle with a mountain still to climb would have been the final irony.

Once back at the tent I lingered awhile, then with some relish packed everything and set off for Glencoe, about five miles to the east. No longer is there any obvious route from Laroch to this best-known of Scottish glens; forestry cover has put paid to that, but the frustrations began with the River Laroch itself. Here in its lower course it was gorge-like and the far bank gave a slightly frantic scramble over moss and clinging birch. From then on the plantation cleverly utilises every decent slope to the bealach, forcing the walker to step goat-fashion around its fringe. With some relief I shook free of the last conifers and strode across the open ground of the bealach. There, below me, was Glencoe, and in an hour or so my long journey would be all but over. It was true that Bidean nam Bian still awaited an ascent, but I was saving this for friends Antony and Ursula who could only join me at the weekend, still some days away.

Glencoe, situated at the apex of high mountains, may not seem the natural place to finish a trek, but, as with Sandwood Bay at the outset, I felt I had reasons enough for being there. Years of visiting and passing through has spawned such a kaleidoscope of memories that, for me at least, this valley has become a microcosm for the entire Western Highlands, representing their every facet. Some of my earliest memories are of grey, rain-drenched screes, towers and mist-filled gullies; these are places I forever carry in my subconscious, recalling them almost with a sense of premonition at every similar landscape.

It was years before I could actually apply names to the shadowy brutes that grew on both sides of the road. Now, an hour before dusk, I gazed beyond the puddle of Loch Achtriochtan to where the Aonach Eagach rose clear, its miles of crest broken like an old saw with missing teeth, then falling sheer to curtains of screes and the ruddy streaks of last year's bracken. I dropped to the valley floor and booked into the bustling youth hostel.

Somehow it wasn't quite the ending I had imagined all those years before; but then what exactly had I imagined? Given the task I had set myself, just making the Great Glen or Blair Atholl was miracle enough; the reality of finishing was something I never dared contemplate, for it always seemed a most unlikely event. There was no great elation or relief, instead I began to be plagued almost by a sense of anticlimax. Perhaps this had been brought on by the recent days of mild spring weather; the storms were gone, my last peak would yield in an unhurried, leisurely manner, and it was now just a case of waiting for the weekend. Also, I was suddenly haunted by the thought of vacuous hours to come once home: the routine of work and traffic, TV and supermarkets, of joining 'civilisation' again. How would I adapt? What would I do next? The future appeared as a void which, just then, I had no wish to enter into, and so the few days of waiting were easy, for it delayed the end.

My fellow hostellers at first seemed distant and immaterial, their words only half-heard, our reference points still far apart. But then I didn't feel particularly sociable. While it was true the only thing I truly missed during my months in the hills was human companionship, particularly that of friends, it was in Glencoe that I realised how far the experience had pulled me away from people, even fellow hill-goers. I attempted to collect my thoughts into some constructive pattern, but as hard as I tried they remained like scattered pieces of a jigsaw, and I knew I would need time for this when I returned home.

Passing a couple of days in Glencoe was easy enough. A dozen short walks fan out from the village and some of the lower peaks are worth a visit, Meall Mòr for instance or Sgorr na Ciche, the Pap of Glencoe, a spectacular afterthought of the Aonach Eagach which gazes down the length of Loch Leven. For a change I explored some of the woods and traced the course of burns uphill, always ending with a drink at the Clachaig.

On one occasion I chatted to a visitor from Ireland, admitting that for me Glencoe was the end of a very long road. Almost inevitably came the question: 'How long did it take you?' I had pretty much lost track of dates so I struggled to give him a precise answer, but 'how long' has always seemed a rather pointless question. Does it really matter how long it took? Are we so lacking in imagination that speed is the only measure of success, whether it be the fastest ascent of Everest or the quickest round of Munros? Surely the longer we spend in the hills the better. By going full tilt and with regular support, I might have shaved two or three weeks off the finish, but that was never the point. It would be like coming home early from a holiday. Racing over the hills is a kind of blasphemy, for surely the degree of enjoyment and personal fulfilment are more relevant; whether you observed dotterel, golden eagle, or wild cat, lingered high to see sunsets, rose early for dawns, stayed up late with strangers; did it nurture love and respect of wild places, provoke your anger at the continuing disfigurement of the wilderness? These things matter: speed, by comparison, doesn't. Only when I arrived home did people ask why on earth I had done it, to my mind a more interesting question. Beyond the lure of freedom, travel and escape—none of which depend upon mountaineering—there are no real answers; for why should an activity demanding huge investments of time and energy, that on any economic or social measure is utterly unproductive, that puts you through considerable discomfort, even danger, be worth while?

At the weekend I left the rather suffocating atmosphere of the hostel and joined Antony and Ursula at the Clachaig. Situated in the heart of Glencoe, the Clachaig Inn has long been a focal point for climbers and the decor admirably reflects this. On the morning of my last day we sat in the comfortable lounge sipping tea. Surrounding us were walls covered, some would say cluttered, with paraphernalia and images from the climbing world: axes and crampons from an almost forgotten era, haunting colour and monochrome studies of Himalayan giants. The photographs show mainly young climbers who pose against backdrops of gleaming white peaks, some even signed by those they depict. At first they seem just gatherings of friends in the mountains, smiles frozen in the thin air, but a closer inspection reveals well-known faces, many of whom never came back, and slowly the room takes on an almost shrine-like aura. But there is no melancholy about the place, rather an understanding that for a select few the normal pattern of work and leisure proved incompatible with their idea of a meaningful life.

There can be few more appropriate peaks to finish on than Bidean nam Bian, at 1,177m the highest in Argyllshire. While only a few would call her beautiful, parting clouds reveal a complexity and magnitude that must have distracted many a motorist. From almost any perspective there is a sense of drama about this mountain, and from my own many fine tussles, an enduring memory is of a glorious June afternoon in 1986 when Bidean was one of many summits topped on a fifteen-hour day of heat and clarity. Never were the flanks, screes and cliffs clothed in finer colours or cleaner light. By contrast, a year earlier I'd climbed Bidean with a friend, Clive Dennier, on a soaking, gale-swept day with snow-melt surging down every conceivable avenue. Having struggled up 'Hidden Valley', we groped our way along the summit ridge, and then were blown into the Lairig Eilde only to find the River Coe white with menace, barring our escape. It was near midnight before we risked a crossing.

From Glencoe there is a good choice of ascent routes, all steep, with perhaps the most dramatic being the climb into 'Hidden Valley'. As this would involve an initial two-mile road walk, in the spirit of the journey we contoured beneath Aonach Dubh and went up Coire nan Lochan instead. We moved up easily, following the red stain of a path, past straggly rowans and over ice-smoothed rock that increasingly won through the thin pasture. The climb steepened and the landscape grew more barren. Straying from the path we entered a tiny hanging valley with boulders and snowfields, and spring water bubbling from a bed of moss, which chilled our throats. It was a mountain day like so many others, more like spring than winter, it was true, but one among a seamless pattern of days which, in a few hours, would have made a complete journey.

After a week of thaw the snow remaining was knee-deep slush, to be avoided where possible. Much of it had disappeared altogether from the main ridge. In such benign conditions and chatting for much of the time, in the end I enjoyed one of the least demanding climbs of the winter. The summit arrived sooner than expected, and we shared our drinks and good humour with a couple already there. Mountain tops are never places to linger for long, whatever the circumstances, and within thirty minutes the swirling mist and chill breeze nudged us back into activity.

And that might have seemed the end of it if the mountain had not spawned one last surprise: I had managed to select the *wrong* descent route. A path of sorts had invited us down but this quickly degenerated into a scrambler's paradise of rocky steps, then gullies and sheer pitches. Hearing the disturbing clatter of loose stones, I led the way back up.

'How did you manage to do it?', Ursula asked.

'Do what?', I replied.

'Climb all those hills in winter?'

I thought for a moment, then said with a shrug and a smile: 'I don't know.'

Appendix: Equipment and Food Parcels

AN OLD saying among mountaineers claims that if you are never cold, tired or hungry then you must be carrying too much weight. I do not subscribe to this. For me, serious hill-walking is about enjoyment, and my preparations were undertaken primarily with this objective in mind. My first criterion, then, was weight.

From long, sometimes bitter experience of lugging heavy rucksacks I knew my comfort threshold to be around 20kg, and this for trail walking. So, despite being subjected to a mind-boggling mix of brands, labels and hype, equipment selection boiled down to a simple question: what does it weigh? Purchasing a rucksack no larger than sixty-five litres that would automatically restrict my load seemed a good start. Certain manufacturers specialise in quality lightweight equipment, notably Macpac, Camp, Patagonia and Rab, and these provided the bulk of my gear. Scepticism about some of the items—particularly the alloy crampons—fortunately proved wrong, and in general the gear was excellent; it did the job. It is worth remembering that despite the great 'advances' in equipment technology in recent years, Hamish Brown managed to walk the Munros in the pre-Gore-Tex and synthetic days of 1974, carrying no more than 12kg—a lesson for us all perhaps.

Keeping weight to a minimum inevitably meant the use of food parcels, and these were placed in twenty-five carefully chosen locations along the route. Even on the odd occasion when mice got there first, there were always enough tins for a day or two, and, unlike on previous trips, I rarely went hungry. A typical day's menu from the parcels went something like this:

Breakfast
Always porridge with condensed milk and sugar. Tea/coffee and biscuits.
Lunch
Tin of fruit, two tins of oily fish, nuts, chocolate, biscuits.
Dinner
Soup followed by either potatoes, mushrooms, pies fried in olive oil
or
tuna, tomato, onion and pasta. Cake and custard to finish.

The parcels were filled with a rich variety of foodstuffs. Each one contained treats, and my only real cravings were for Irn Bru and vegetable samosas, which of course I indulged whenever I passed village stores.

A walk in the hills is a panacea for many things, and my general health throughout was excellent. Occasional days were lost through migraine, though I reckoned I suffered rather less than usual. My bad knee, too, gave no problems. One thousand six hundred and seven miles of rough walking, it seems, was just what it needed.

Further Reading

Brown, Hamish, *Hamish's Mountain Walk* (London, 1978)
Brown, Hamish, *Poems of the Scottish Hills* (Aberdeen, 1982)
Brown, D. & Mitchell I., *A View from the Ridge* (Glasgow, 1991)
Crumley, Jim, *A High and Lonely Place* (London, 1991)
Crumley, Jim, *Among Mountains* (Edinburgh, 1993)
Cherry-Garrard, Apsley, *The Worst Journey in the World* (London, 1922)
Gray, Affleck, *The Big Grey Man of Ben Macdhui* (Edinburgh, 1994)
Herzog, Maurice, *Annapurna* (London, 1952)
Hillaby, John, *Journey through Britain* (London, 1968)
Moran, Martin, *The Munros in Winter* (London, 1986)
Murray, W. H, *Mountaineering in Scotland* (London, 1947)
Prebble, John, *Glencoe* (London, 1966)
Ramsey, Paul, *Revival of the Land* (Perth, 1997)
Rawicz, Slavomir, *The Long Walk* (London, 1956)
Scroggie, Sydney, *The Cairngorms Scene and Unseen* (Edinburgh, 1989)
Theroux, Paul, *The Kingdom by the Sea* (London, 1983)
Tompkins, Steve, *Theft of the Hills* (London, 1986)
Weir, Tom, *Highland Days* (London, 1948)
Wightman, Andy, *Who Owns Scotland?* (Edinburgh, 1996)

Index